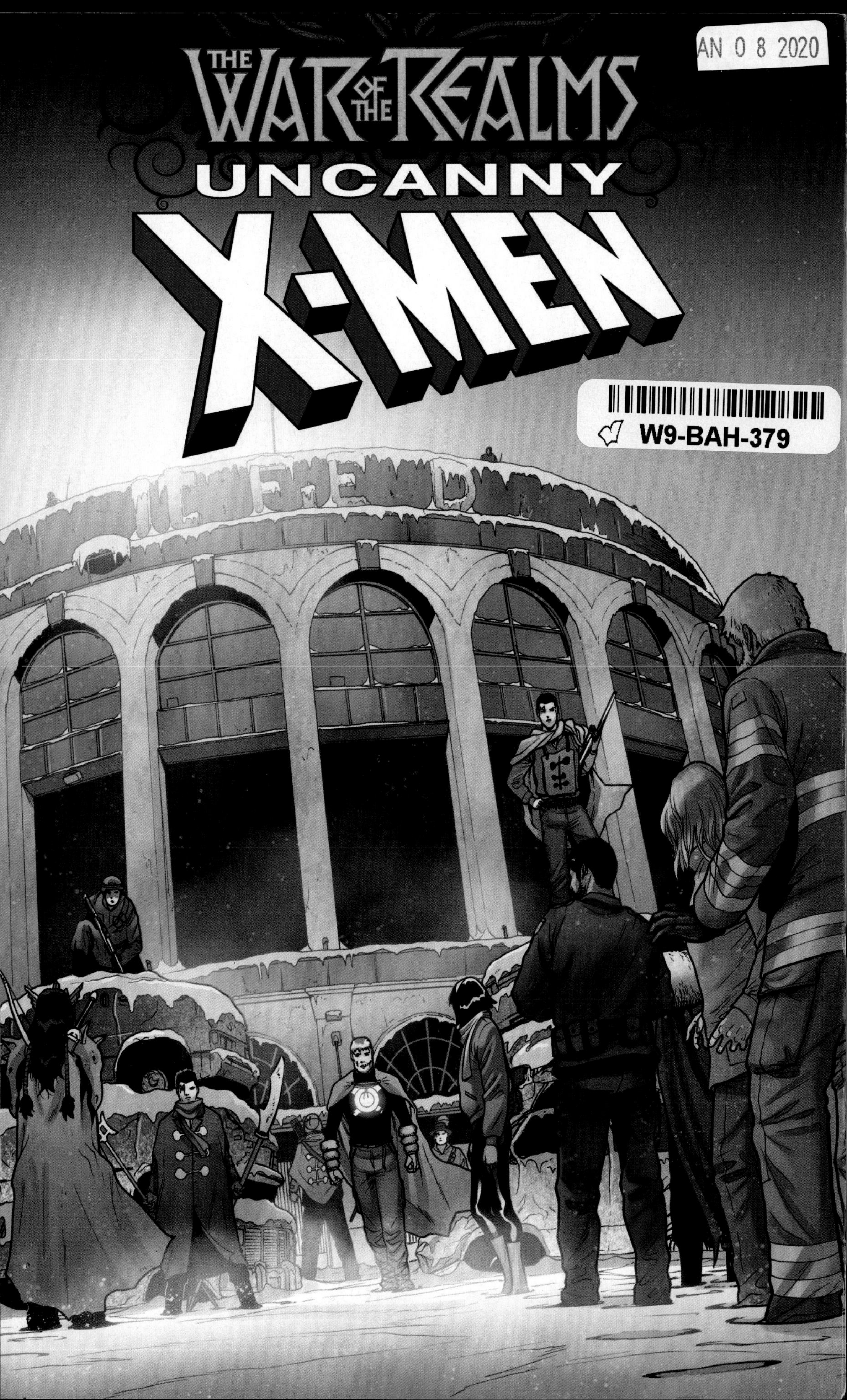
THE WAR OF THE REALMS
UNCANNY
X-MEN

THE WAR OF THE REALMS

After laying waste to nine of the Ten Realms, the Dark Elf
King Malekith and his powerful allies have finally brought
the War of the Realms to Midgard – the last realm standing!

Recently, Cyclops and Wolverine banded together as the last
X-Men with Magik, Wolfsbane, Mirage, Karma, Havok,
Multiple Man and Chamber. Together they hunt down
lingering threats to mutantkind!

COLLECTION EDITOR **JENNIFER GRÜNWALD**   **CAITLIN O'CONNELL** ASSISTANT EDITOR
ASSOCIATE MANAGING EDITOR **KATERI WOODY**   **MARK D. BEAZLEY** EDITOR, SPECIAL PROJECTS
VP PRODUCTION & SPECIAL PROJECTS **JEFF YOUNGQUIST**   **JAY BOWEN** BOOK DESIGNER

SVP PRINT, SALES & MARKETING **DAVID GABRIEL**   **SVEN LARSEN** DIRECTOR, LICENSED PUBLISHING
EDITOR IN CHIEF **C.B. CEBULSKI**   **JOE QUESADA** CHIEF CREATIVE OFFICER
PRESIDENT **DAN BUCKLEY**   **ALAN FINE** EXECUTIVE PRODUCER

WAR OF THE REALMS: UNCANNY X-MEN. Contains material originally published in magazine form as WAR OF THE REALMS: UNCANNY X-MEN #1-3, UNCANNY X-MEN #17 and WAR OF THE REALMS: WAR SCROLLS #2. First printing 2019. ISBN 978-1-302-91919-1. Published by MARVEL WORLDWIDE, INC., a subsidiary of MARVEL ENTERTAINMENT, LLC. OFFICE OF PUBLICATION: 135 West 50th Street, New York, NY 10020. © 2019 MARVEL No similarity between any of the names, characters, persons, and/or institutions in this magazine with those of any living or dead person or institution is intended, and any such similarity which may exist is purely coincidental. **Printed in Canada.** DAN BUCKLEY, President, Marvel Entertainment; JOHN NEE, Publisher; JOE QUESADA, Chief Creative Officer; TOM BREVOORT, SVP of Publishing; DAVID BOGART, Associate Publisher & SVP of Talent Affairs; DAVID GABRIEL, SVP of Sales & Marketing, Publishing; JEFF YOUNGQUIST, VP of Production & Special Projects; DAN CARR, Executive Director of Publishing Technology; ALEX MORALES, Director of Publishing Operations; DAN EDINGTON, Managing Editor; SUSAN CRESPI, Production Manager; STAN LEE, Chairman Emeritus. For information regarding advertising in Marvel Comics or on Marvel.com, please contact Vit DeBellis, Custom Solutions & Integrated Advertising Manager, at vdebellis@marvel.com. For Marvel subscription inquiries, please call 888-511-5480. **Manufactured between 9/6/2019 and 10/8/2019 by SOLISCO PRINTERS, SCOTT, QC, CANADA.**

10 9 8 7 6 5 4 3 2 1

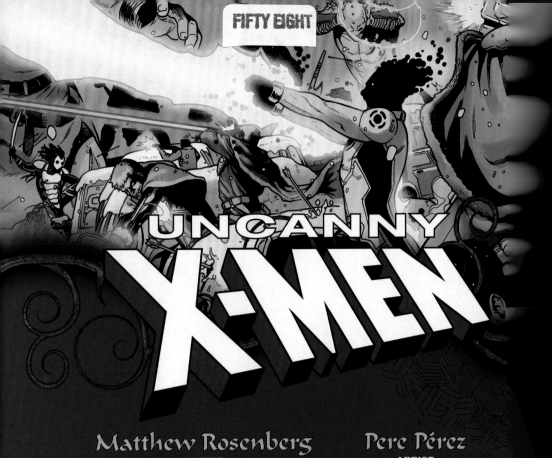

FIFTY EIGHT

UNCANNY X·MEN

Matthew Rosenberg
WRITER

Pere Pérez
ARTIST

Rachelle Rosenberg
COLOR ARTIST

VC's Travis Lanha
LETTERER

David Yardin
COVER ART

Chris Robinson
EDITOR

Jordan D. White
CONSULTING EDITOR

SPECIAL THANKS TO WIL MOSS & SARAH BRUNSTAD

X-MEN CREATED BY STAN LEE & JACK KIRBY

UNCANNY X-MEN #17

Matthew Rosenberg
WRITER

Carlos Gómez
ARTIST

Guru-eFX
COLOR ARTIST

Joe Caramagna
LETTERER

Paul Davidson
COVER ART

Chris Robinson
ASSISTANT EDITOR

Jordan D. White
EDITOR

WAR OF THE REALMS: WAR SCROLLS #2

DOCTOR STRANGE IN "AGENCY"

Devin Grayson
WRITER

Paul Davidson
ARTIST

Andres Mossa
COLOR ARTIST

WICCAN & HULKLING IN "MY DRAG BRUNCH WITH LOKI"

Anthony Oliveira
WRITER

Nick Robles
ARTIST

Cris Peter
COLOR ARTIST

VC's Joe Sabino
LETTERER

Sarah Brunstad
ASSOCIATE EDITOR

Wil Moss
EDITOR

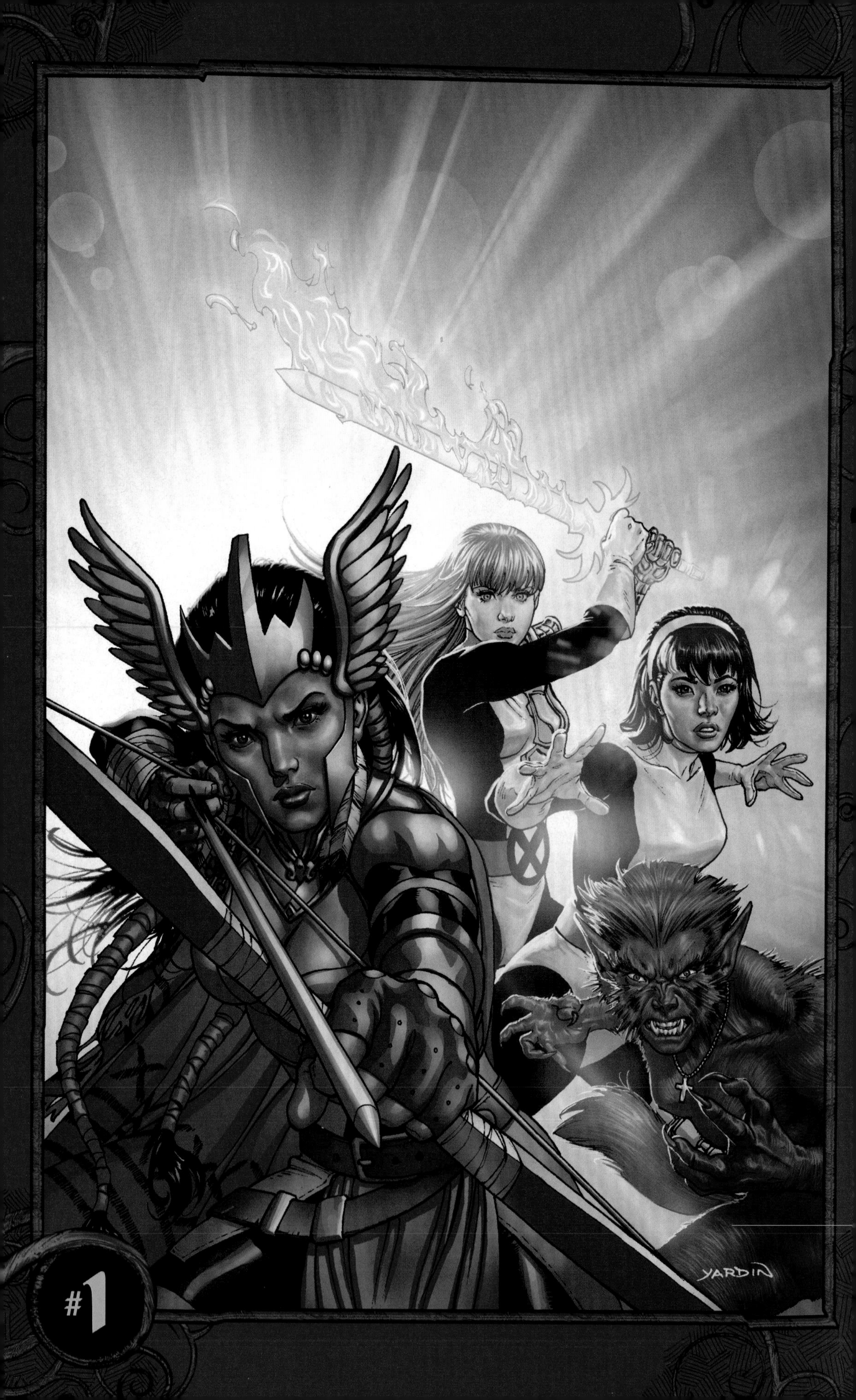

#1
YARDIN

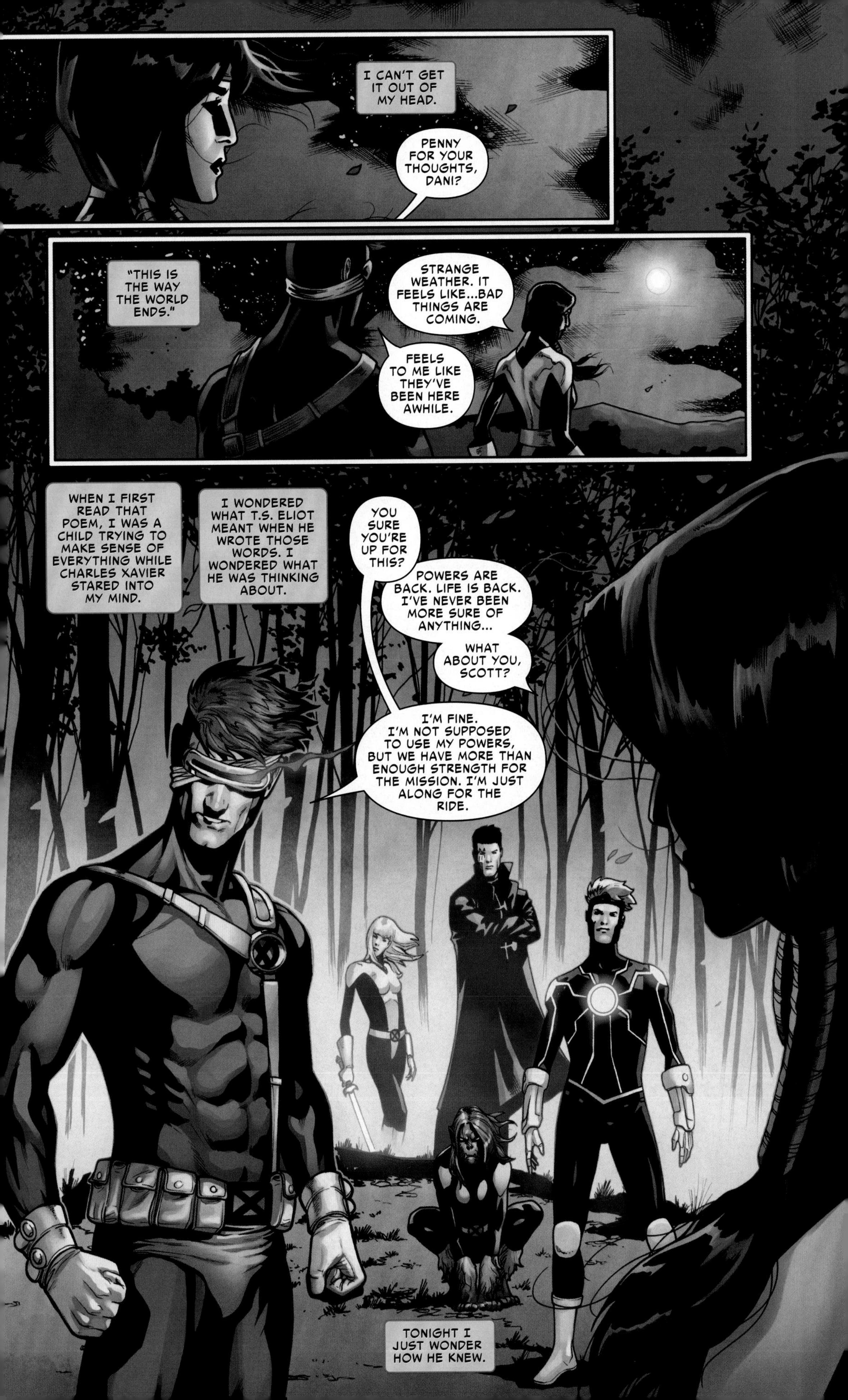

I CAN'T GET IT OUT OF MY HEAD.
PENNY FOR YOUR THOUGHTS, DANI?
"THIS IS THE WAY THE WORLD ENDS."
STRANGE WEATHER. IT FEELS LIKE...BAD THINGS ARE COMING.
FEELS TO ME LIKE THEY'VE BEEN HERE AWHILE.
WHEN I FIRST READ THAT POEM, I WAS A CHILD TRYING TO MAKE SENSE OF EVERYTHING WHILE CHARLES XAVIER STARED INTO MY MIND.
I WONDERED WHAT T.S. ELIOT MEANT WHEN HE WROTE THOSE WORDS. I WONDERED WHAT HE WAS THINKING ABOUT.
YOU SURE YOU'RE UP FOR THIS?
POWERS ARE BACK. LIFE IS BACK. I'VE NEVER BEEN MORE SURE OF ANYTHING...
WHAT ABOUT YOU, SCOTT?
I'M FINE. I'M NOT SUPPOSED TO USE MY POWERS, BUT WE HAVE MORE THAN ENOUGH STRENGTH FOR THE MISSION. I'M JUST ALONG FOR THE RIDE.
TONIGHT I JUST WONDER HOW HE KNEW.

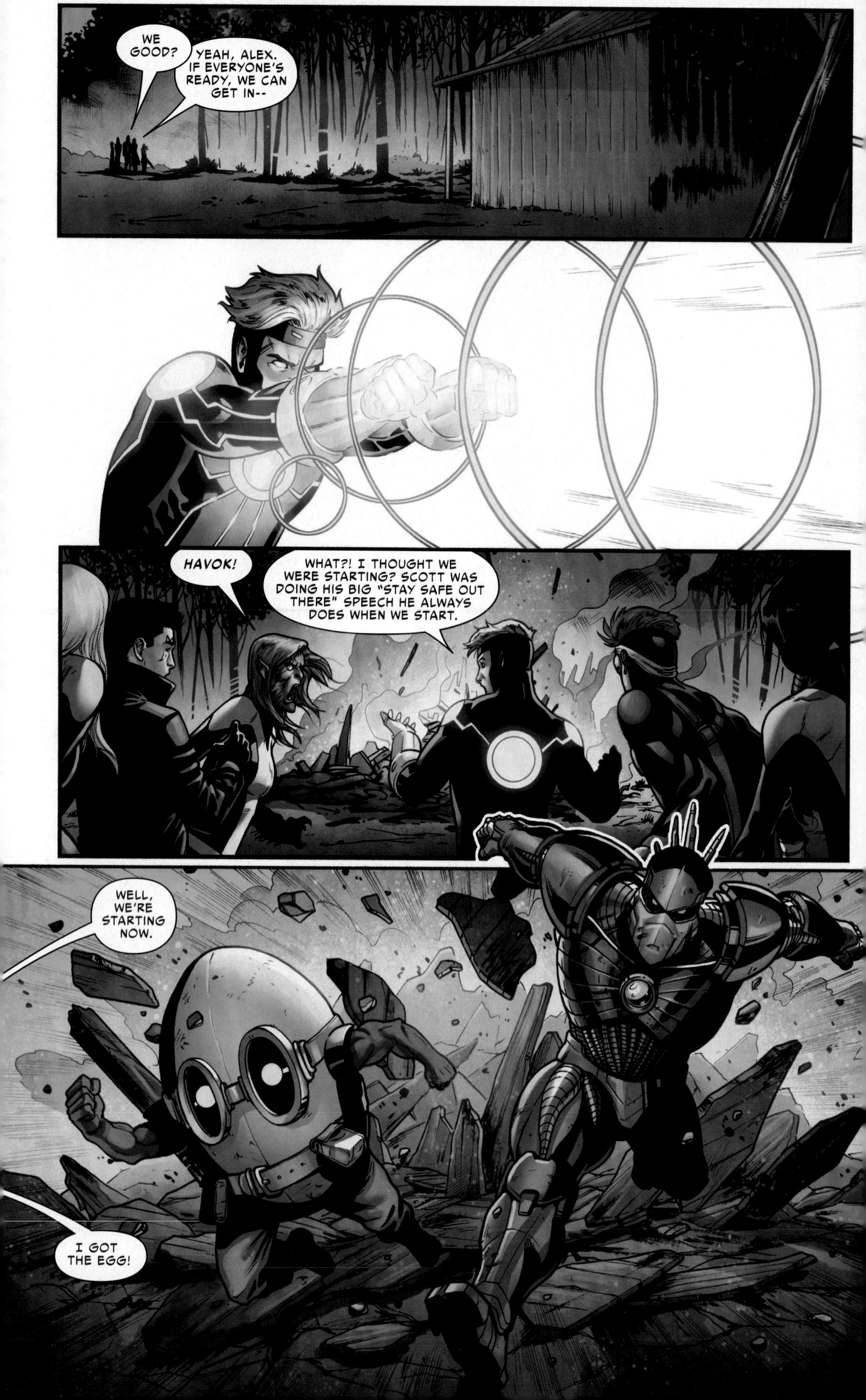
WE GOOD?
YEAH, ALEX. IF EVERYONE'S READY, WE CAN GET IN--
HAVOK!
WHAT?! I THOUGHT WE WERE STARTING? SCOTT WAS DOING HIS BIG "STAY SAFE OUT THERE" SPEECH HE ALWAYS DOES WHEN WE START.
WELL, WE'RE STARTING NOW.
I GOT THE EGG!

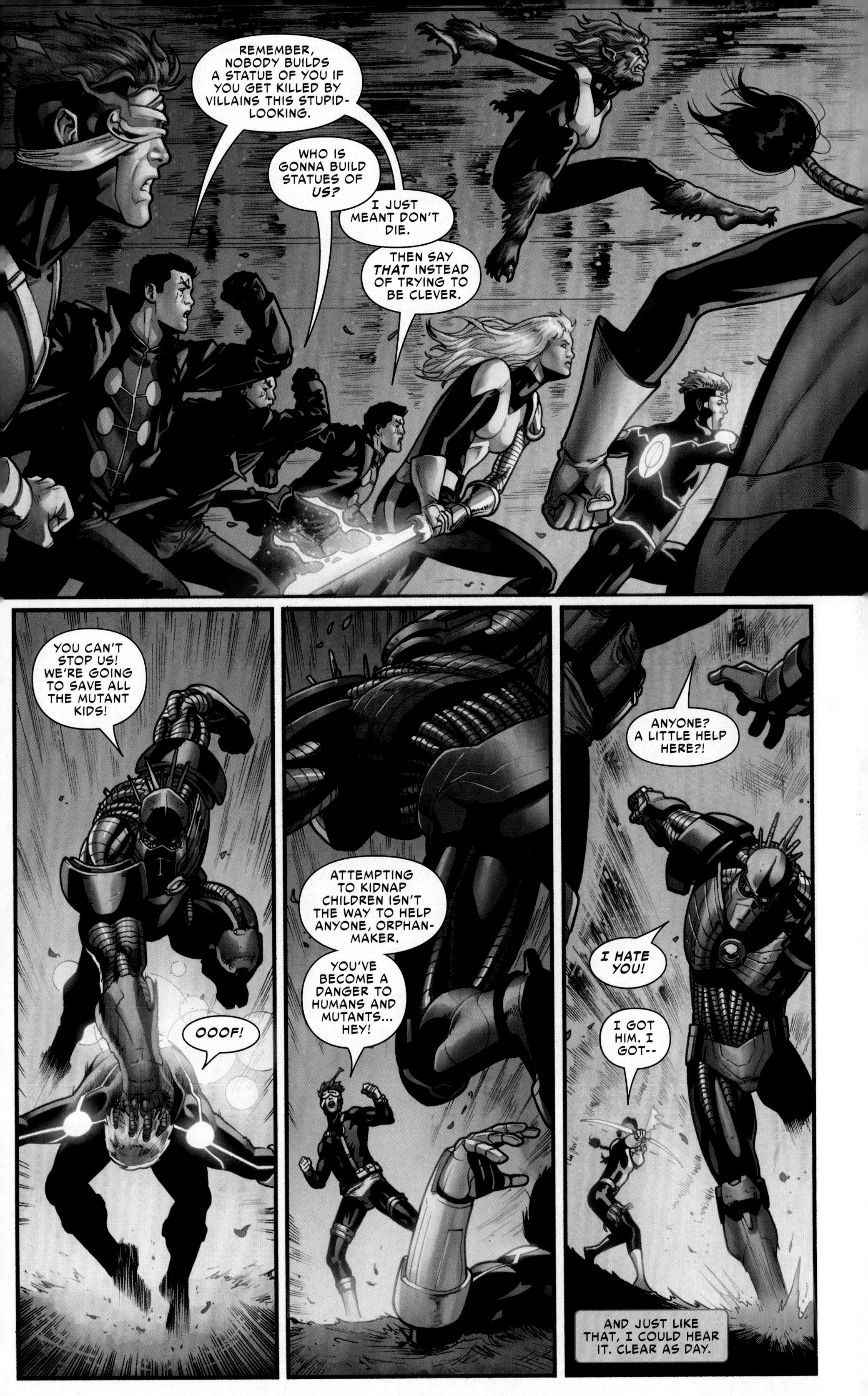
REMEMBER, NOBODY BUILDS A STATUE OF YOU IF YOU GET KILLED BY VILLAINS THIS STUPID-LOOKING.
WHO IS GONNA BUILD STATUES OF *US?*
I JUST MEANT DON'T DIE.
THEN SAY *THAT* INSTEAD OF TRYING TO BE CLEVER.
YOU CAN'T STOP US! WE'RE GOING TO SAVE ALL THE MUTANT KIDS!
OOOF!
ATTEMPTING TO KIDNAP CHILDREN ISN'T THE WAY TO HELP ANYONE, ORPHAN-MAKER.
YOU'VE BECOME A DANGER TO HUMANS AND MUTANTS... HEY!
ANYONE? A LITTLE HELP HERE?!
I HATE YOU!
I GOT HIM. I GOT--
AND JUST LIKE THAT, I COULD HEAR IT. CLEAR AS DAY.

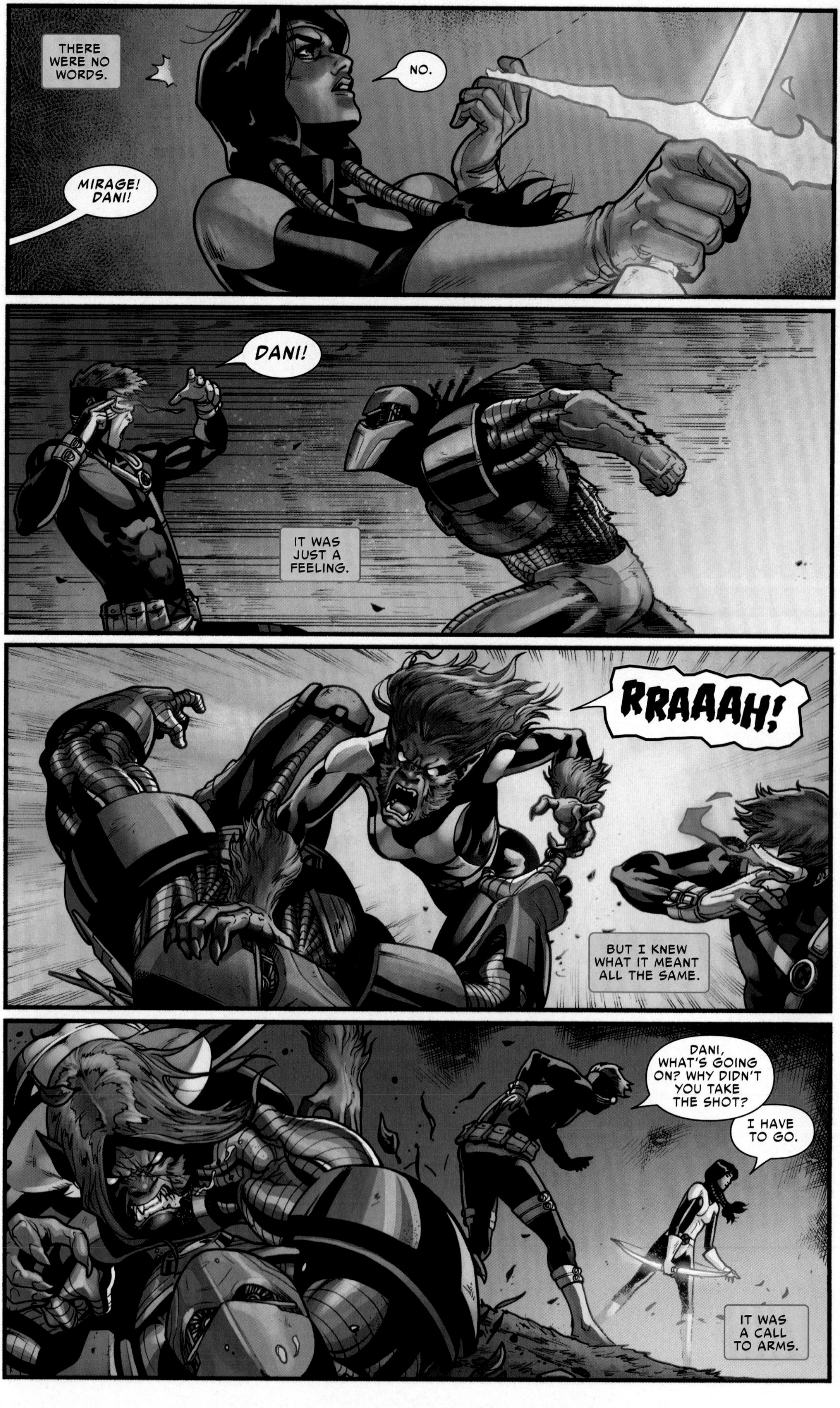
THERE WERE NO WORDS.
NO.
MIRAGE! DANI!
DANI!
IT WAS JUST A FEELING.
RRAAAH!
BUT I KNEW WHAT IT MEANT ALL THE SAME.
DANI, WHAT'S GOING ON? WHY DIDN'T YOU TAKE THE SHOT?
I HAVE TO GO.
IT WAS A CALL TO ARMS.

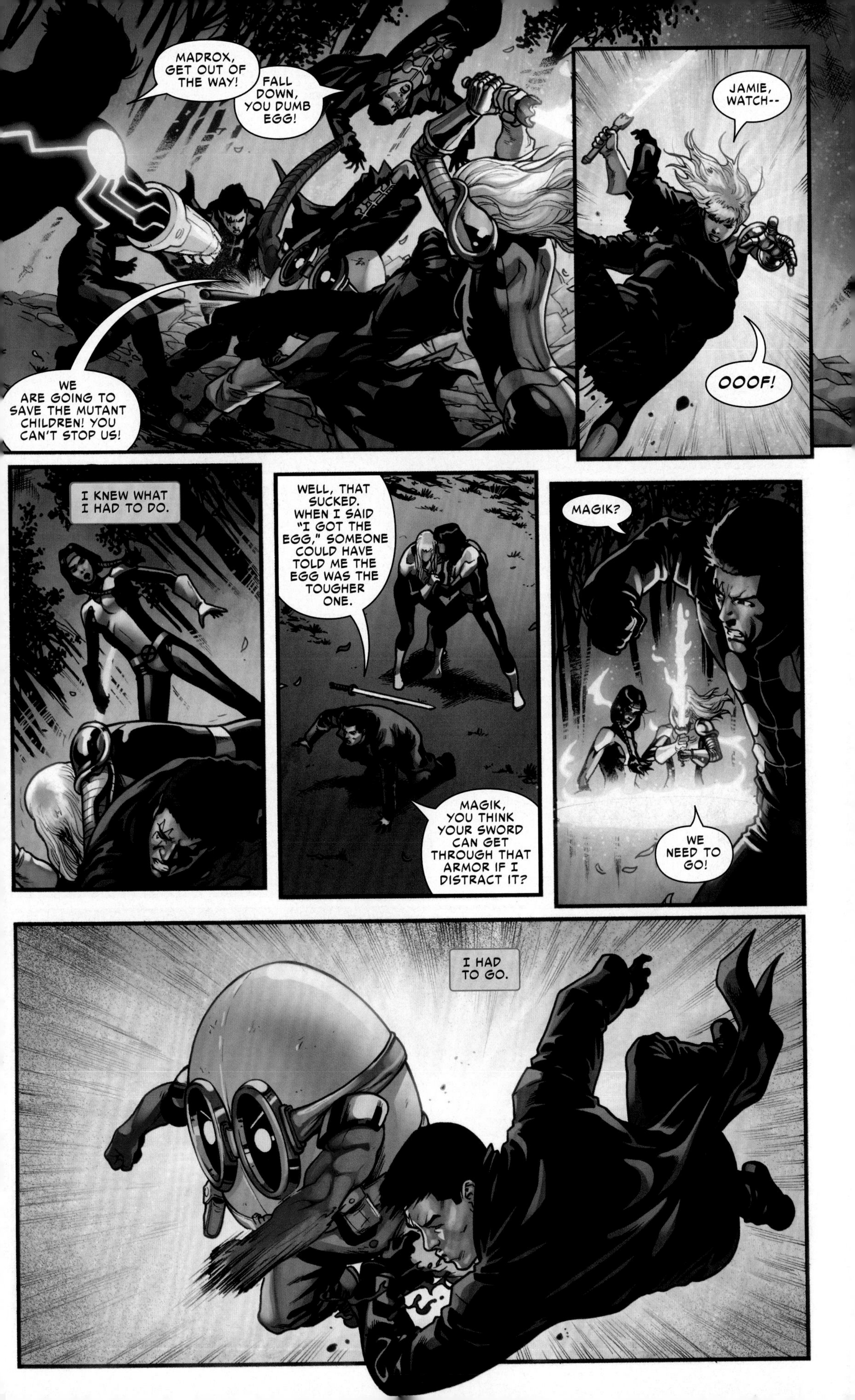

MADROX, GET OUT OF THE WAY!
FALL DOWN, YOU DUMB EGG!
WE ARE GOING TO SAVE THE MUTANT CHILDREN! YOU CAN'T STOP US!
JAMIE, WATCH--
OOOF!
I KNEW WHAT I HAD TO DO.
WELL, THAT SUCKED. WHEN I SAID "I GOT THE EGG," SOMEONE COULD HAVE TOLD ME THE EGG WAS THE TOUGHER ONE.
MAGIK, YOU THINK YOUR SWORD CAN GET THROUGH THAT ARMOR IF I DISTRACT IT?
MAGIK?
WE NEED TO GO!
I HAD TO GO.

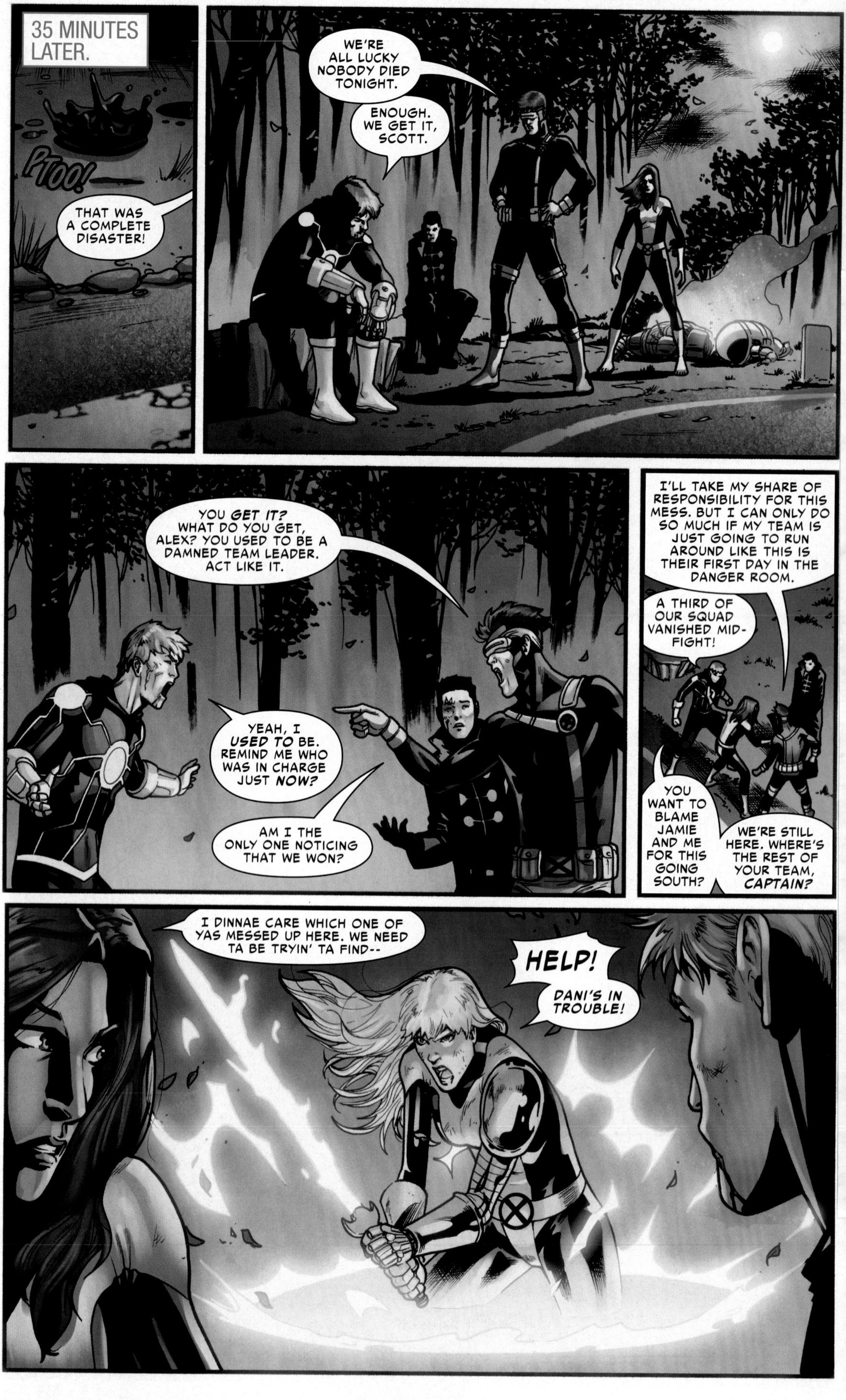
35 MINUTES LATER.
PTOO!
THAT WAS A COMPLETE DISASTER!
WE'RE ALL LUCKY NOBODY DIED TONIGHT.
ENOUGH. WE GET IT, SCOTT.
YOU GET IT? WHAT DO YOU GET, ALEX? YOU USED TO BE A DAMNED TEAM LEADER. ACT LIKE IT.
YEAH, I USED TO BE. REMIND ME WHO WAS IN CHARGE JUST NOW?
AM I THE ONLY ONE NOTICING THAT WE WON?
I'LL TAKE MY SHARE OF RESPONSIBILITY FOR THIS MESS. BUT I CAN ONLY DO SO MUCH IF MY TEAM IS JUST GOING TO RUN AROUND LIKE THIS IS THEIR FIRST DAY IN THE DANGER ROOM.
A THIRD OF OUR SQUAD VANISHED MID-FIGHT!
YOU WANT TO BLAME JAMIE AND ME FOR THIS GOING SOUTH?
WE'RE STILL HERE. WHERE'S THE REST OF YOUR TEAM, CAPTAIN?
I DINNAE CARE WHICH ONE OF YAS MESSED UP HERE. WE NEED TA BE TRYIN' TA FIND--
HELP!
DANI'S IN TROUBLE!

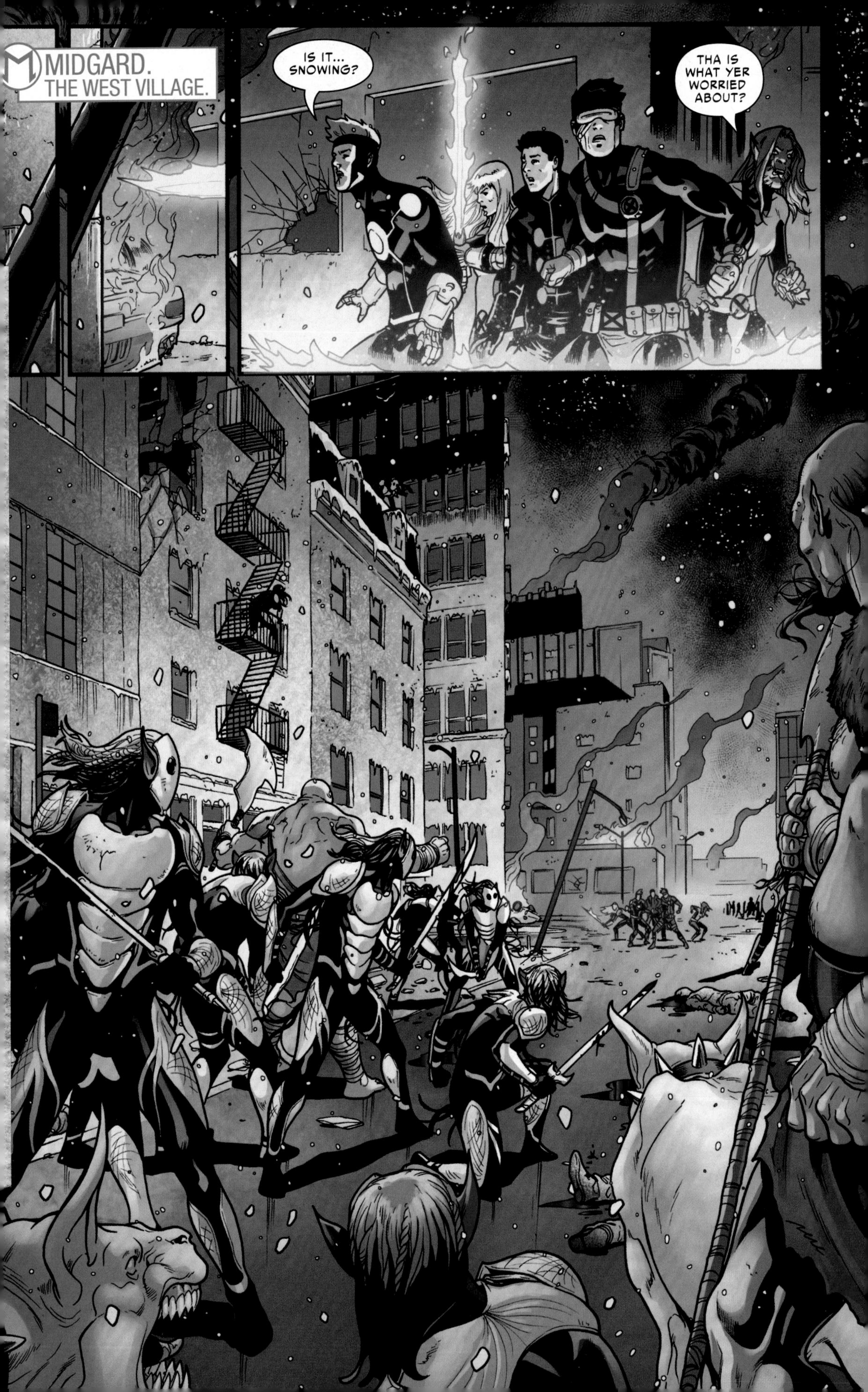
MIDGARD.
THE WEST VILLAGE.
IS IT... SNOWING?
THA IS WHAT YER WORRIED ABOUT?

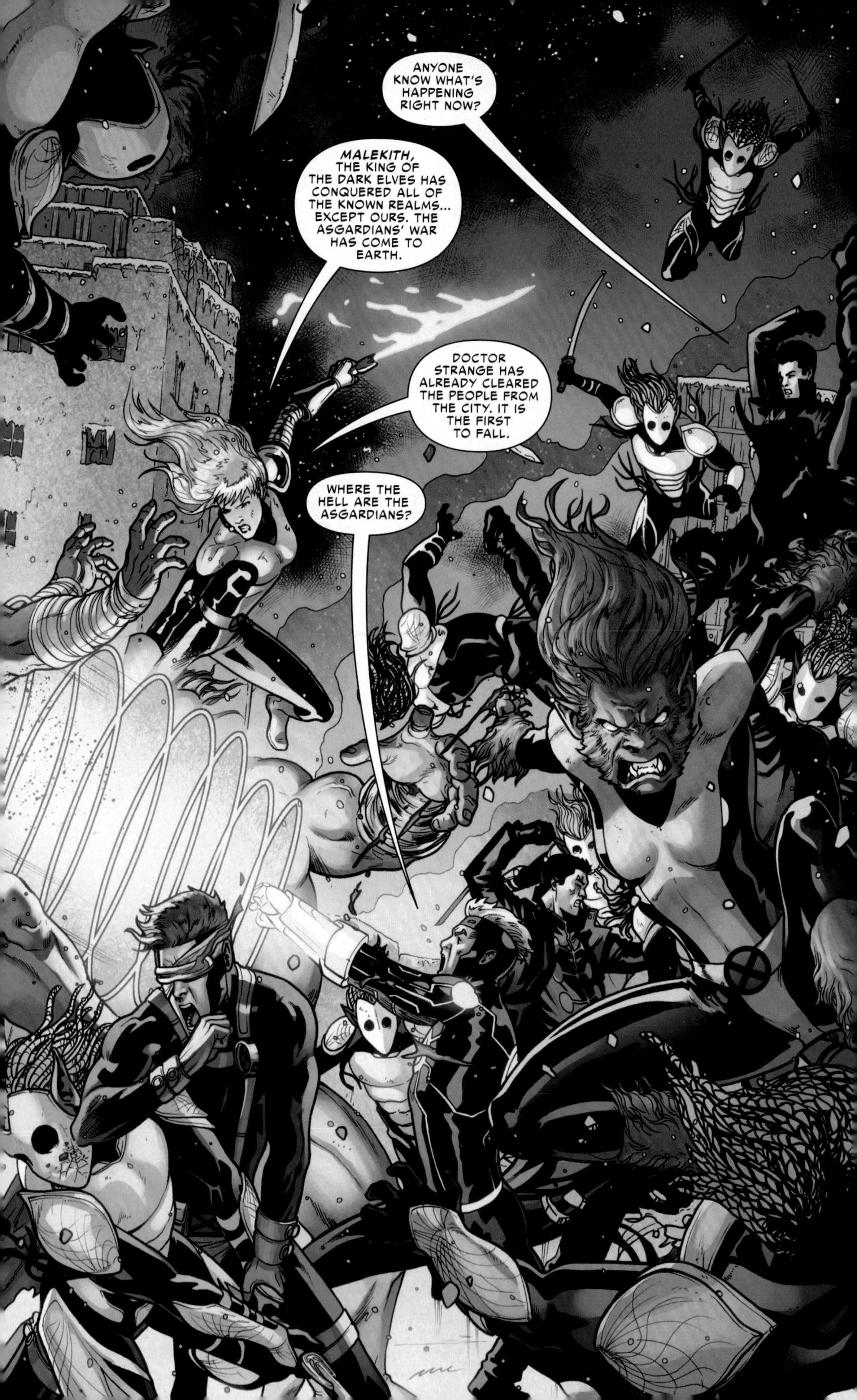
ANYONE KNOW WHAT'S HAPPENING RIGHT NOW?
MALEKITH, THE KING OF THE DARK ELVES HAS CONQUERED ALL OF THE KNOWN REALMS... EXCEPT OURS. THE ASGARDIANS' WAR HAS COME TO EARTH.
DOCTOR STRANGE HAS ALREADY CLEARED THE PEOPLE FROM THE CITY. IT IS THE FIRST TO FALL.
WHERE THE HELL ARE THE ASGARDIANS?

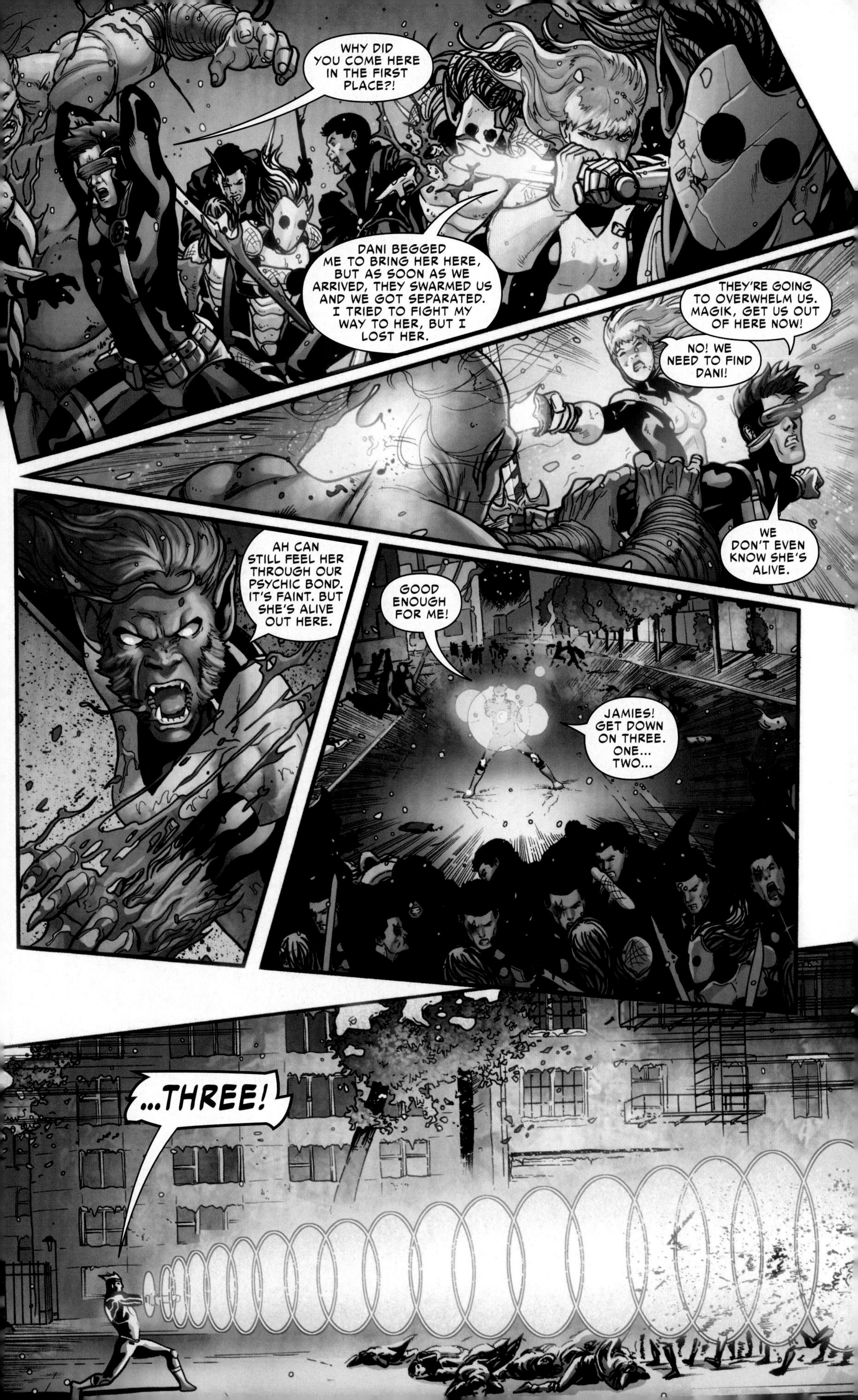
WHY DID YOU COME HERE IN THE FIRST PLACE?!
DANI BEGGED ME TO BRING HER HERE, BUT AS SOON AS WE ARRIVED, THEY SWARMED US AND WE GOT SEPARATED. I TRIED TO FIGHT MY WAY TO HER, BUT I LOST HER.
THEY'RE GOING TO OVERWHELM US. MAGIK, GET US OUT OF HERE NOW!
NO! WE NEED TO FIND DANI!
WE DON'T EVEN KNOW SHE'S ALIVE.
AH CAN STILL FEEL HER THROUGH OUR PSYCHIC BOND. IT'S FAINT. BUT SHE'S ALIVE OUT HERE.
GOOD ENOUGH FOR ME!
JAMIES! GET DOWN ON THREE. ONE... TWO...
...THREE!

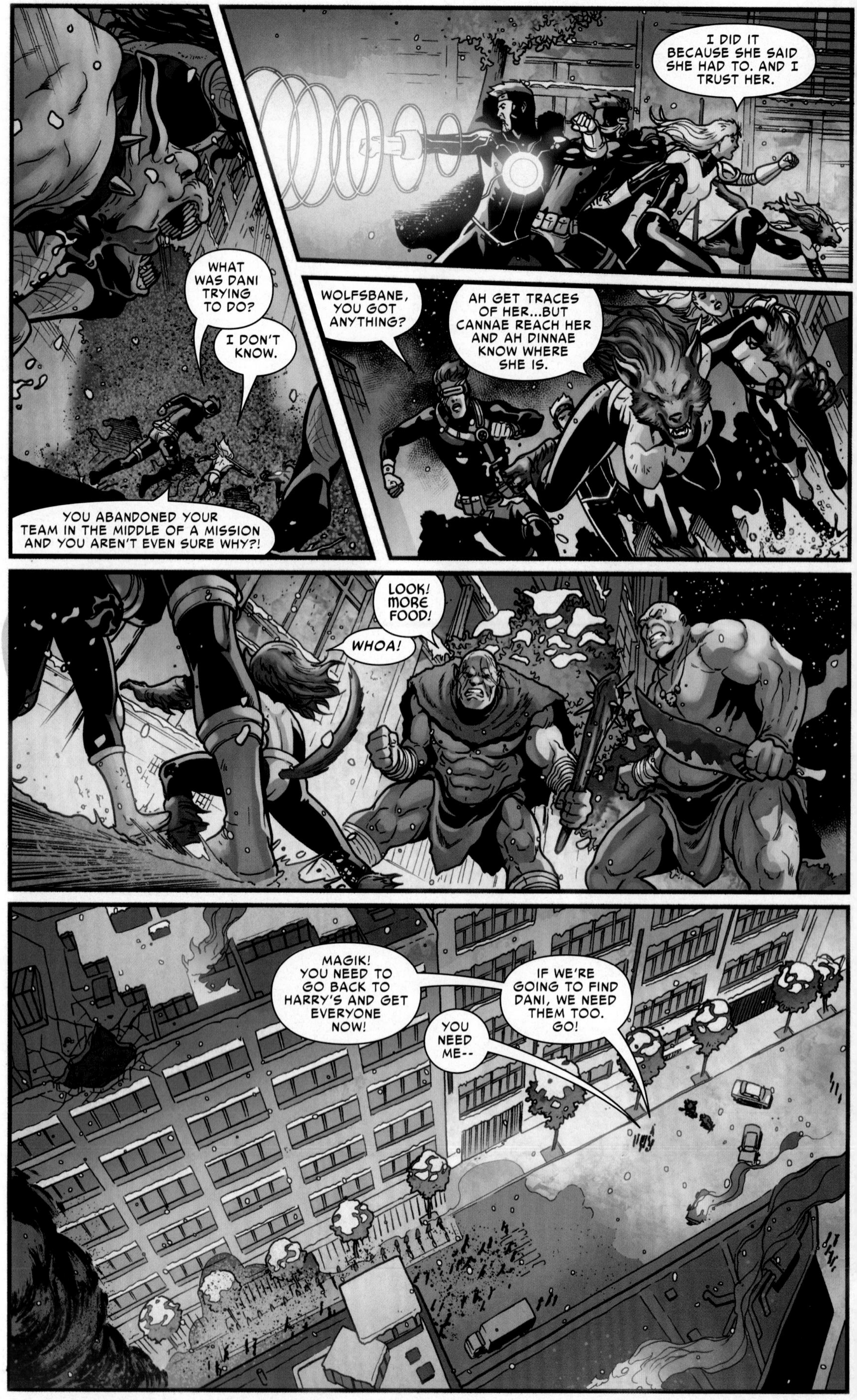
I DID IT BECAUSE SHE SAID SHE HAD TO. AND I TRUST HER.
WHAT WAS DANI TRYING TO DO?
I DON'T KNOW.
YOU ABANDONED YOUR TEAM IN THE MIDDLE OF A MISSION AND YOU AREN'T EVEN SURE WHY?!
WOLFSBANE, YOU GOT ANYTHING?
AH GET TRACES OF HER...BUT CANNAE REACH HER AND AH DINNAE KNOW WHERE SHE IS.
LOOK! MORE FOOD!
WHOA!
MAGIK! YOU NEED TO GO BACK TO HARRY'S AND GET EVERYONE NOW!
YOU NEED ME--
IF WE'RE GOING TO FIND DANI, WE NEED THEM TOO. GO!

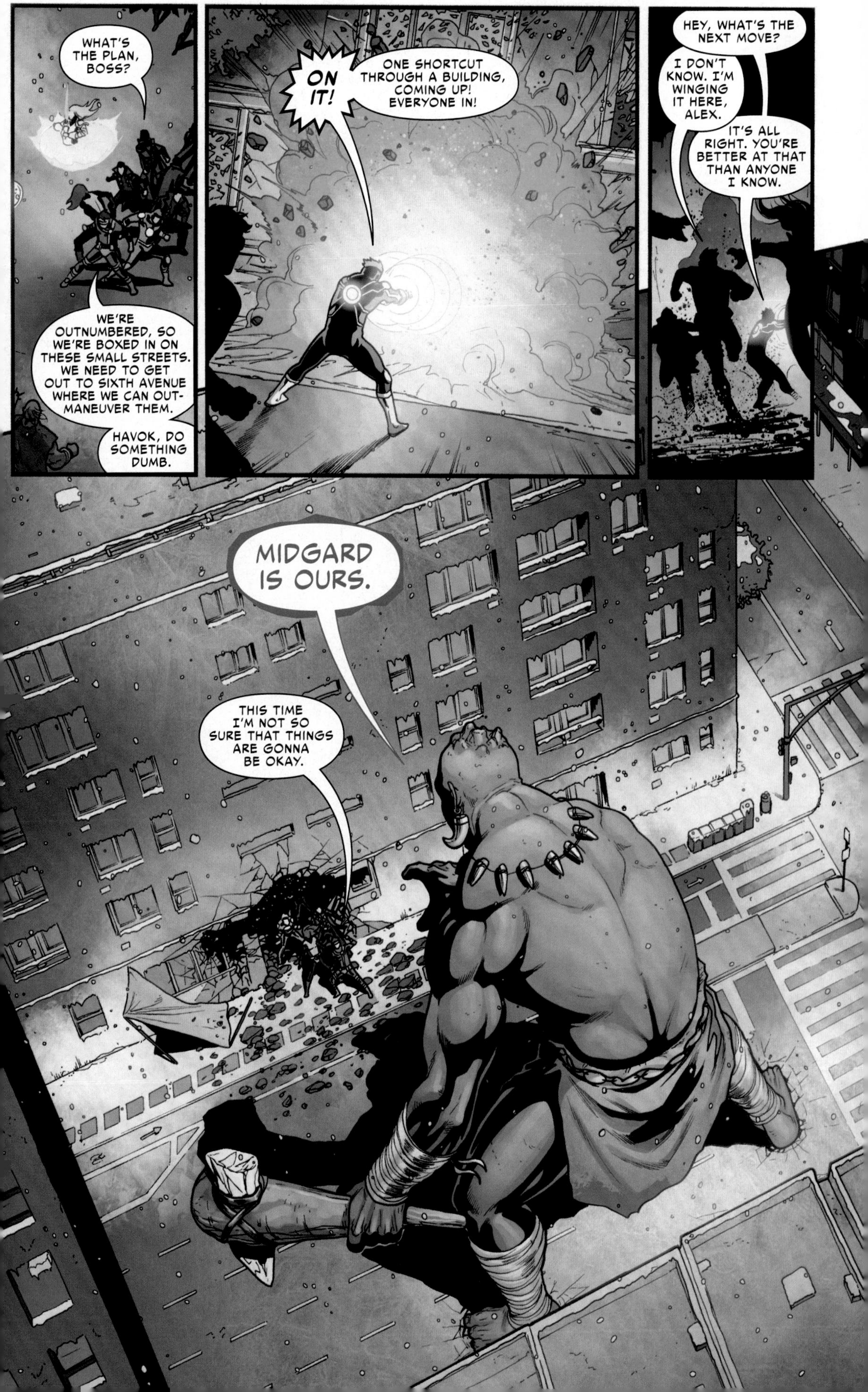
WHAT'S THE PLAN, BOSS?
WE'RE OUTNUMBERED, SO WE'RE BOXED IN ON THESE SMALL STREETS. WE NEED TO GET OUT TO SIXTH AVENUE WHERE WE CAN OUT-MANEUVER THEM.
HAVOK, DO SOMETHING DUMB.
ON IT!
ONE SHORTCUT THROUGH A BUILDING, COMING UP! EVERYONE IN!
HEY, WHAT'S THE NEXT MOVE?
I DON'T KNOW. I'M WINGING IT HERE, ALEX.
IT'S ALL RIGHT. YOU'RE BETTER AT THAT THAN ANYONE I KNOW.
MIDGARD IS OURS.
THIS TIME I'M NOT SO SURE THAT THINGS ARE GONNA BE OKAY.

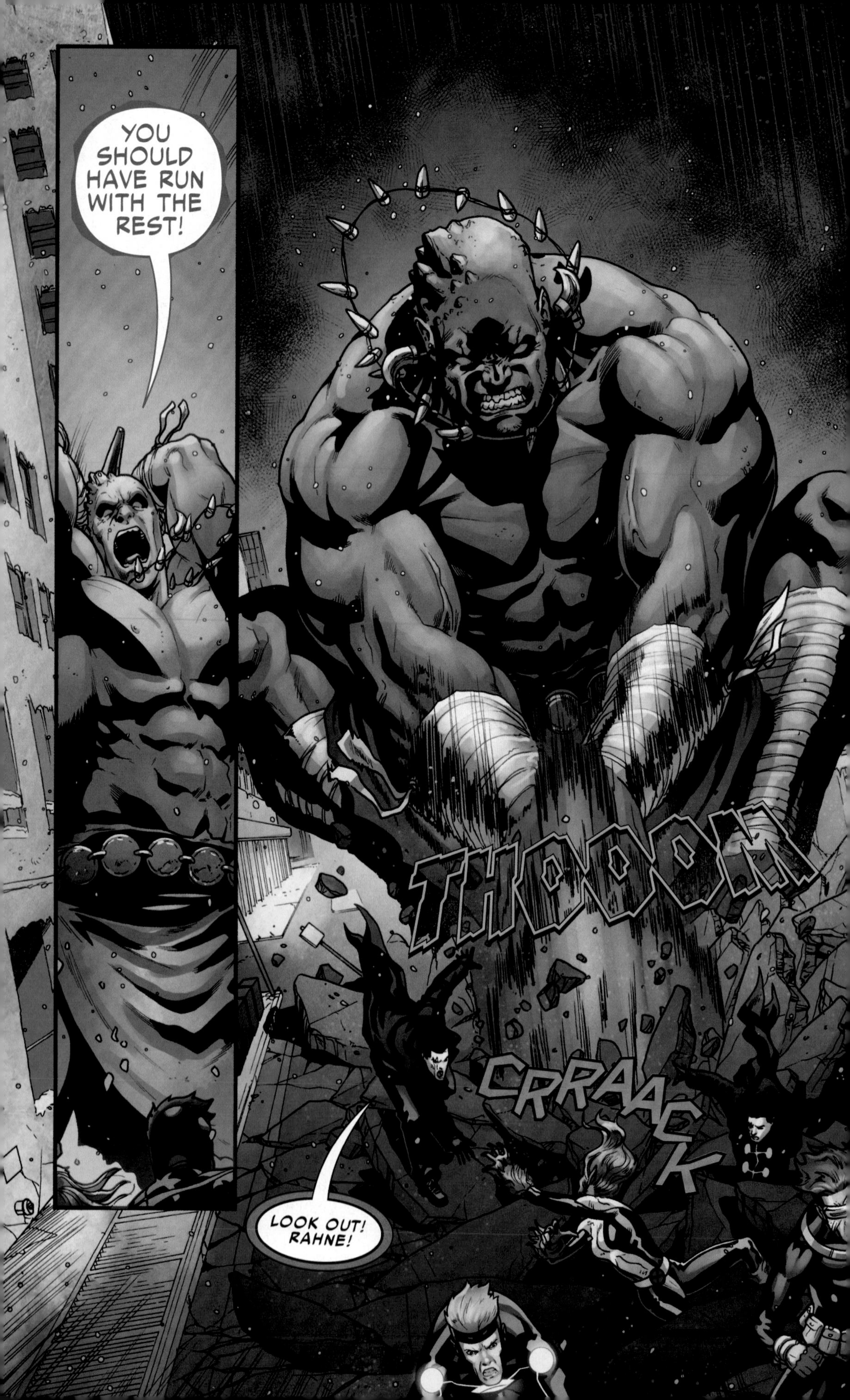
YOU SHOULD HAVE RUN WITH THE REST!
THOOOM
CRRAACK
LOOK OUT! RAHNE!

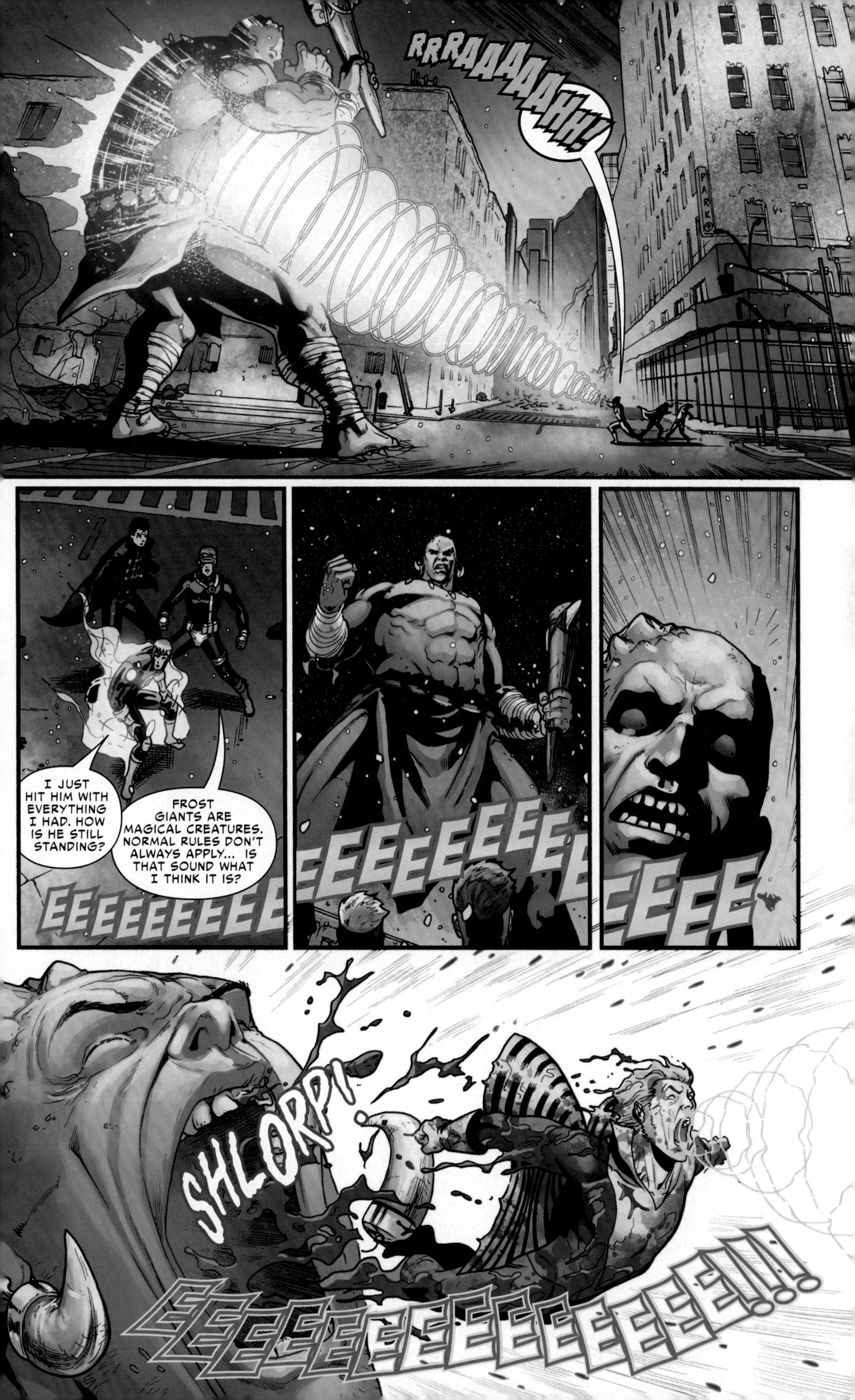
RRRAAAAAAHH!
PARK
I JUST HIT HIM WITH EVERYTHING I HAD. HOW IS HE STILL STANDING?
FROST GIANTS ARE MAGICAL CREATURES. NORMAL RULES DON'T ALWAYS APPLY... IS THAT SOUND WHAT I THINK IT IS?
EEEEEEEEEEEEEEEEEEEEEEEEEEEEE
SHLORP!
EEEEEEEEEEEEEEEEEEE!!!

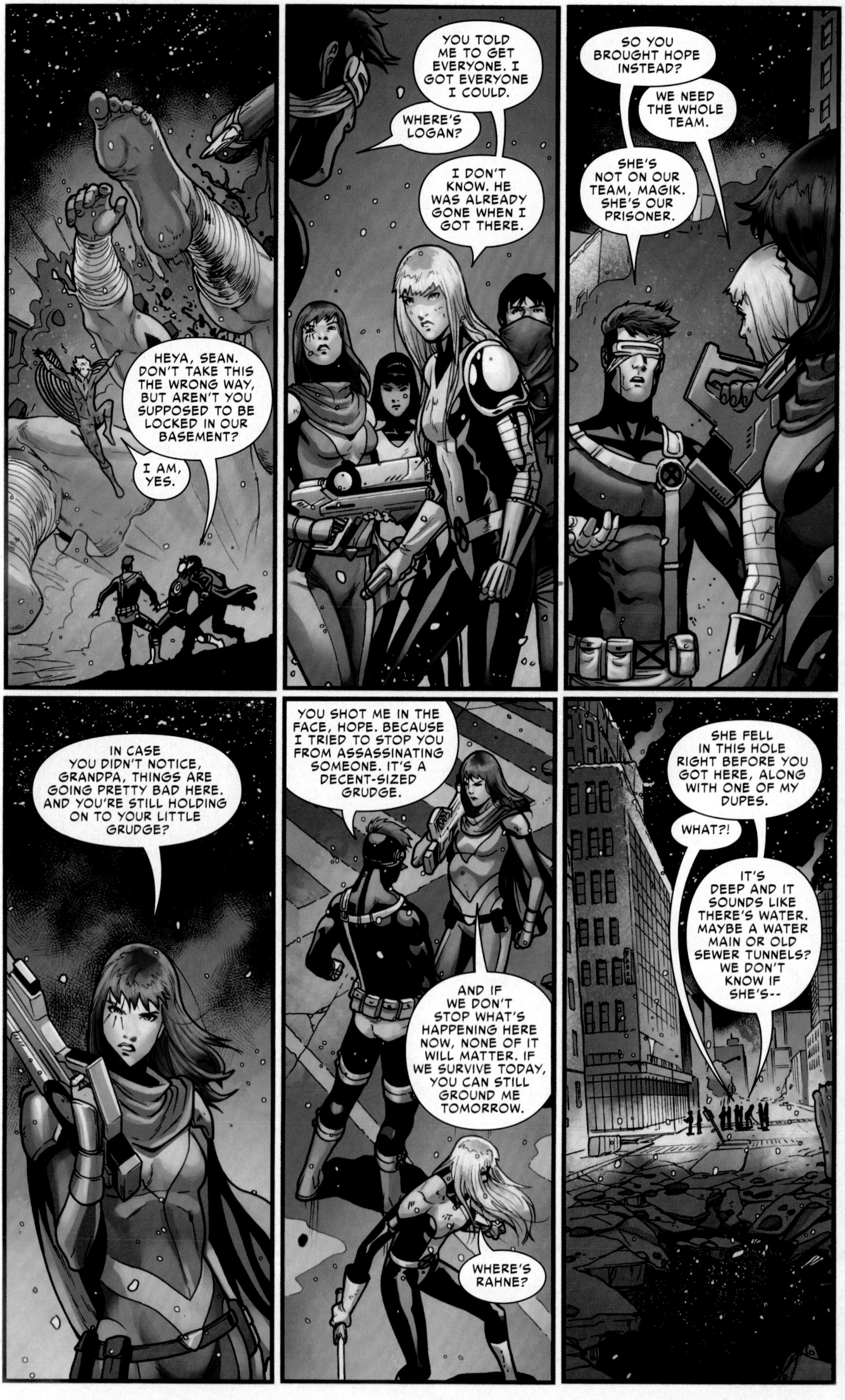
HEYA, SEAN. DON'T TAKE THIS THE WRONG WAY, BUT AREN'T YOU SUPPOSED TO BE LOCKED IN OUR BASEMENT?
I AM, YES.
YOU TOLD ME TO GET EVERYONE. I GOT EVERYONE I COULD.
WHERE'S LOGAN?
I DON'T KNOW. HE WAS ALREADY GONE WHEN I GOT THERE.
SO YOU BROUGHT HOPE INSTEAD?
WE NEED THE WHOLE TEAM.
SHE'S NOT ON OUR TEAM, MAGIK. SHE'S OUR PRISONER.
IN CASE YOU DIDN'T NOTICE, GRANDPA, THINGS ARE GOING PRETTY BAD HERE. AND YOU'RE STILL HOLDING ON TO YOUR LITTLE GRUDGE?
YOU SHOT ME IN THE FACE, HOPE. BECAUSE I TRIED TO STOP YOU FROM ASSASSINATING SOMEONE. IT'S A DECENT-SIZED GRUDGE.
AND IF WE DON'T STOP WHAT'S HAPPENING HERE NOW, NONE OF IT WILL MATTER. IF WE SURVIVE TODAY, YOU CAN STILL GROUND ME TOMORROW.
WHERE'S RAHNE?
SHE FELL IN THIS HOLE RIGHT BEFORE YOU GOT HERE, ALONG WITH ONE OF MY DUPES.
WHAT?!
IT'S DEEP AND IT SOUNDS LIKE THERE'S WATER. MAYBE A WATER MAIN OR OLD SEWER TUNNELS? WE DON'T KNOW IF SHE'S--

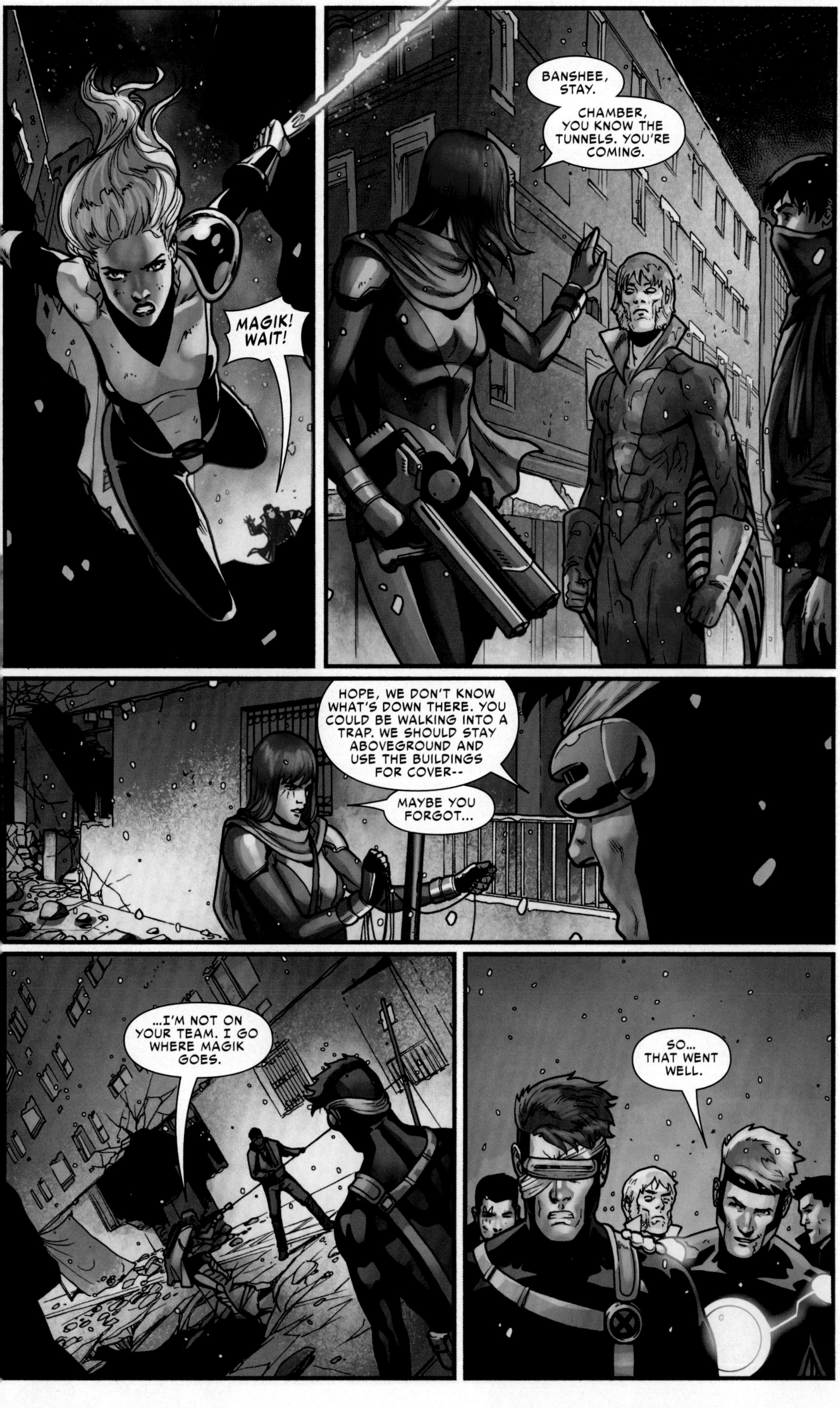
MAGIK! WAIT!
BANSHEE, STAY.
CHAMBER, YOU KNOW THE TUNNELS. YOU'RE COMING.
HOPE, WE DON'T KNOW WHAT'S DOWN THERE. YOU COULD BE WALKING INTO A TRAP. WE SHOULD STAY ABOVEGROUND AND USE THE BUILDINGS FOR COVER--
MAYBE YOU FORGOT...
...I'M NOT ON YOUR TEAM. I GO WHERE MAGIK GOES.
SO... THAT WENT WELL.

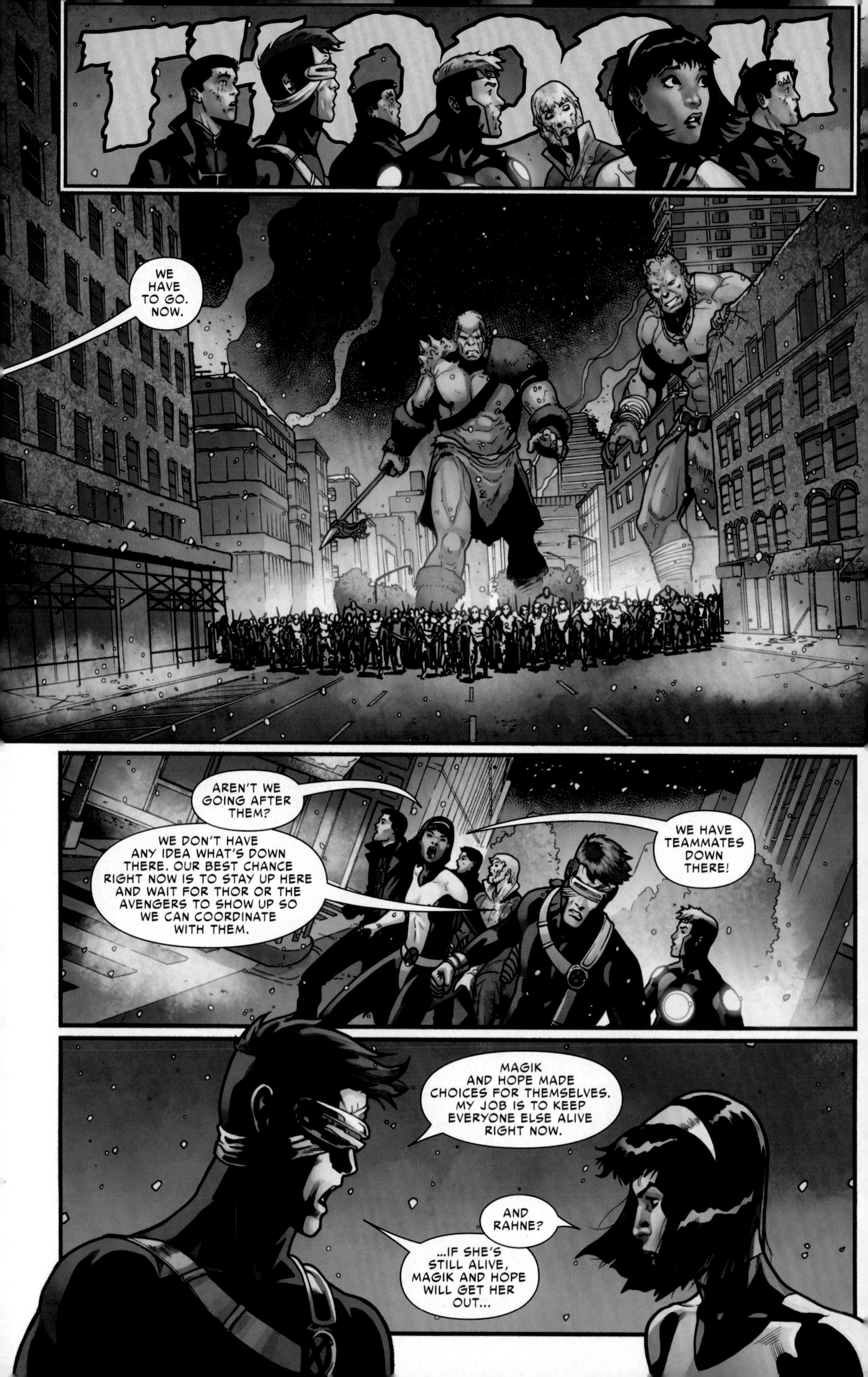
WE HAVE TO GO. NOW.
AREN'T WE GOING AFTER THEM?
WE DON'T HAVE ANY IDEA WHAT'S DOWN THERE. OUR BEST CHANCE RIGHT NOW IS TO STAY UP HERE AND WAIT FOR THOR OR THE AVENGERS TO SHOW UP SO WE CAN COORDINATE WITH THEM.
WE HAVE TEAMMATES DOWN THERE!
MAGIK AND HOPE MADE CHOICES FOR THEMSELVES. MY JOB IS TO KEEP EVERYONE ELSE ALIVE RIGHT NOW.
AND RAHNE?
...IF SHE'S STILL ALIVE, MAGIK AND HOPE WILL GET HER OUT...

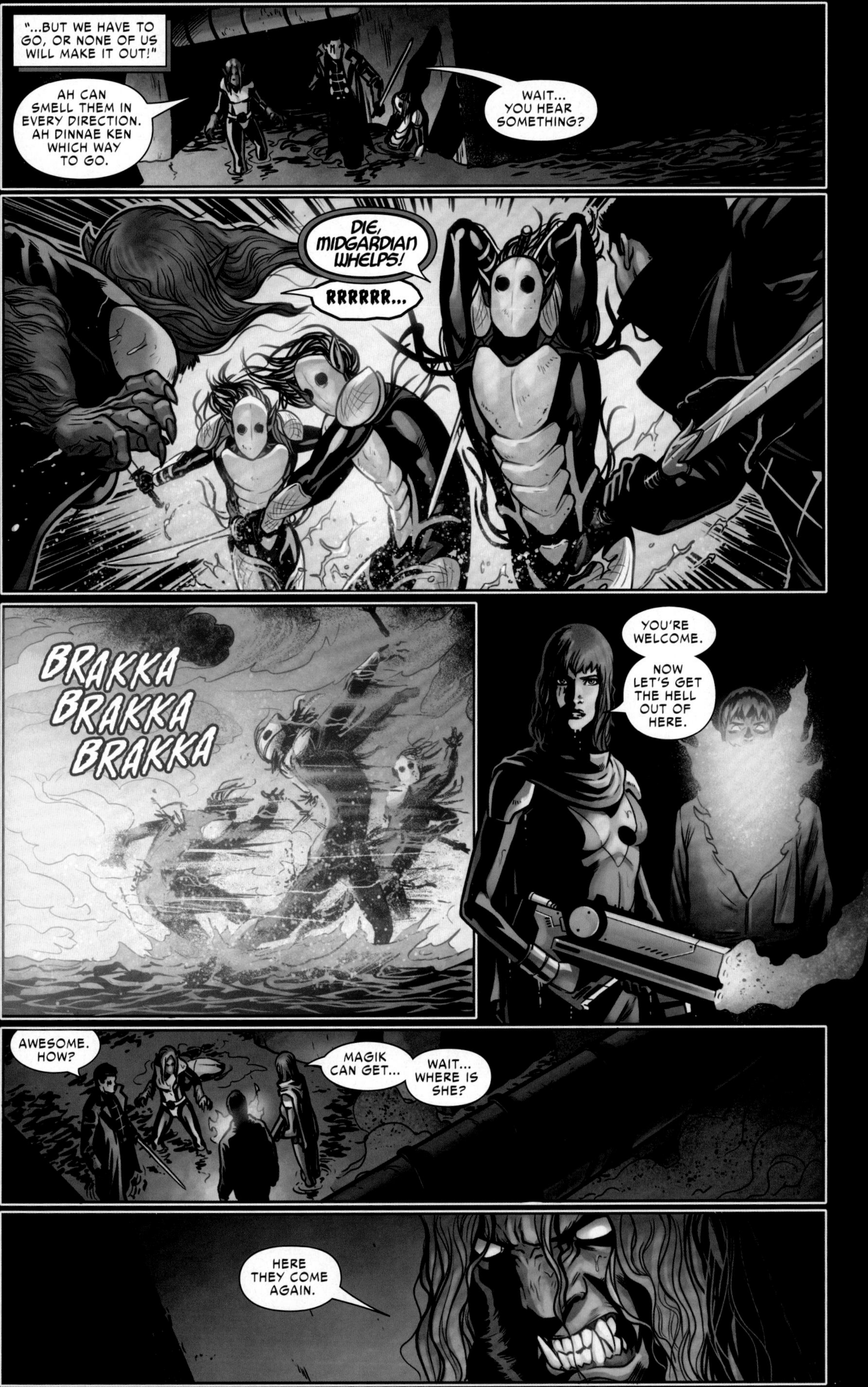
"...BUT WE HAVE TO GO, OR NONE OF US WILL MAKE IT OUT!"
AH CAN SMELL THEM IN EVERY DIRECTION. AH DINNAE KEN WHICH WAY TO GO.
WAIT... YOU HEAR SOMETHING?
DIE, MIDGARDIAN WHELPS!
RRRRRR...
BRAKKA BRAKKA BRAKKA
YOU'RE WELCOME.
NOW LET'S GET THE HELL OUT OF HERE.
AWESOME. HOW?
MAGIK CAN GET...
WAIT... WHERE IS SHE?
HERE THEY COME AGAIN.

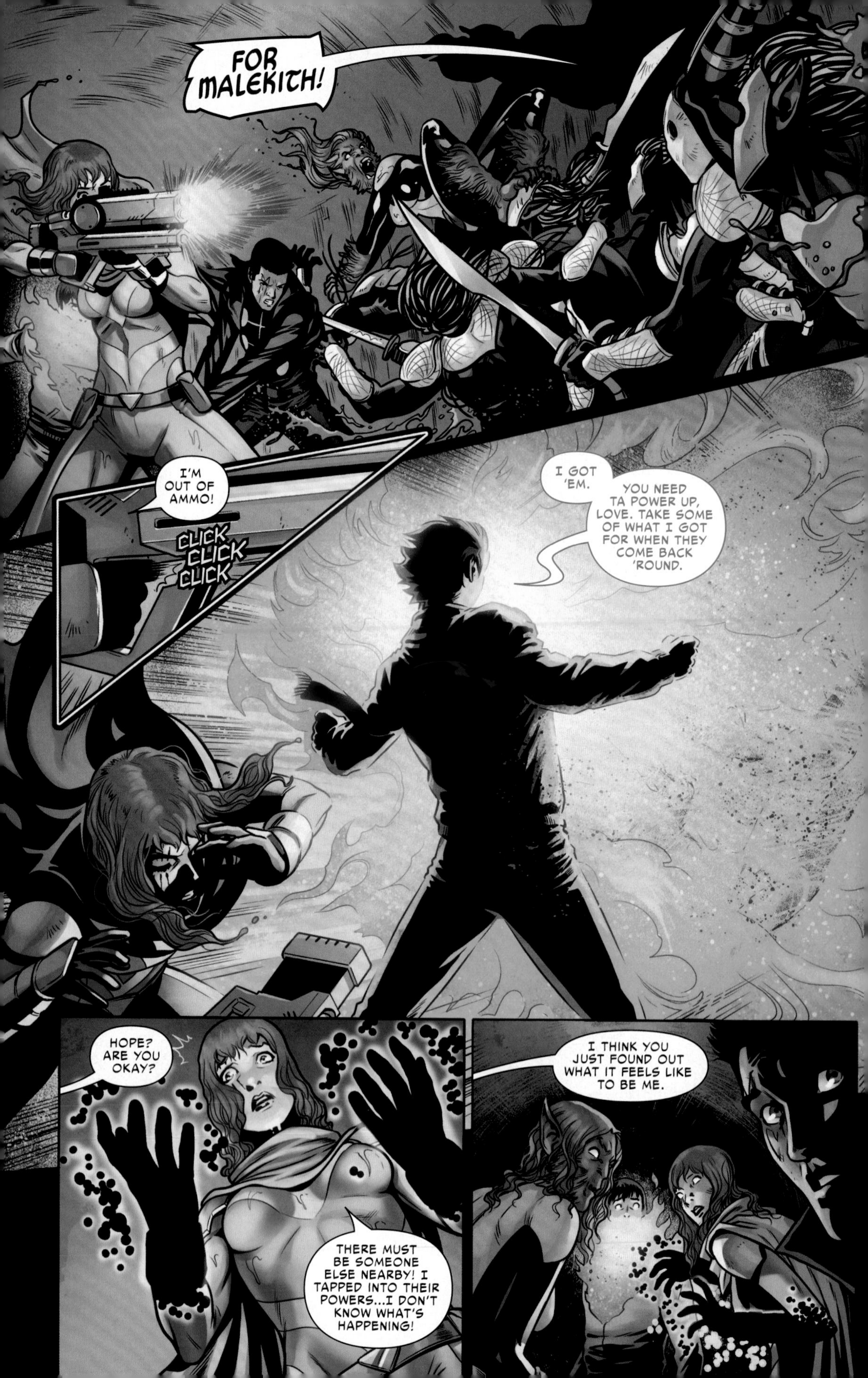
FOR MALEKITH!
I'M OUT OF AMMO!
CLICK CLICK CLICK
I GOT 'EM.
YOU NEED TA POWER UP, LOVE. TAKE SOME OF WHAT I GOT FOR WHEN THEY COME BACK 'ROUND.
HOPE? ARE YOU OKAY?
THERE MUST BE SOMEONE ELSE NEARBY! I TAPPED INTO THEIR POWERS...I DON'T KNOW WHAT'S HAPPENING!
I THINK YOU JUST FOUND OUT WHAT IT FEELS LIKE TO BE ME.

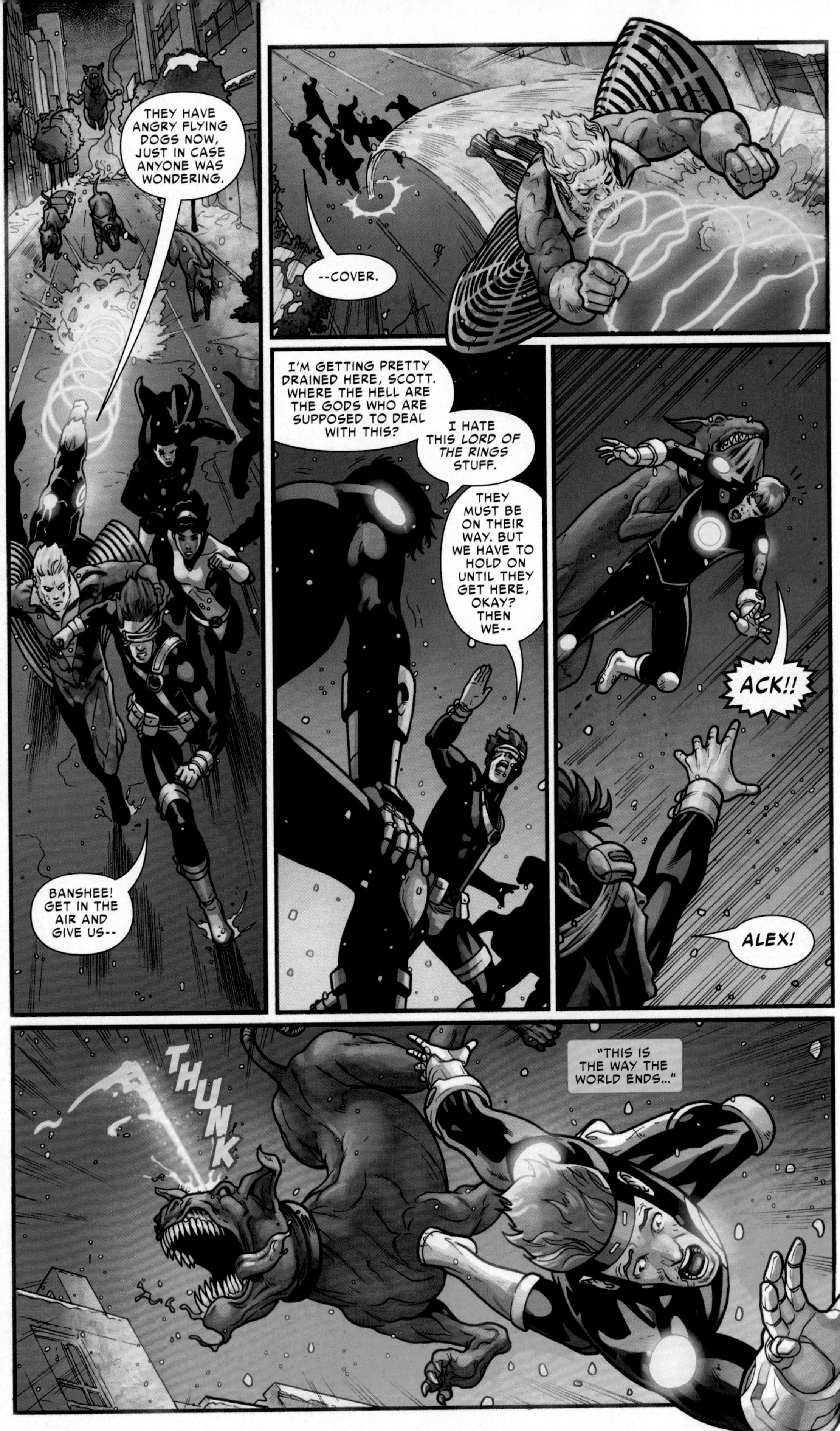
THEY HAVE ANGRY FLYING DOGS NOW, JUST IN CASE ANYONE WAS WONDERING.
BANSHEE! GET IN THE AIR AND GIVE US--
--COVER.
I'M GETTING PRETTY DRAINED HERE, SCOTT. WHERE THE HELL ARE THE GODS WHO ARE SUPPOSED TO DEAL WITH THIS?
I HATE THIS LORD OF THE RINGS STUFF.
THEY MUST BE ON THEIR WAY. BUT WE HAVE TO HOLD ON UNTIL THEY GET HERE, OKAY? THEN WE--
ACK!!
ALEX!
THUNK
"THIS IS THE WAY THE WORLD ENDS..."

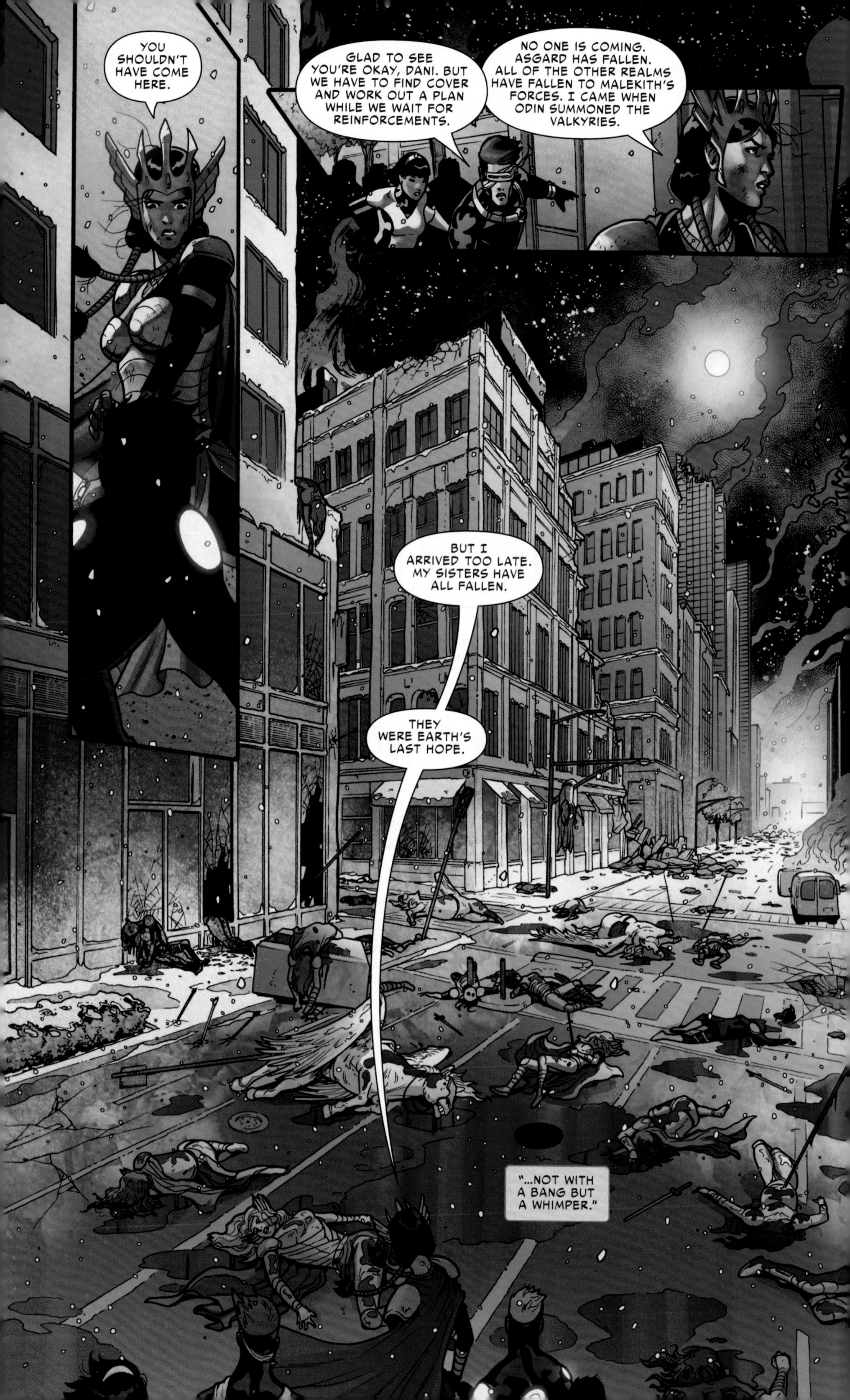
YOU SHOULDN'T HAVE COME HERE.
GLAD TO SEE YOU'RE OKAY, DANI. BUT WE HAVE TO FIND COVER AND WORK OUT A PLAN WHILE WE WAIT FOR REINFORCEMENTS.
NO ONE IS COMING. ASGARD HAS FALLEN. ALL OF THE OTHER REALMS HAVE FALLEN TO MALEKITH'S FORCES. I CAME WHEN ODIN SUMMONED THE VALKYRIES.
BUT I ARRIVED TOO LATE. MY SISTERS HAVE ALL FALLEN.
THEY WERE EARTH'S LAST HOPE.
"...NOT WITH A BANG BUT A WHIMPER."

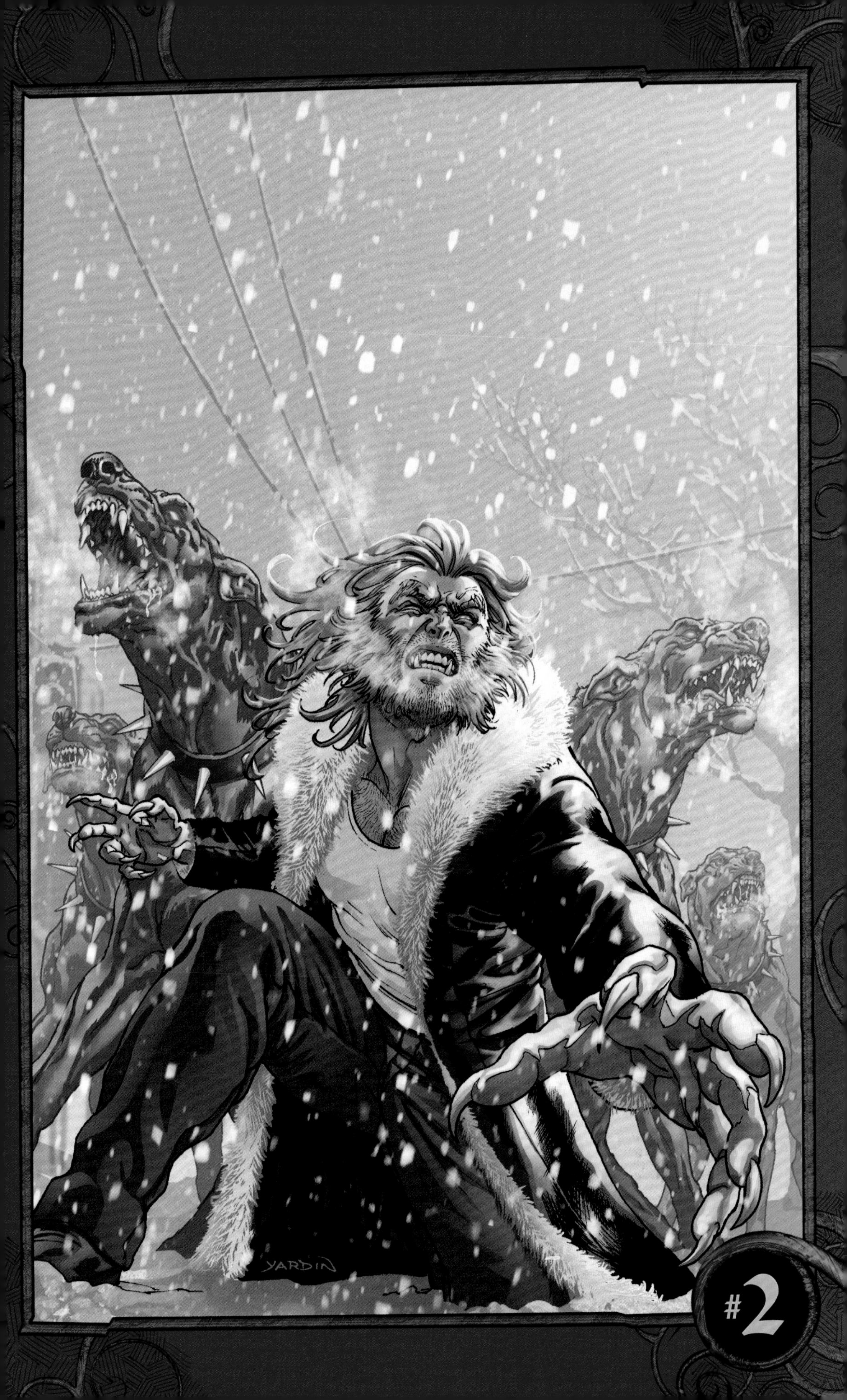
YARDIN
#2

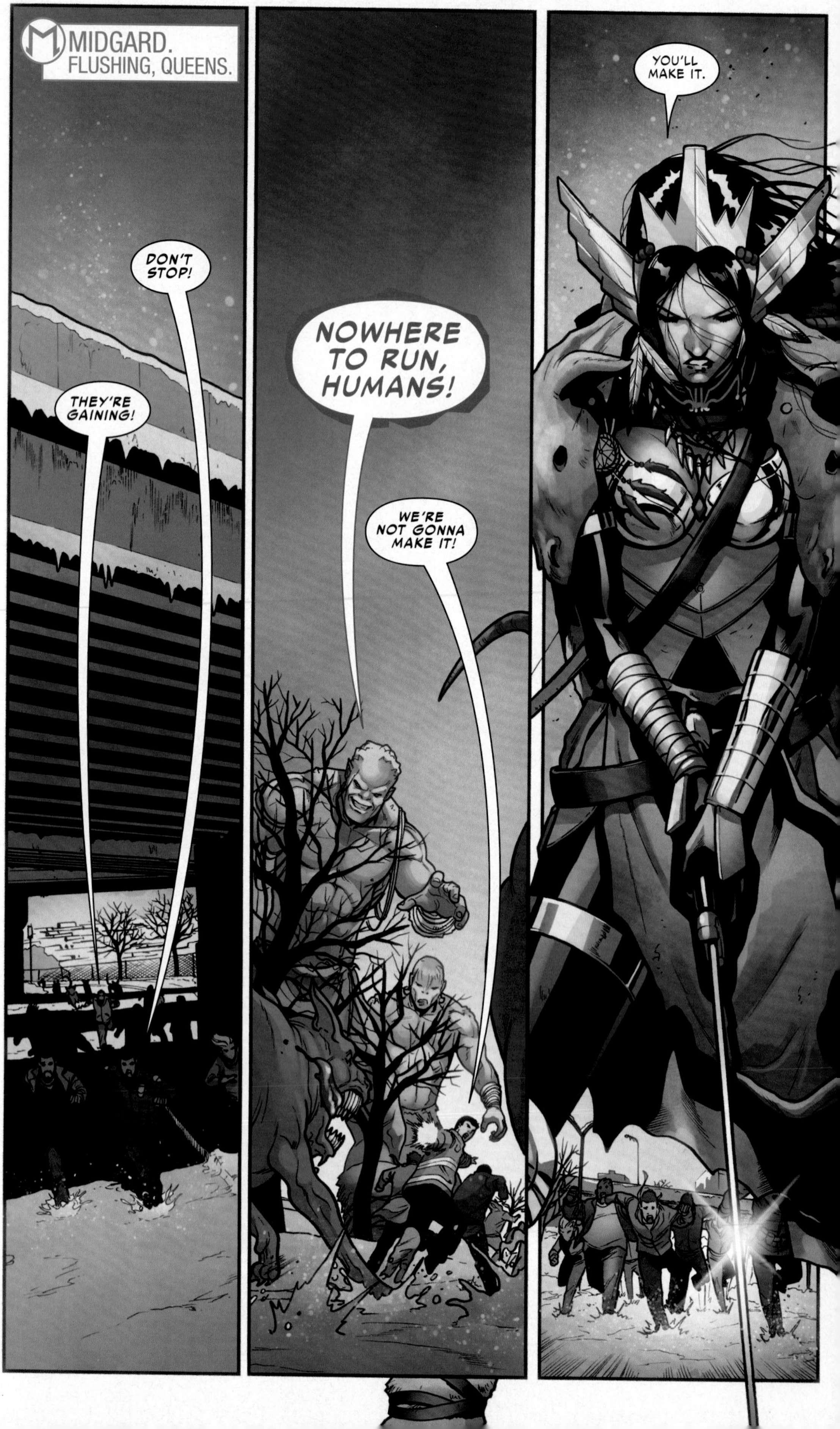
MIDGARD.
FLUSHING, QUEENS.
DON'T STOP!
THEY'RE GAINING!
NOWHERE TO RUN, HUMANS!
WE'RE NOT GONNA MAKE IT!
YOU'LL MAKE IT.

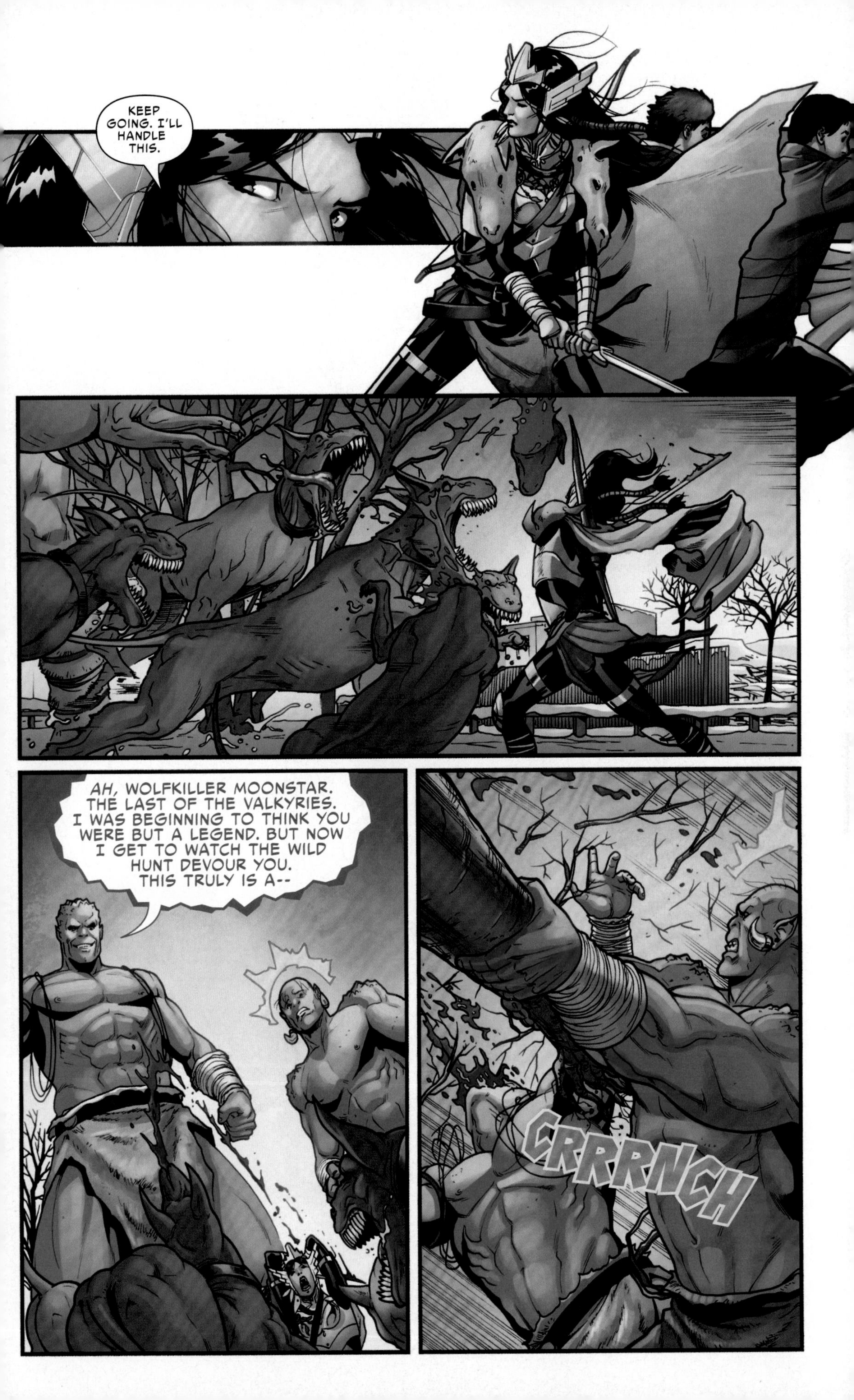
KEEP GOING. I'LL HANDLE THIS.
AH, WOLFKILLER MOONSTAR. THE LAST OF THE VALKYRIES. I WAS BEGINNING TO THINK YOU WERE BUT A LEGEND. BUT NOW I GET TO WATCH THE WILD HUNT DEVOUR YOU. THIS TRULY IS A--
CRRRNCH

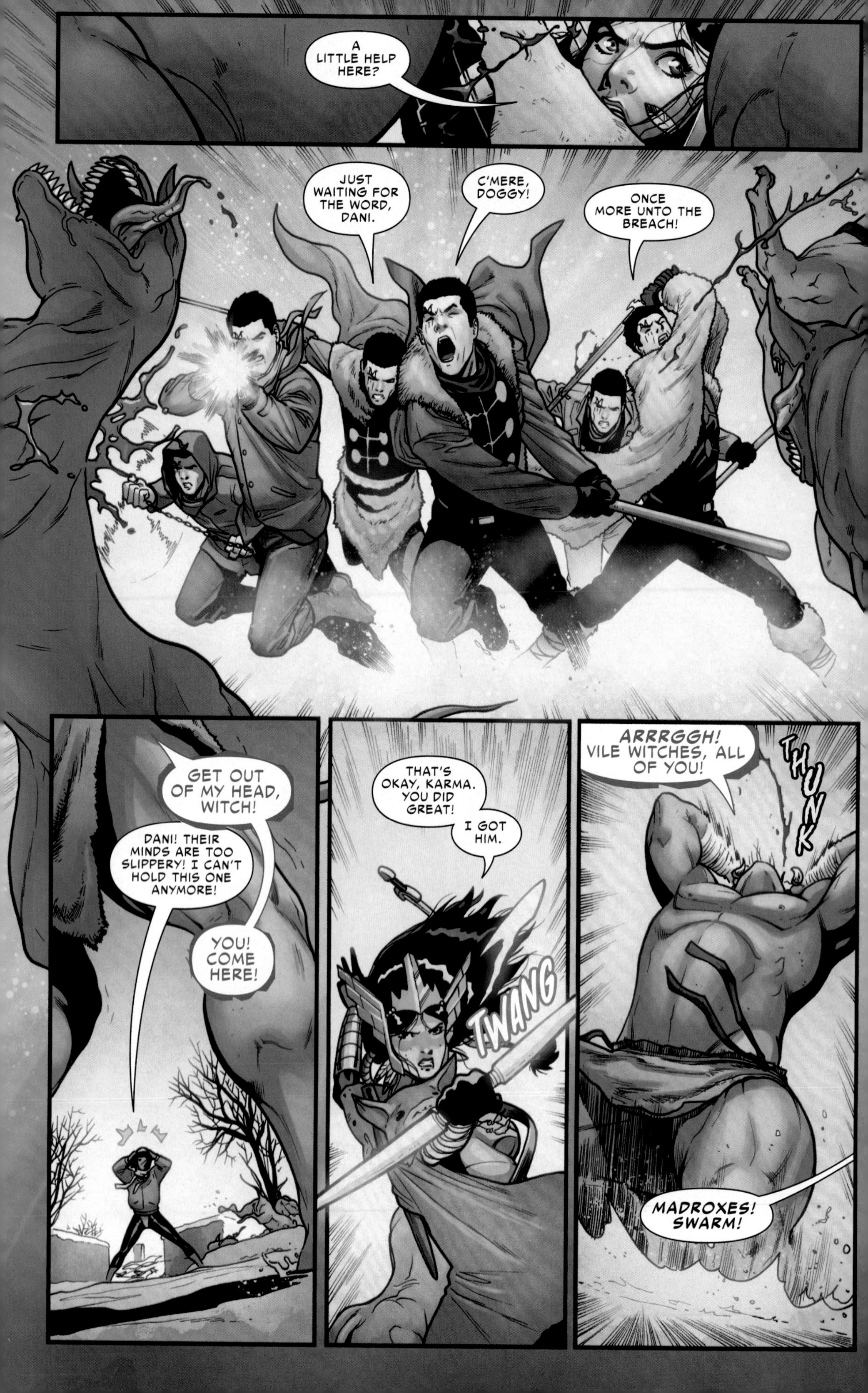
A LITTLE HELP HERE?
JUST WAITING FOR THE WORD, DANI.
C'MERE, DOGGY!
ONCE MORE UNTO THE BREACH!
GET OUT OF MY HEAD, WITCH!
DANI! THEIR MINDS ARE TOO SLIPPERY! I CAN'T HOLD THIS ONE ANYMORE!
YOU! COME HERE!
THAT'S OKAY, KARMA. YOU DID GREAT!
I GOT HIM.
TWANG
ARRRGGH! VILE WITCHES, ALL OF YOU!
THUNK
MADROXES! SWARM!

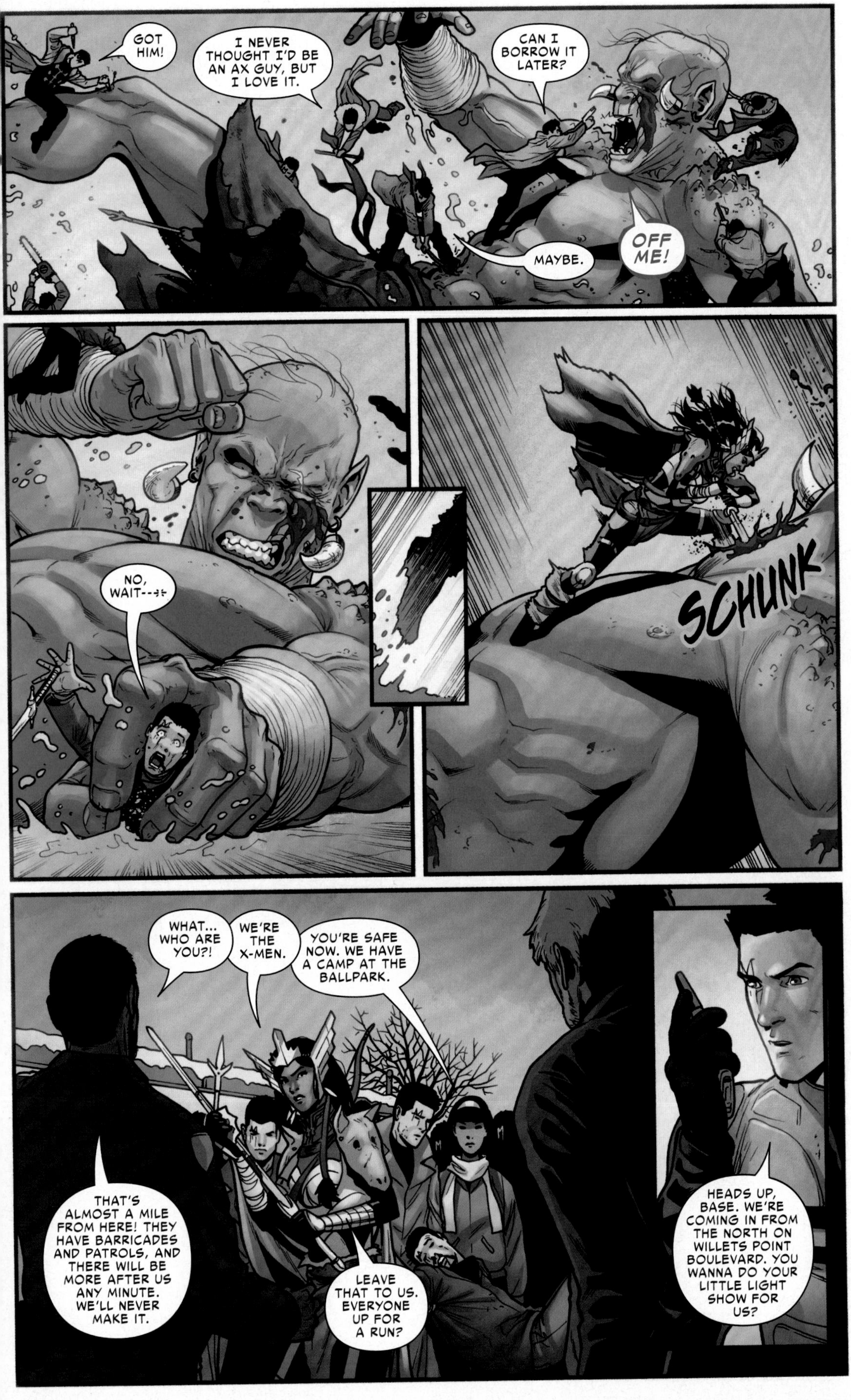
GOT HIM!
I NEVER THOUGHT I'D BE AN AX GUY, BUT I LOVE IT.
CAN I BORROW IT LATER?
MAYBE.
OFF ME!
NO, WAIT--
SCHUNK
WHAT... WHO ARE YOU?!
WE'RE THE X-MEN.
YOU'RE SAFE NOW. WE HAVE A CAMP AT THE BALLPARK.
THAT'S ALMOST A MILE FROM HERE! THEY HAVE BARRICADES AND PATROLS, AND THERE WILL BE MORE AFTER US ANY MINUTE. WE'LL NEVER MAKE IT.
LEAVE THAT TO US. EVERYONE UP FOR A RUN?
HEADS UP, BASE. WE'RE COMING IN FROM THE NORTH ON WILLETS POINT BOULEVARD. YOU WANNA DO YOUR LITTLE LIGHT SHOW FOR US?

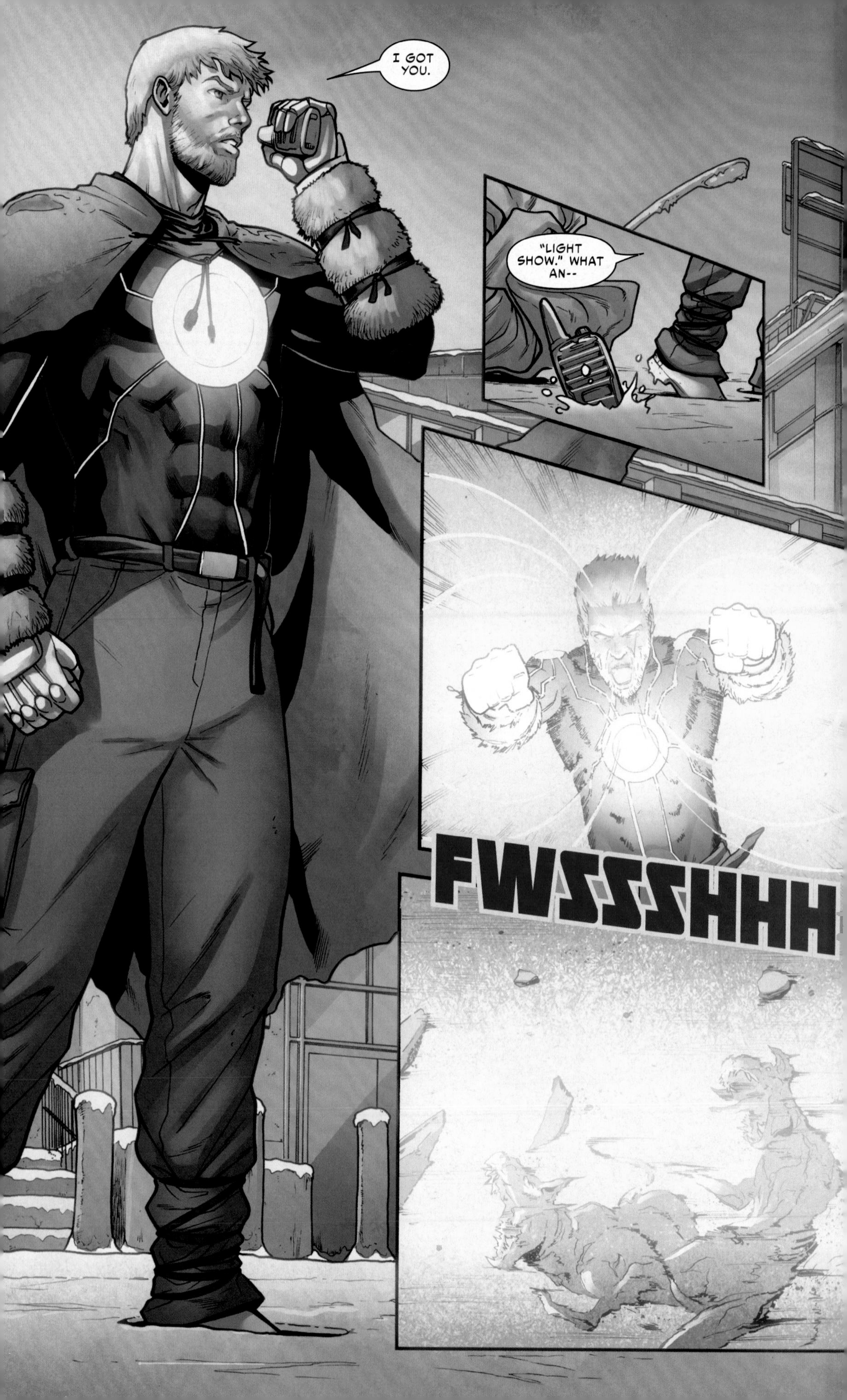
I GOT YOU.
"LIGHT SHOW." WHAT AN--
FWSSSHHH

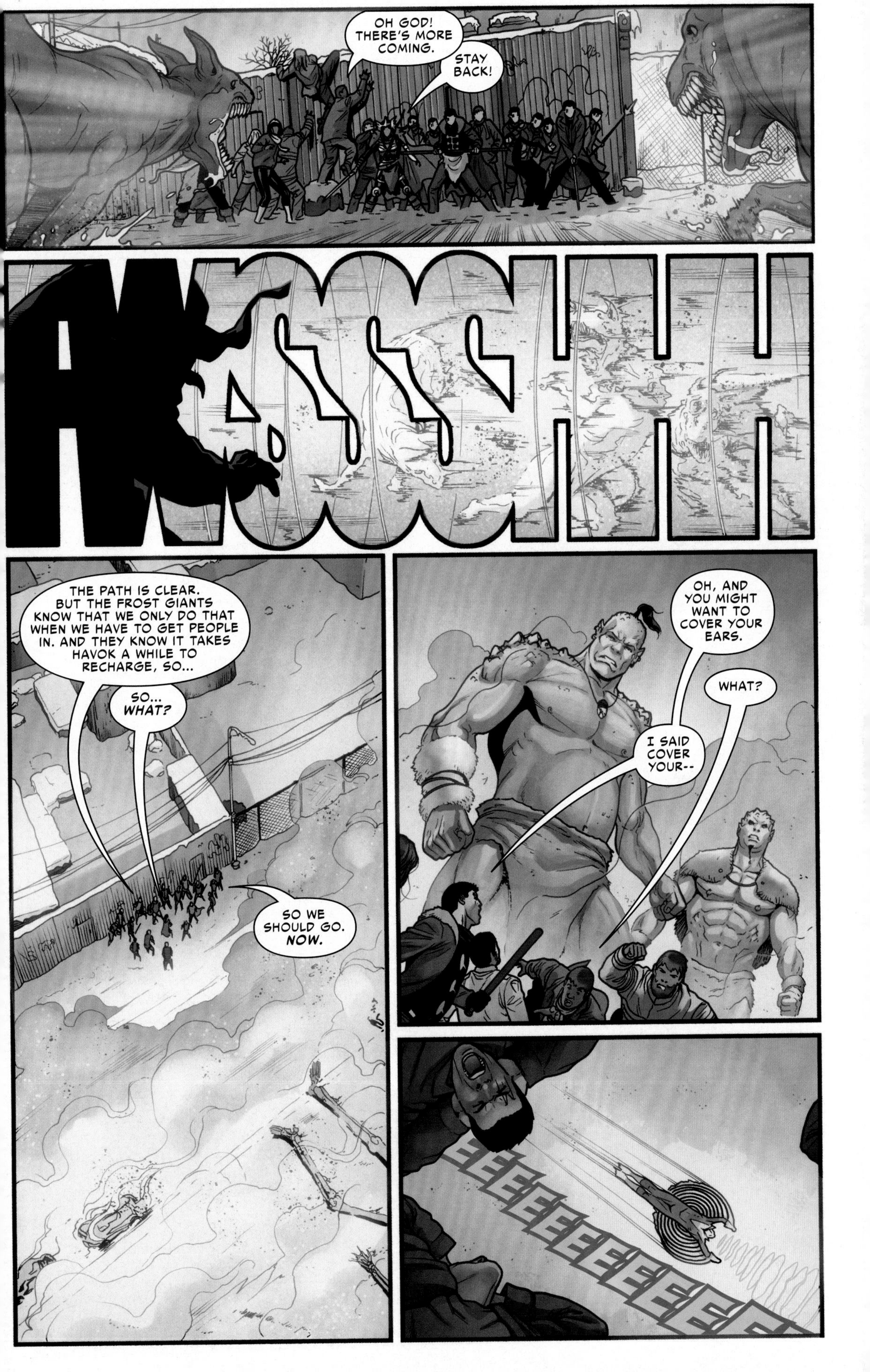
OH GOD! THERE'S MORE COMING.
STAY BACK!
THE PATH IS CLEAR. BUT THE FROST GIANTS KNOW THAT WE ONLY DO THAT WHEN WE HAVE TO GET PEOPLE IN. AND THEY KNOW IT TAKES HAVOK A WHILE TO RECHARGE, SO...
SO... *WHAT?*
SO WE SHOULD GO. *NOW.*
OH, AND YOU MIGHT WANT TO COVER YOUR EARS.
WHAT?
I SAID COVER YOUR--

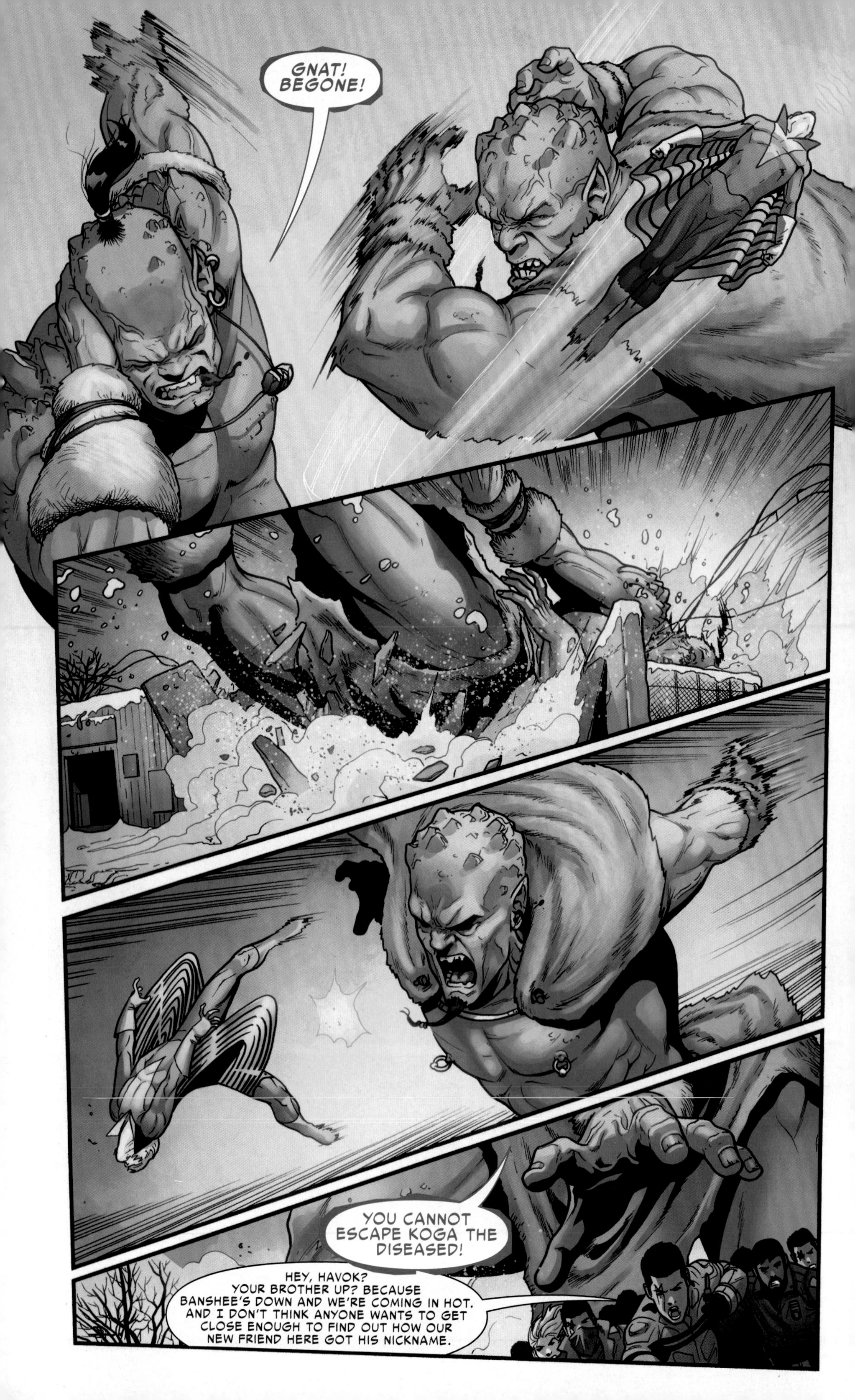
GNAT! BEGONE!
YOU CANNOT ESCAPE KOGA THE DISEASED!
HEY, HAVOK? YOUR BROTHER UP? BECAUSE BANSHEE'S DOWN AND WE'RE COMING IN HOT. AND I DON'T THINK ANYONE WANTS TO GET CLOSE ENOUGH TO FIND OUT HOW OUR NEW FRIEND HERE GOT HIS NICKNAME.

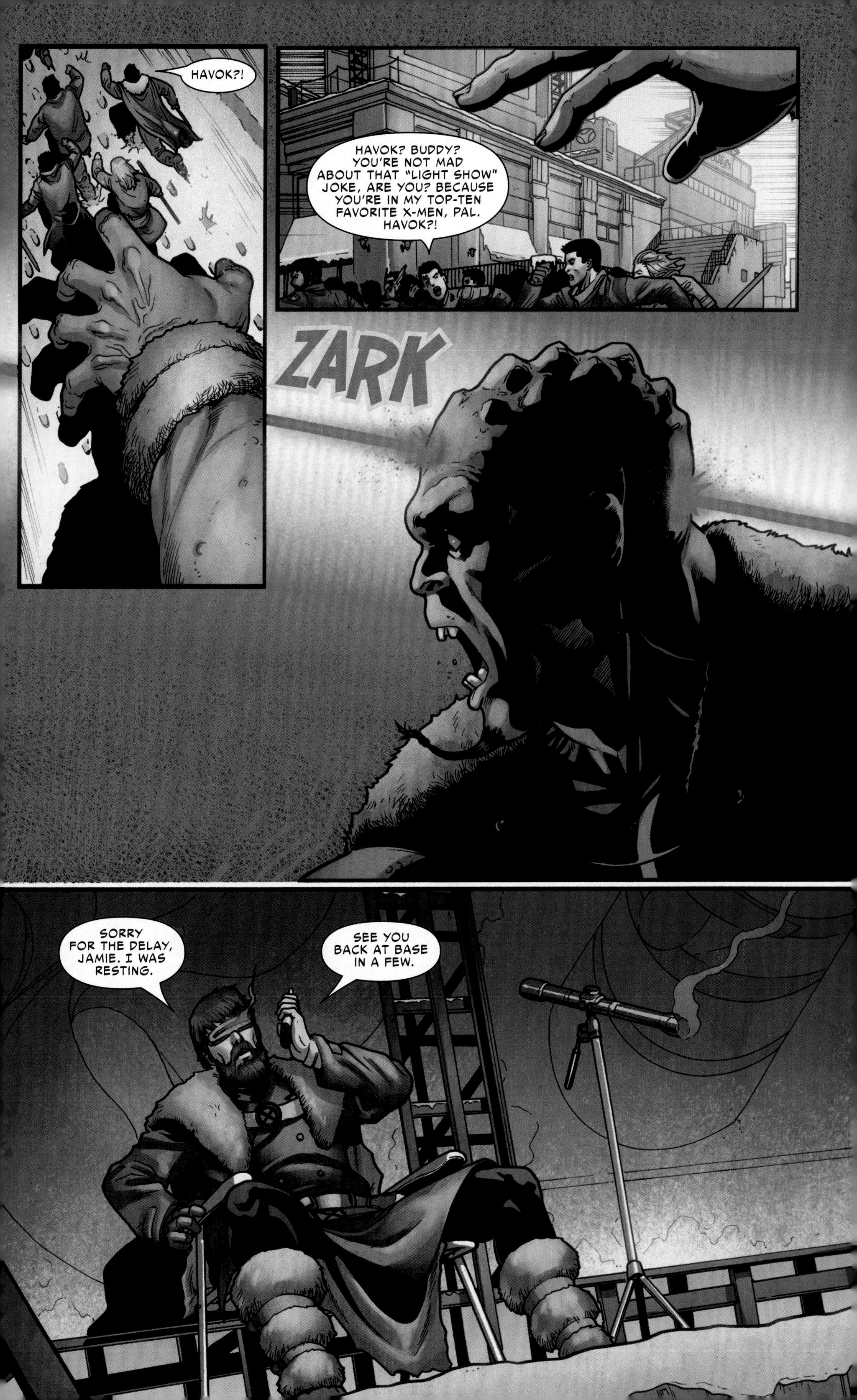
HAVOK?!
HAVOK? BUDDY? YOU'RE NOT MAD ABOUT THAT "LIGHT SHOW" JOKE, ARE YOU? BECAUSE YOU'RE IN MY TOP-TEN FAVORITE X-MEN, PAL. HAVOK?!
ZARK
SORRY FOR THE DELAY, JAMIE. I WAS RESTING.
SEE YOU BACK AT BASE IN A FEW.

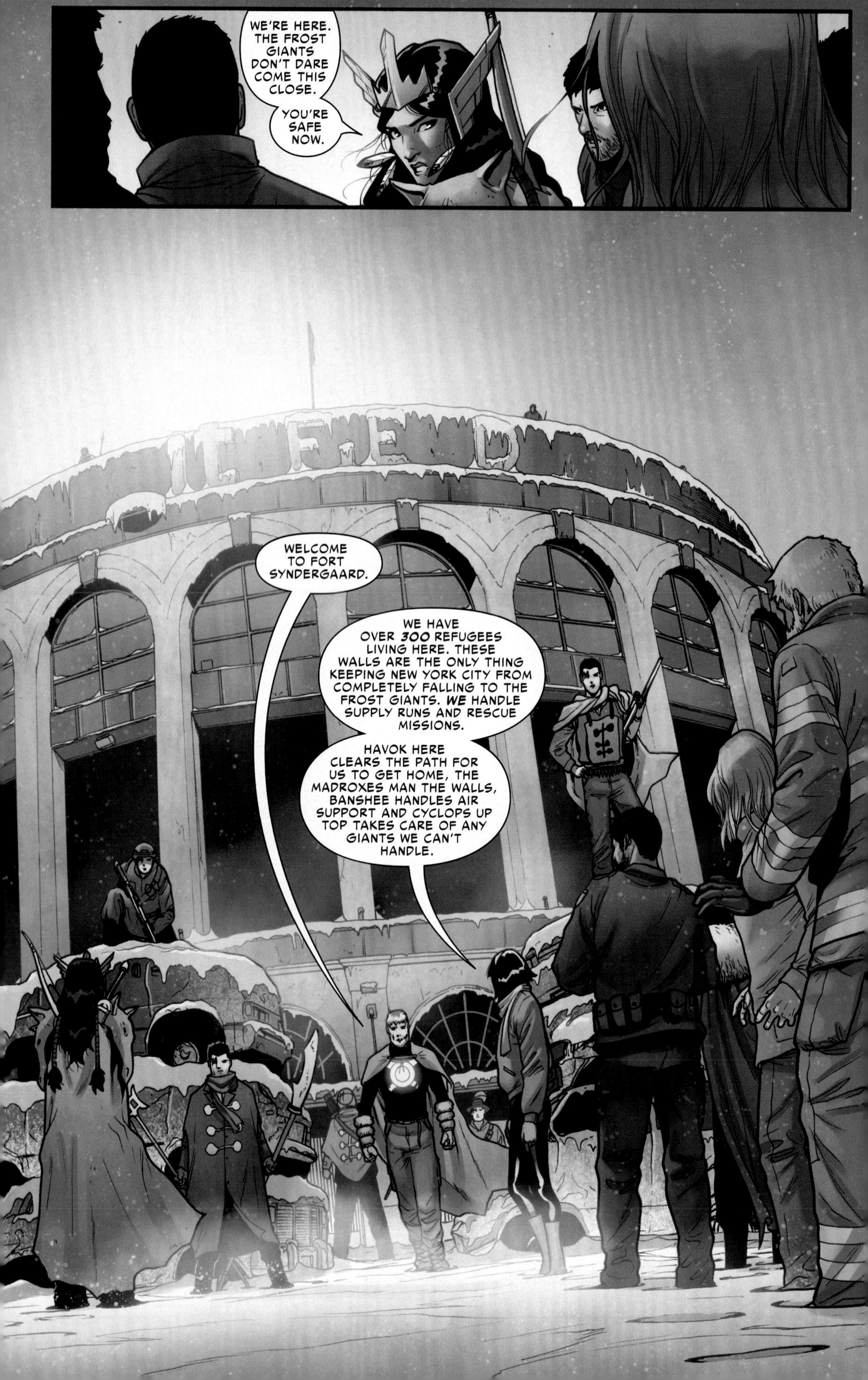
WE'RE HERE. THE FROST GIANTS DON'T DARE COME THIS CLOSE.
YOU'RE SAFE NOW.
WELCOME TO FORT SYNDERGAARD.
WE HAVE OVER *300* REFUGEES LIVING HERE. THESE WALLS ARE THE ONLY THING KEEPING NEW YORK CITY FROM COMPLETELY FALLING TO THE FROST GIANTS. *WE* HANDLE SUPPLY RUNS AND RESCUE MISSIONS.
HAVOK HERE CLEARS THE PATH FOR US TO GET HOME, THE MADROXES MAN THE WALLS, BANSHEE HANDLES AIR SUPPORT AND CYCLOPS UP TOP TAKES CARE OF ANY GIANTS WE CAN'T HANDLE.

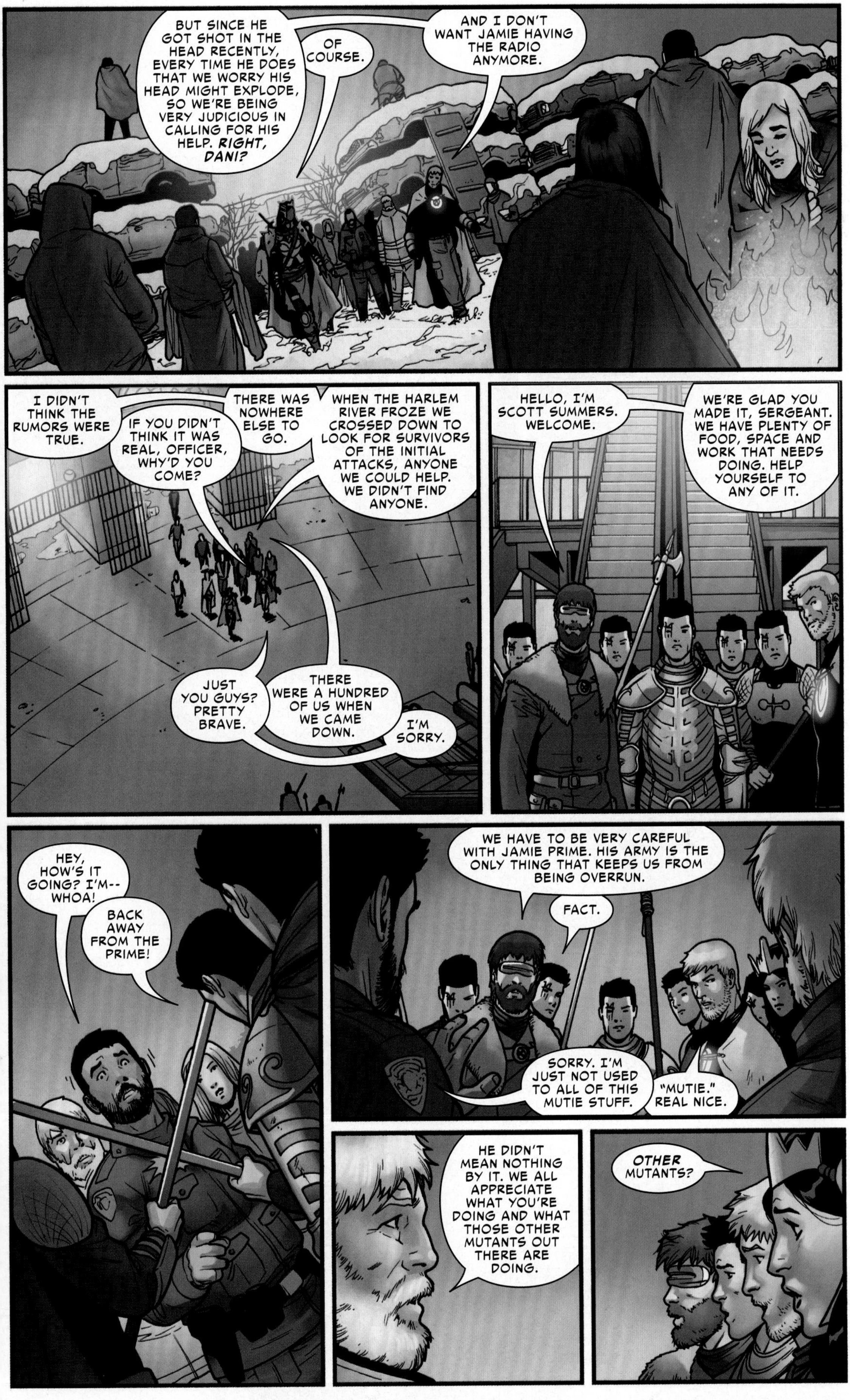

BUT SINCE HE GOT SHOT IN THE HEAD RECENTLY, EVERY TIME HE DOES THAT WE WORRY HIS HEAD MIGHT EXPLODE, SO WE'RE BEING VERY JUDICIOUS IN CALLING FOR HIS HELP. *RIGHT, DANI?*
OF COURSE.
AND I DON'T WANT JAMIE HAVING THE RADIO ANYMORE.
I DIDN'T THINK THE RUMORS WERE TRUE.
IF YOU DIDN'T THINK IT WAS REAL, OFFICER, WHY'D YOU COME?
THERE WAS NOWHERE ELSE TO GO.
WHEN THE HARLEM RIVER FROZE WE CROSSED DOWN TO LOOK FOR SURVIVORS OF THE INITIAL ATTACKS, ANYONE WE COULD HELP. WE DIDN'T FIND ANYONE.
JUST YOU GUYS? PRETTY BRAVE.
THERE WERE A HUNDRED OF US WHEN WE CAME DOWN.
I'M SORRY.
HELLO, I'M SCOTT SUMMERS. WELCOME.
WE'RE GLAD YOU MADE IT, SERGEANT. WE HAVE PLENTY OF FOOD, SPACE AND WORK THAT NEEDS DOING. HELP YOURSELF TO ANY OF IT.
HEY, HOW'S IT GOING? I'M-- WHOA!
BACK AWAY FROM THE PRIME!
WE HAVE TO BE VERY CAREFUL WITH JAMIE PRIME. HIS ARMY IS THE ONLY THING THAT KEEPS US FROM BEING OVERRUN.
FACT.
SORRY. I'M JUST NOT USED TO ALL OF THIS MUTIE STUFF.
"MUTIE." REAL NICE.
HE DIDN'T MEAN NOTHING BY IT. WE ALL APPRECIATE WHAT YOU'RE DOING AND WHAT THOSE OTHER MUTANTS OUT THERE ARE DOING.
OTHER MUTANTS?

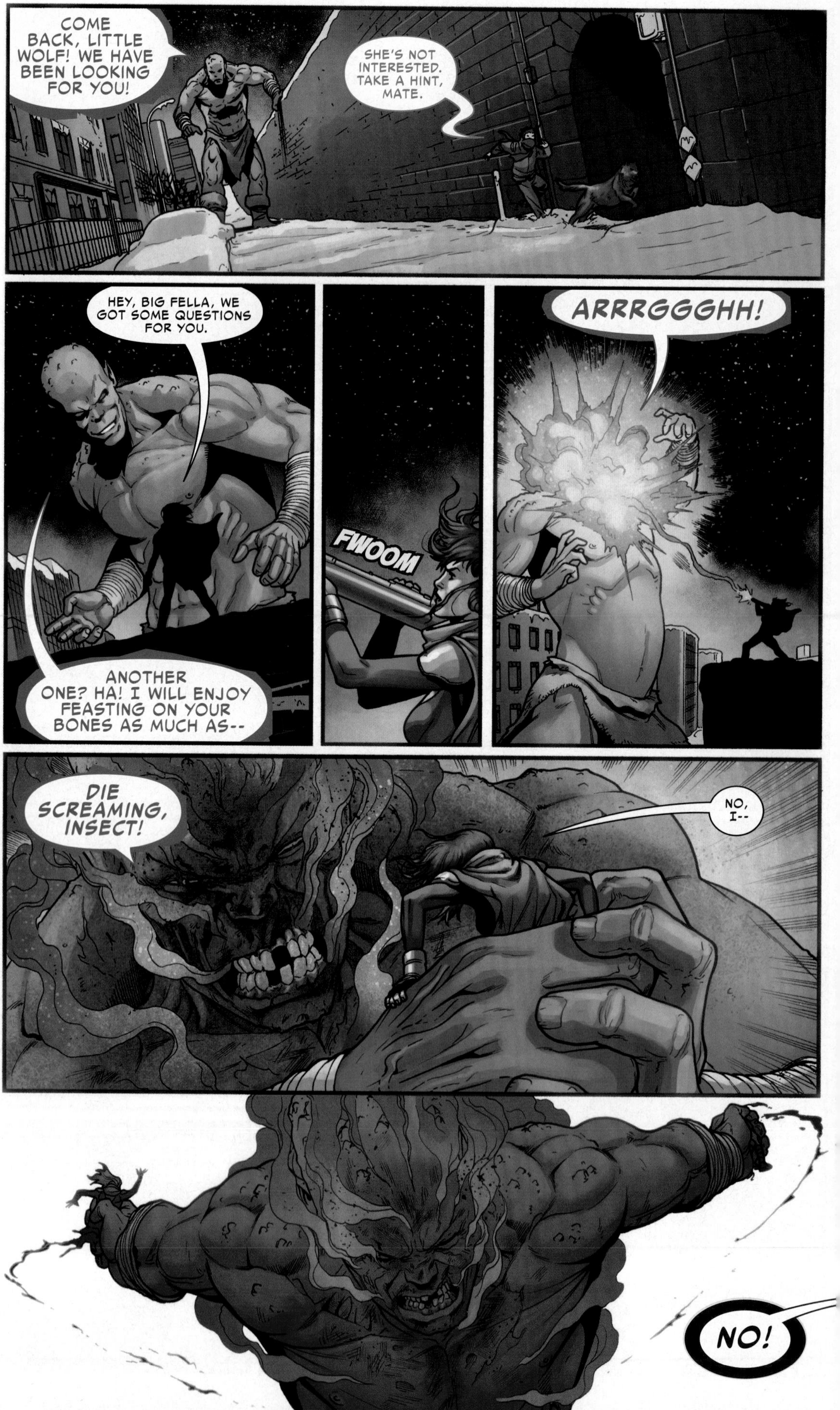
COME BACK, LITTLE WOLF! WE HAVE BEEN LOOKING FOR YOU!
SHE'S NOT INTERESTED. TAKE A HINT, MATE.
HEY, BIG FELLA, WE GOT SOME QUESTIONS FOR YOU.
ANOTHER ONE? HA! I WILL ENJOY FEASTING ON YOUR BONES AS MUCH AS--
FWOOM
ARRRGGGHH!
DIE SCREAMING, INSECT!
NO, I--
NO!

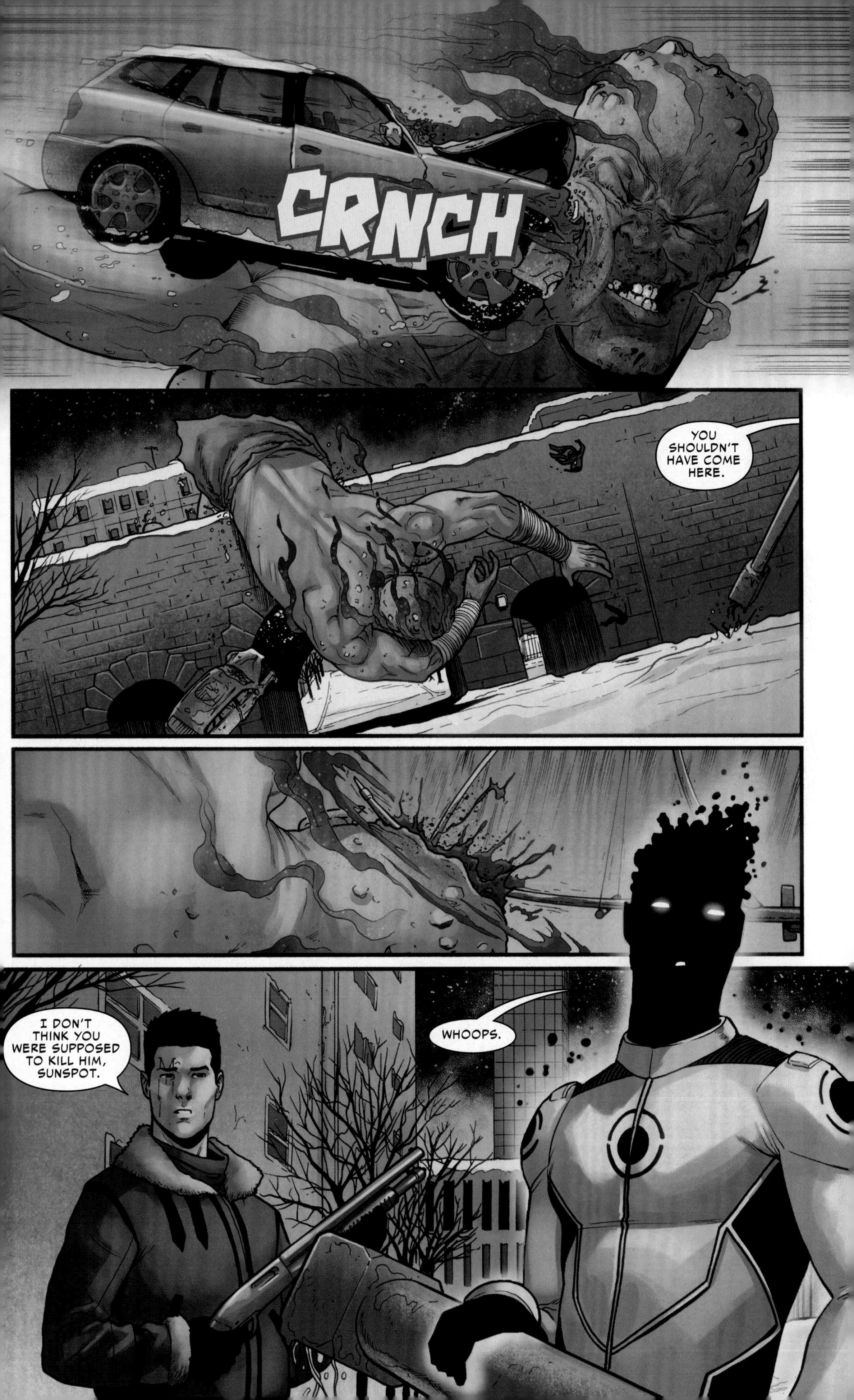
CRNCH
YOU SHOULDN'T HAVE COME HERE.
I DON'T THINK YOU WERE SUPPOSED TO KILL HIM, SUNSPOT.
WHOOPS.

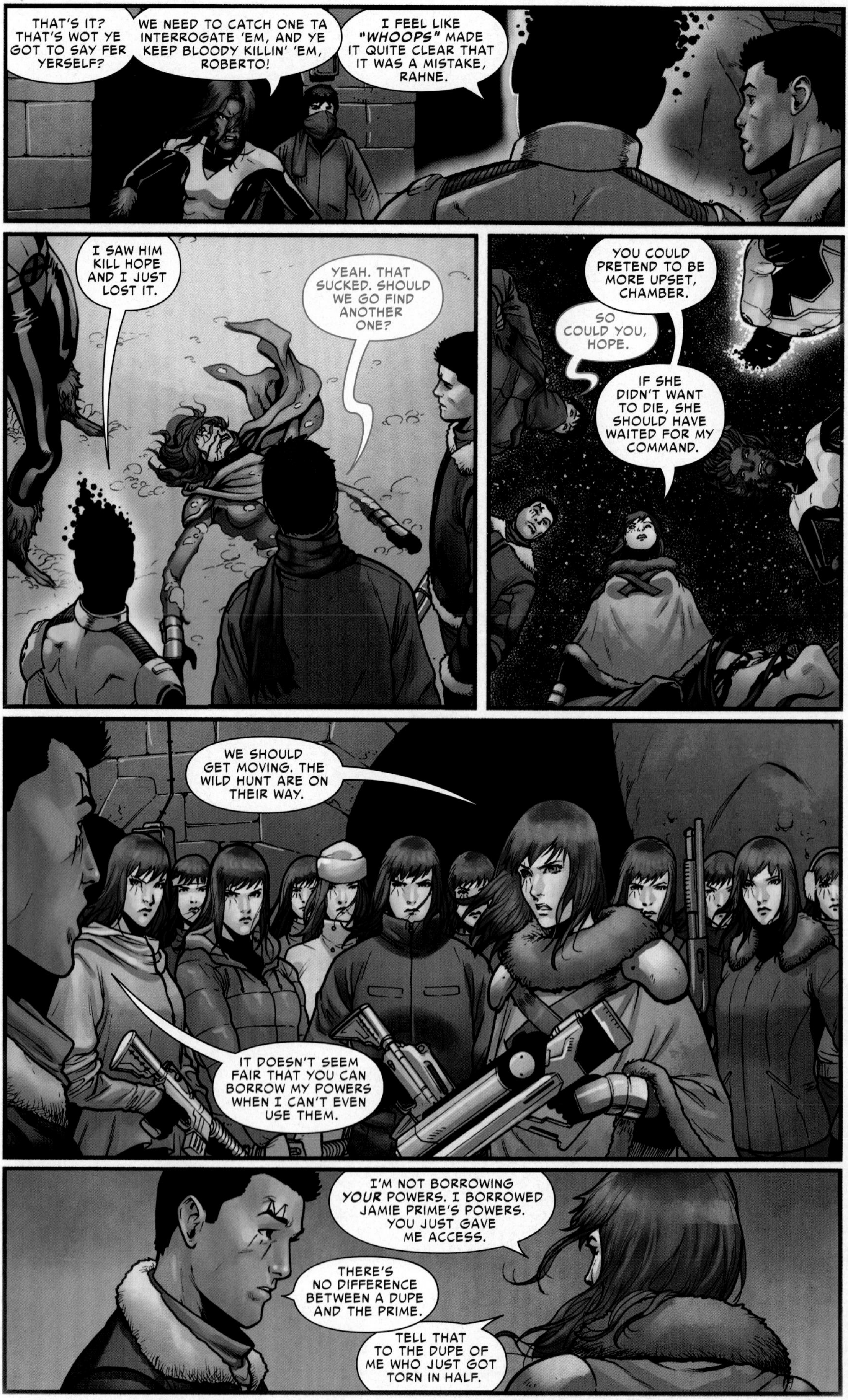
THAT'S IT? THAT'S WOT YE GOT TO SAY FER YERSELF?
WE NEED TO CATCH ONE TA INTERROGATE 'EM, AND YE KEEP BLOODY KILLIN' 'EM, ROBERTO!
I FEEL LIKE "WHOOPS" MADE IT QUITE CLEAR THAT IT WAS A MISTAKE, RAHNE.
I SAW HIM KILL HOPE AND I JUST LOST IT.
YEAH. THAT SUCKED. SHOULD WE GO FIND ANOTHER ONE?
YOU COULD PRETEND TO BE MORE UPSET, CHAMBER.
SO COULD YOU, HOPE.
IF SHE DIDN'T WANT TO DIE, SHE SHOULD HAVE WAITED FOR MY COMMAND.
WE SHOULD GET MOVING. THE WILD HUNT ARE ON THEIR WAY.
IT DOESN'T SEEM FAIR THAT YOU CAN BORROW MY POWERS WHEN I CAN'T EVEN USE THEM.
I'M NOT BORROWING YOUR POWERS. I BORROWED JAMIE PRIME'S POWERS. YOU JUST GAVE ME ACCESS.
THERE'S NO DIFFERENCE BETWEEN A DUPE AND THE PRIME.
TELL THAT TO THE DUPE OF ME WHO JUST GOT TORN IN HALF.

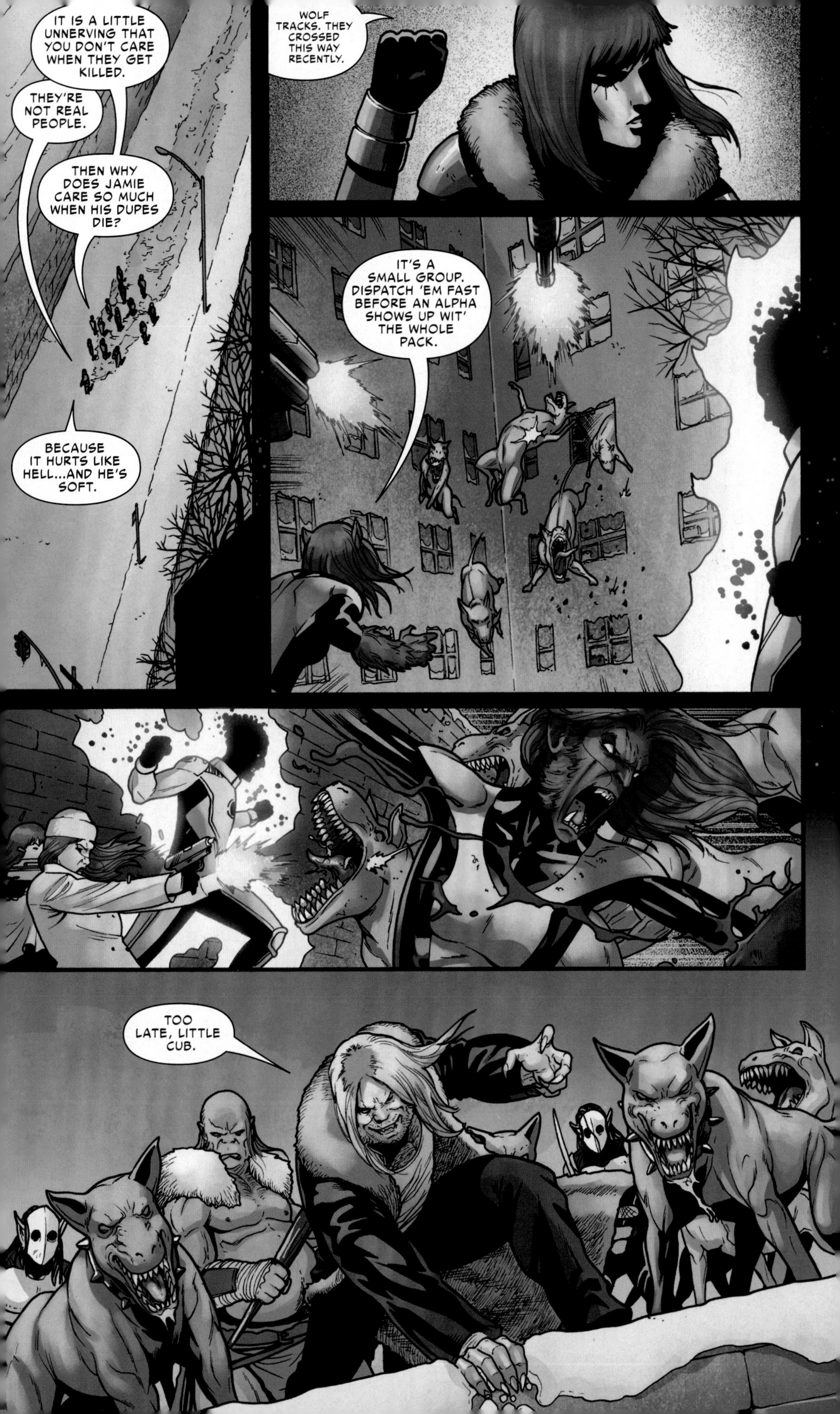
IT IS A LITTLE UNNERVING THAT YOU DON'T CARE WHEN THEY GET KILLED.
THEY'RE NOT REAL PEOPLE.
THEN WHY DOES JAMIE CARE SO MUCH WHEN HIS DUPES DIE?
BECAUSE IT HURTS LIKE HELL...AND HE'S SOFT.
WOLF TRACKS. THEY CROSSED THIS WAY RECENTLY.
IT'S A SMALL GROUP. DISPATCH 'EM FAST BEFORE AN ALPHA SHOWS UP WIT' THE WHOLE PACK.
TOO LATE, LITTLE CUB.

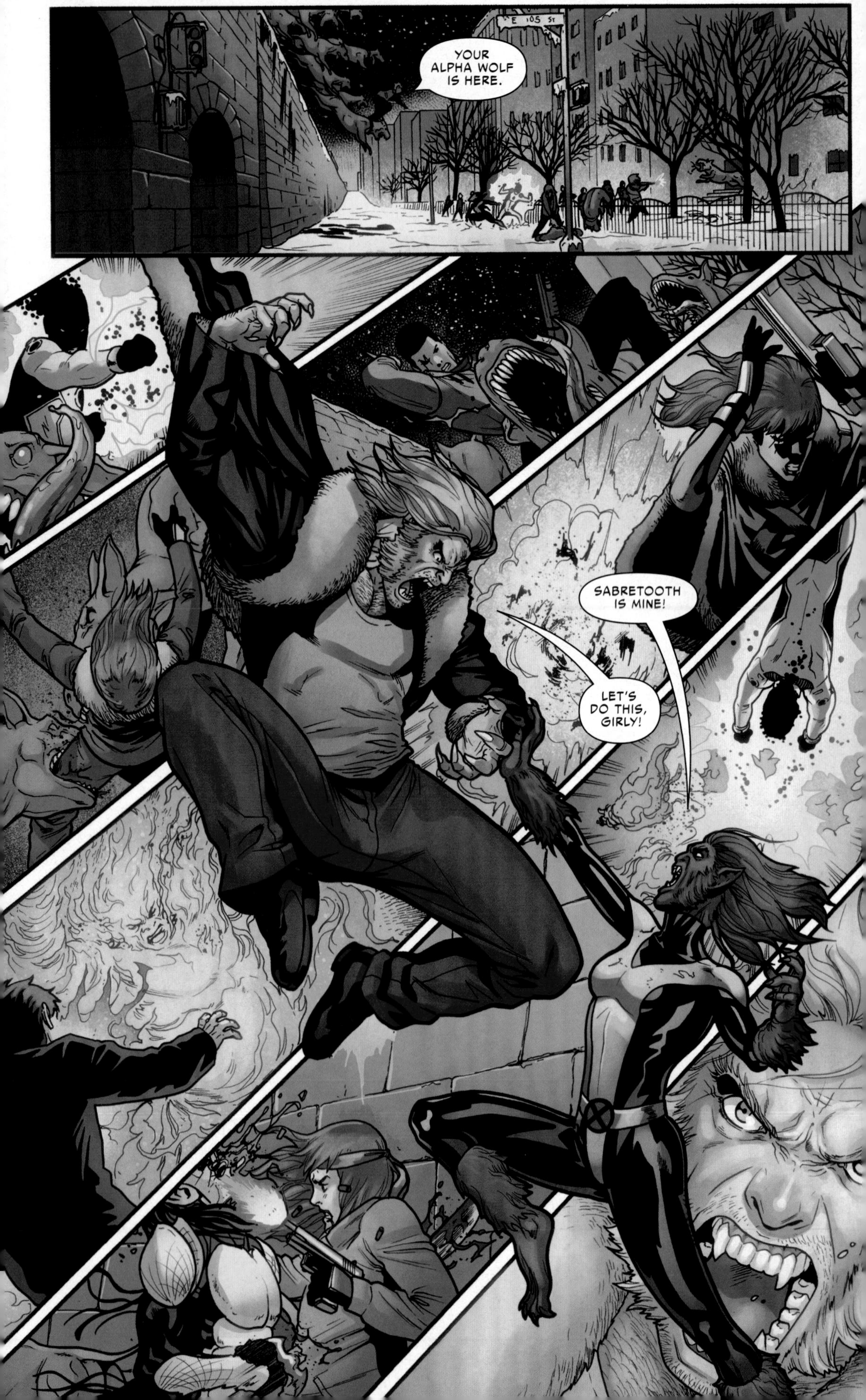
E 105 ST
YOUR ALPHA WOLF IS HERE.
SABRETOOTH IS MINE!
LET'S DO THIS, GIRLY!

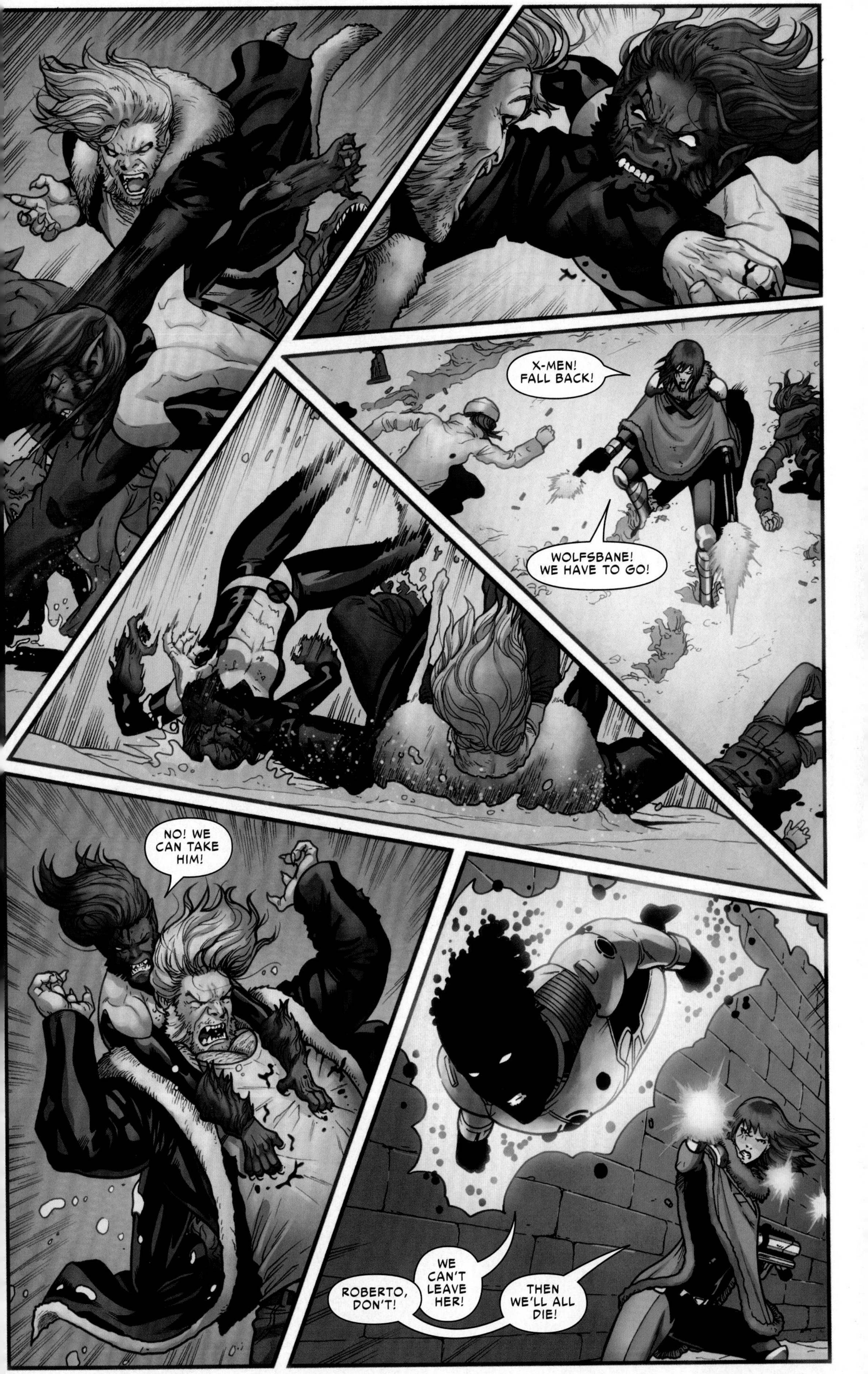
X-MEN! FALL BACK!
WOLFSBANE! WE HAVE TO GO!
NO! WE CAN TAKE HIM!
ROBERTO, DON'T!
WE CAN'T LEAVE HER!
THEN WE'LL ALL DIE!

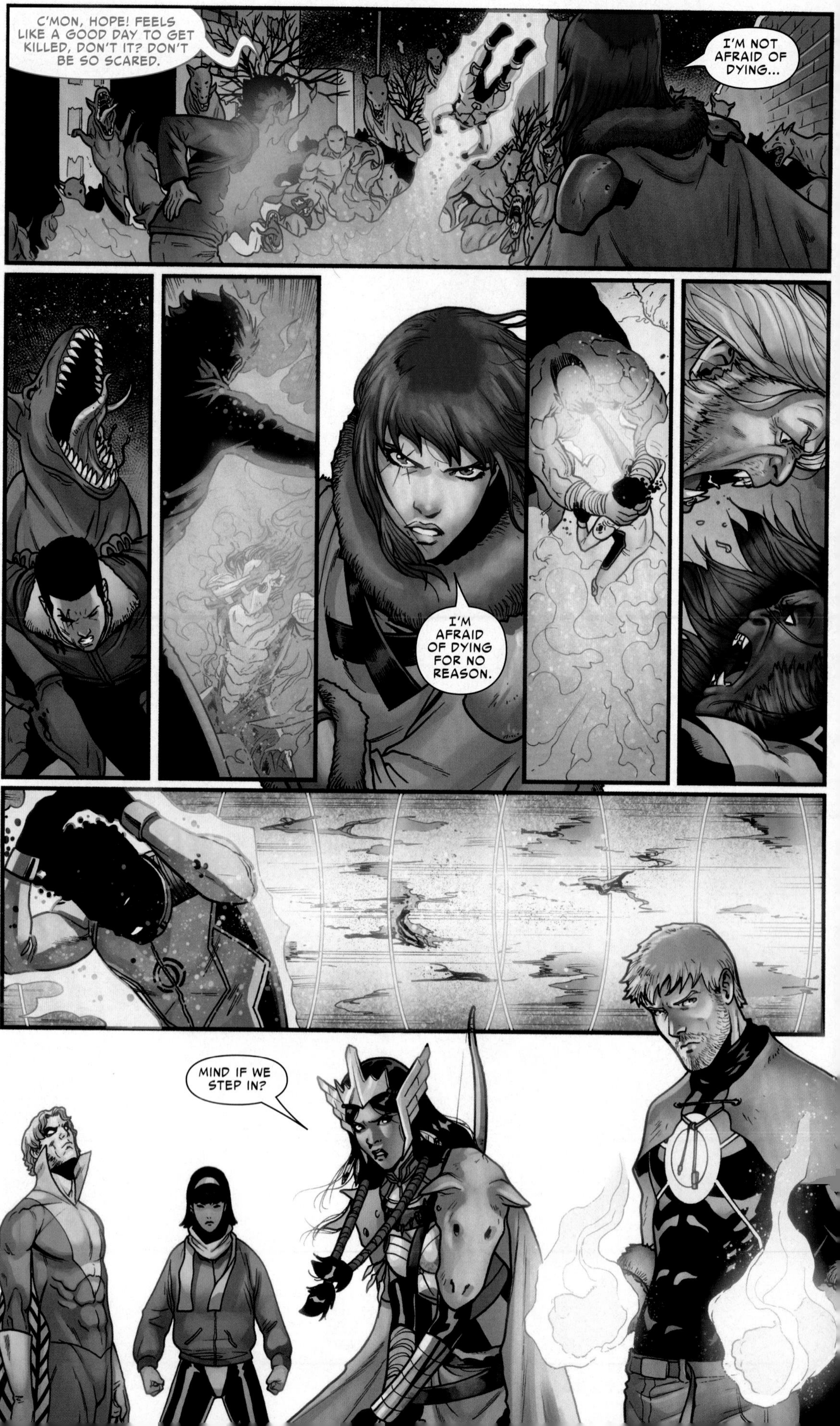
C'MON, HOPE! FEELS LIKE A GOOD DAY TO GET KILLED, DON'T IT? DON'T BE SO SCARED.
I'M NOT AFRAID OF DYING...
I'M AFRAID OF DYING FOR NO REASON.
MIND IF WE STEP IN?

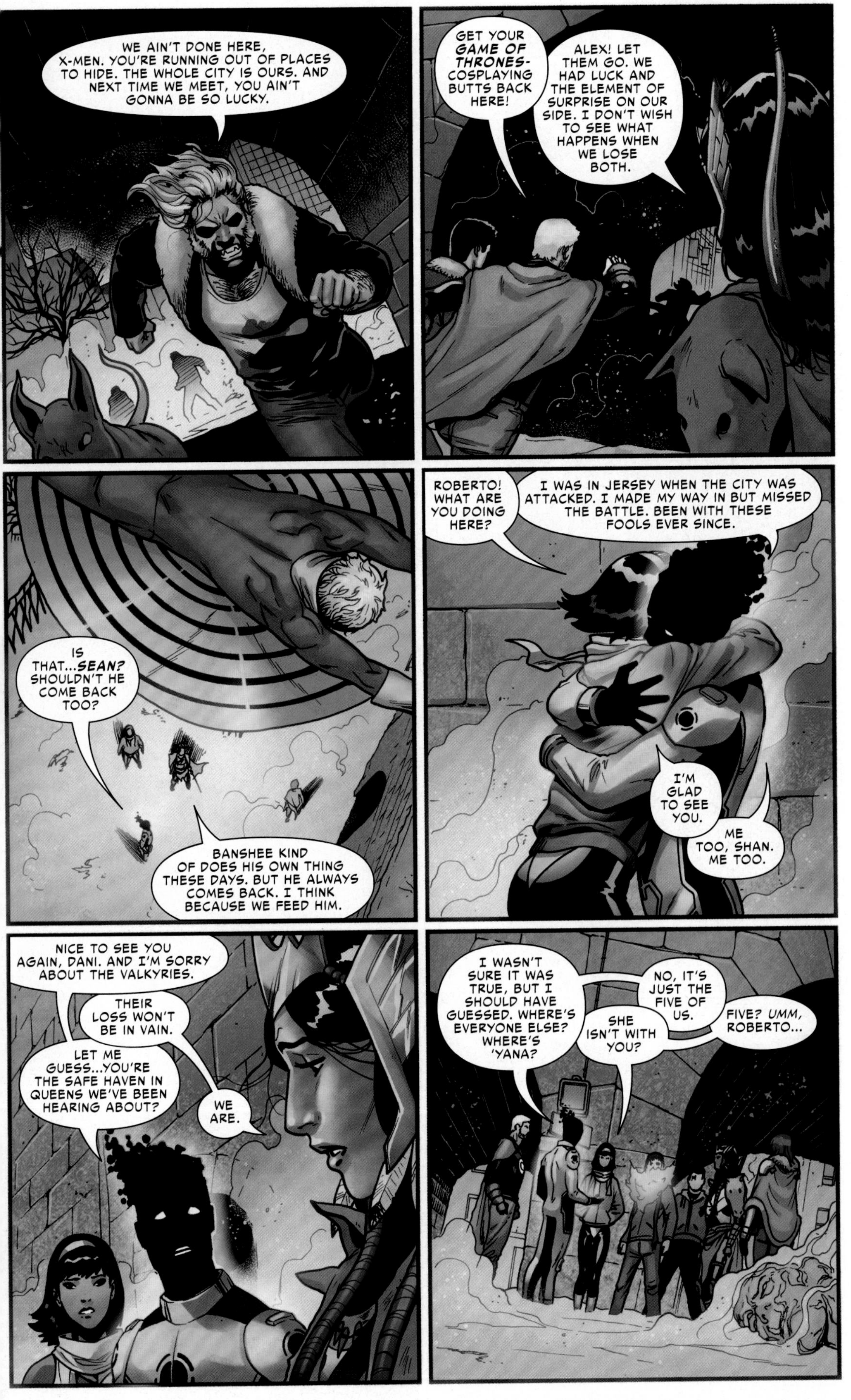
WE AIN'T DONE HERE, X-MEN. YOU'RE RUNNING OUT OF PLACES TO HIDE. THE WHOLE CITY IS OURS. AND NEXT TIME WE MEET, YOU AIN'T GONNA BE SO LUCKY.
GET YOUR *GAME OF THRONES*-COSPLAYING BUTTS BACK HERE!
ALEX! LET THEM GO. WE HAD LUCK AND THE ELEMENT OF SURPRISE ON OUR SIDE. I DON'T WISH TO SEE WHAT HAPPENS WHEN WE LOSE BOTH.
IS THAT...*SEAN?* SHOULDN'T HE COME BACK TOO?
BANSHEE KIND OF DOES HIS OWN THING THESE DAYS. BUT HE ALWAYS COMES BACK. I THINK BECAUSE WE FEED HIM.
ROBERTO! WHAT ARE YOU DOING HERE?
I WAS IN JERSEY WHEN THE CITY WAS ATTACKED. I MADE MY WAY IN BUT MISSED THE BATTLE. BEEN WITH THESE FOOLS EVER SINCE.
I'M GLAD TO SEE YOU.
ME TOO, SHAN. ME TOO.
NICE TO SEE YOU AGAIN, DANI. AND I'M SORRY ABOUT THE VALKYRIES.
THEIR LOSS WON'T BE IN VAIN.
LET ME GUESS...YOU'RE THE SAFE HAVEN IN QUEENS WE'VE BEEN HEARING ABOUT?
WE ARE.
I WASN'T SURE IT WAS TRUE, BUT I SHOULD HAVE GUESSED. WHERE'S EVERYONE ELSE? WHERE'S 'YANA?
NO, IT'S JUST THE FIVE OF US.
SHE ISN'T WITH YOU?
FIVE? *UMM,* ROBERTO...

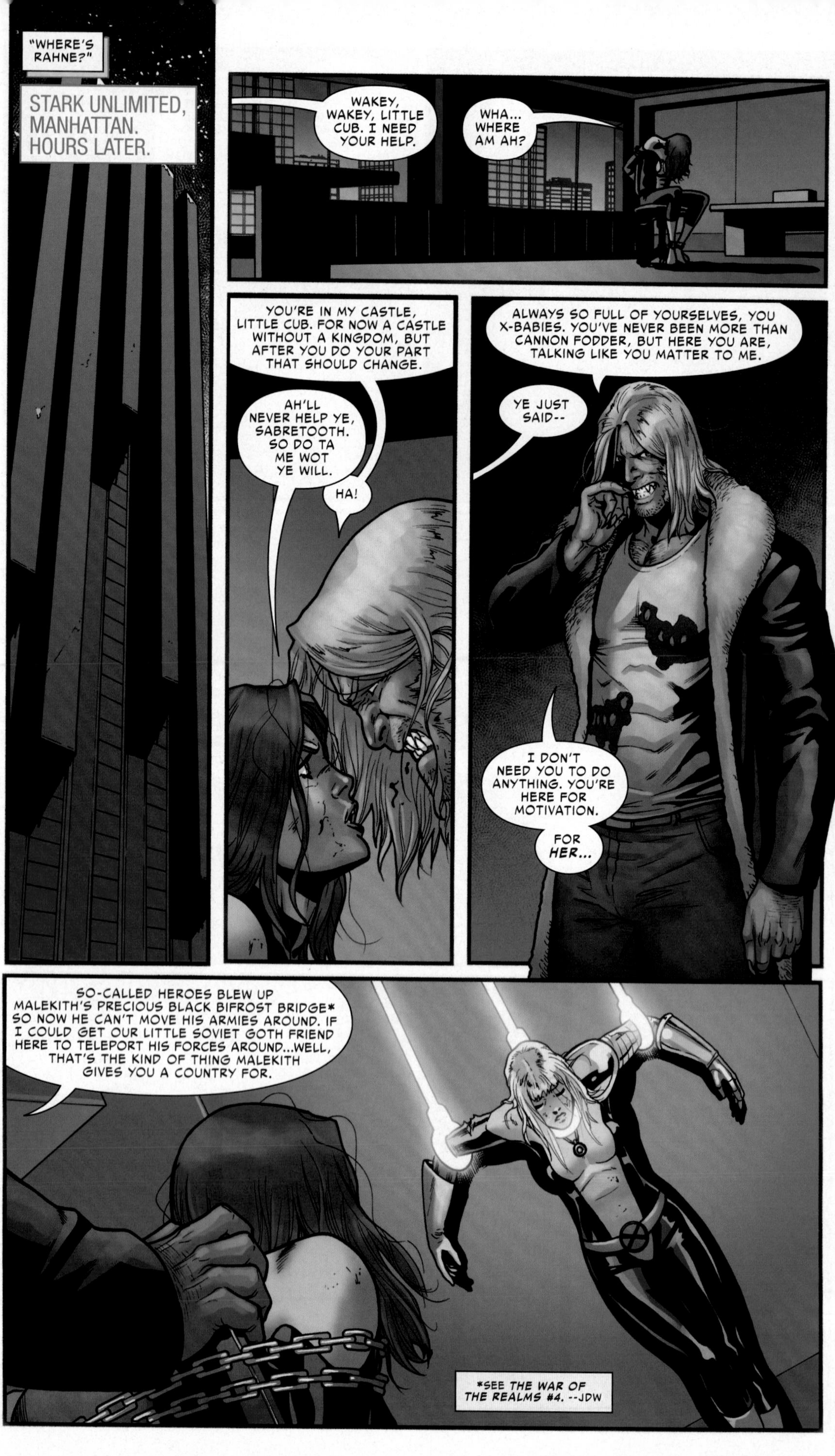
"WHERE'S RAHNE?"
STARK UNLIMITED, MANHATTAN. HOURS LATER.
WAKEY, WAKEY, LITTLE CUB. I NEED YOUR HELP.
WHA... WHERE AM AH?
YOU'RE IN MY CASTLE, LITTLE CUB. FOR NOW A CASTLE WITHOUT A KINGDOM, BUT AFTER YOU DO YOUR PART THAT SHOULD CHANGE.
AH'LL NEVER HELP YE, SABRETOOTH. SO DO TA ME WOT YE WILL.
HA!
ALWAYS SO FULL OF YOURSELVES, YOU X-BABIES. YOU'VE NEVER BEEN MORE THAN CANNON FODDER, BUT HERE YOU ARE, TALKING LIKE YOU MATTER TO ME.
YE JUST SAID--
I DON'T NEED YOU TO DO ANYTHING. YOU'RE HERE FOR MOTIVATION.
FOR *HER*...
SO-CALLED HEROES BLEW UP MALEKITH'S PRECIOUS BLACK BIFROST BRIDGE* SO NOW HE CAN'T MOVE HIS ARMIES AROUND. IF I COULD GET OUR LITTLE SOVIET GOTH FRIEND HERE TO TELEPORT HIS FORCES AROUND...WELL, THAT'S THE KIND OF THING MALEKITH GIVES YOU A COUNTRY FOR.
*SEE *THE WAR OF THE REALMS #4*. --JDW

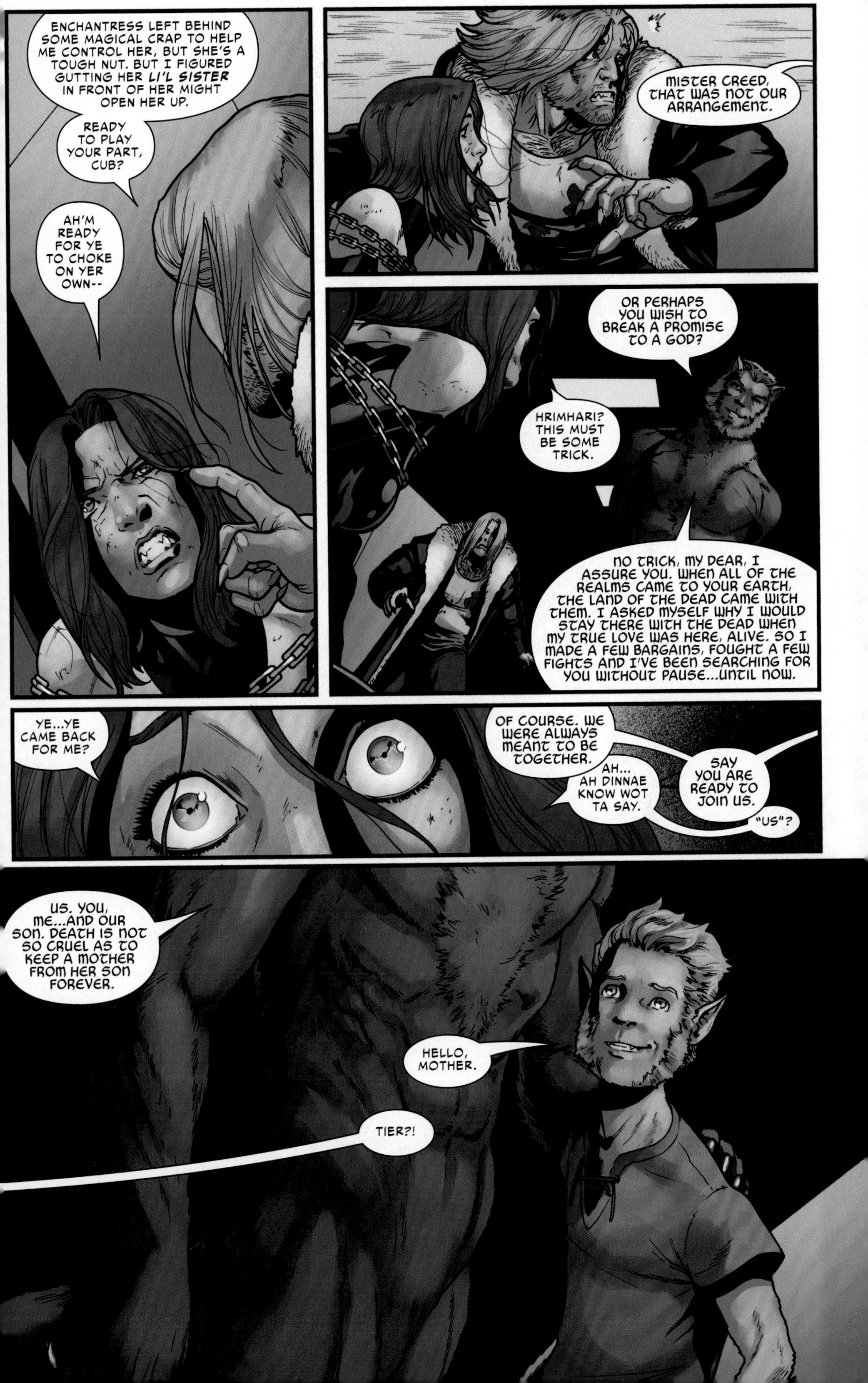
ENCHANTRESS LEFT BEHIND SOME MAGICAL CRAP TO HELP ME CONTROL HER, BUT SHE'S A TOUGH NUT. BUT I FIGURED GUTTING HER LI'L SISTER IN FRONT OF HER MIGHT OPEN HER UP.
READY TO PLAY YOUR PART, CUB?
AH'M READY FOR YE TO CHOKE ON YER OWN--
MISTER CREED, THAT WAS NOT OUR ARRANGEMENT.
OR PERHAPS YOU WISH TO BREAK A PROMISE TO A GOD?
HRIMHARI? THIS MUST BE SOME TRICK.
NO TRICK, MY DEAR, I ASSURE YOU. WHEN ALL OF THE REALMS CAME TO YOUR EARTH, THE LAND OF THE DEAD CAME WITH THEM. I ASKED MYSELF WHY I WOULD STAY THERE WITH THE DEAD WHEN MY TRUE LOVE WAS HERE, ALIVE. SO I MADE A FEW BARGAINS, FOUGHT A FEW FIGHTS AND I'VE BEEN SEARCHING FOR YOU WITHOUT PAUSE...UNTIL NOW.
YE...YE CAME BACK FOR ME?
OF COURSE. WE WERE ALWAYS MEANT TO BE TOGETHER.
AH... AH DINNAE KNOW WOT TA SAY.
SAY YOU ARE READY TO JOIN US.
"US"?
US. YOU, ME...AND OUR SON. DEATH IS NOT SO CRUEL AS TO KEEP A MOTHER FROM HER SON FOREVER.
HELLO, MOTHER.
TIER?!

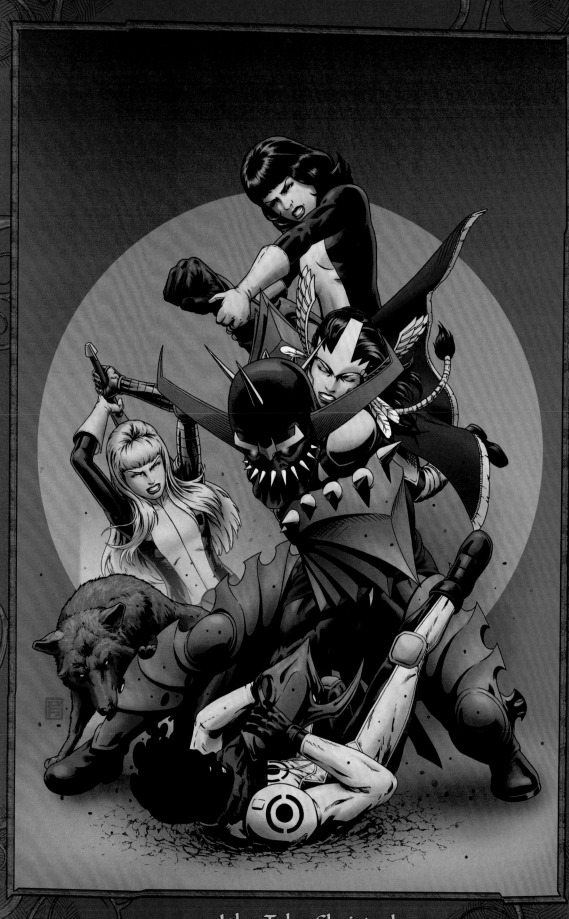

1 VARIANT BY John Tyler Christopher

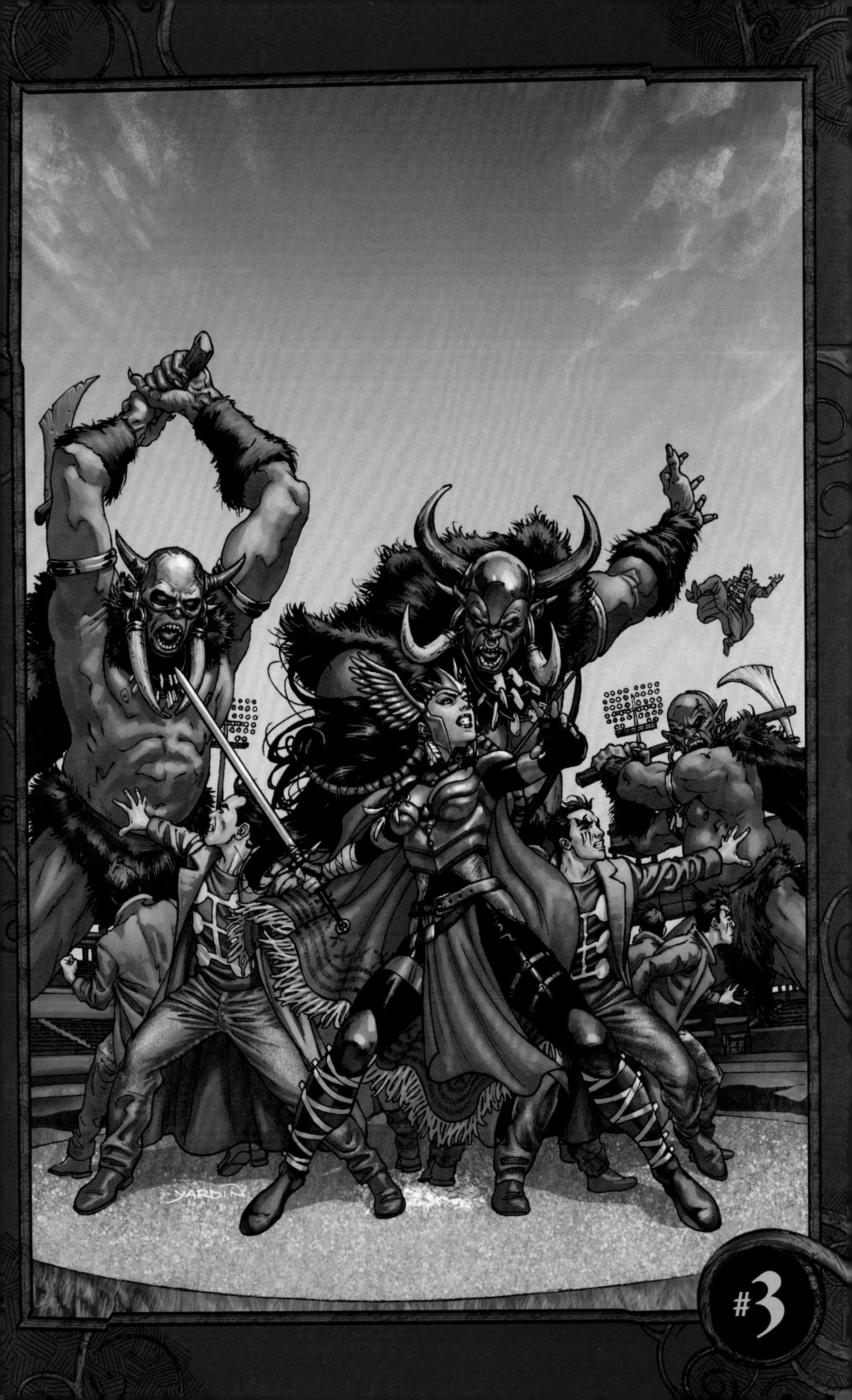
YARDIN
#3

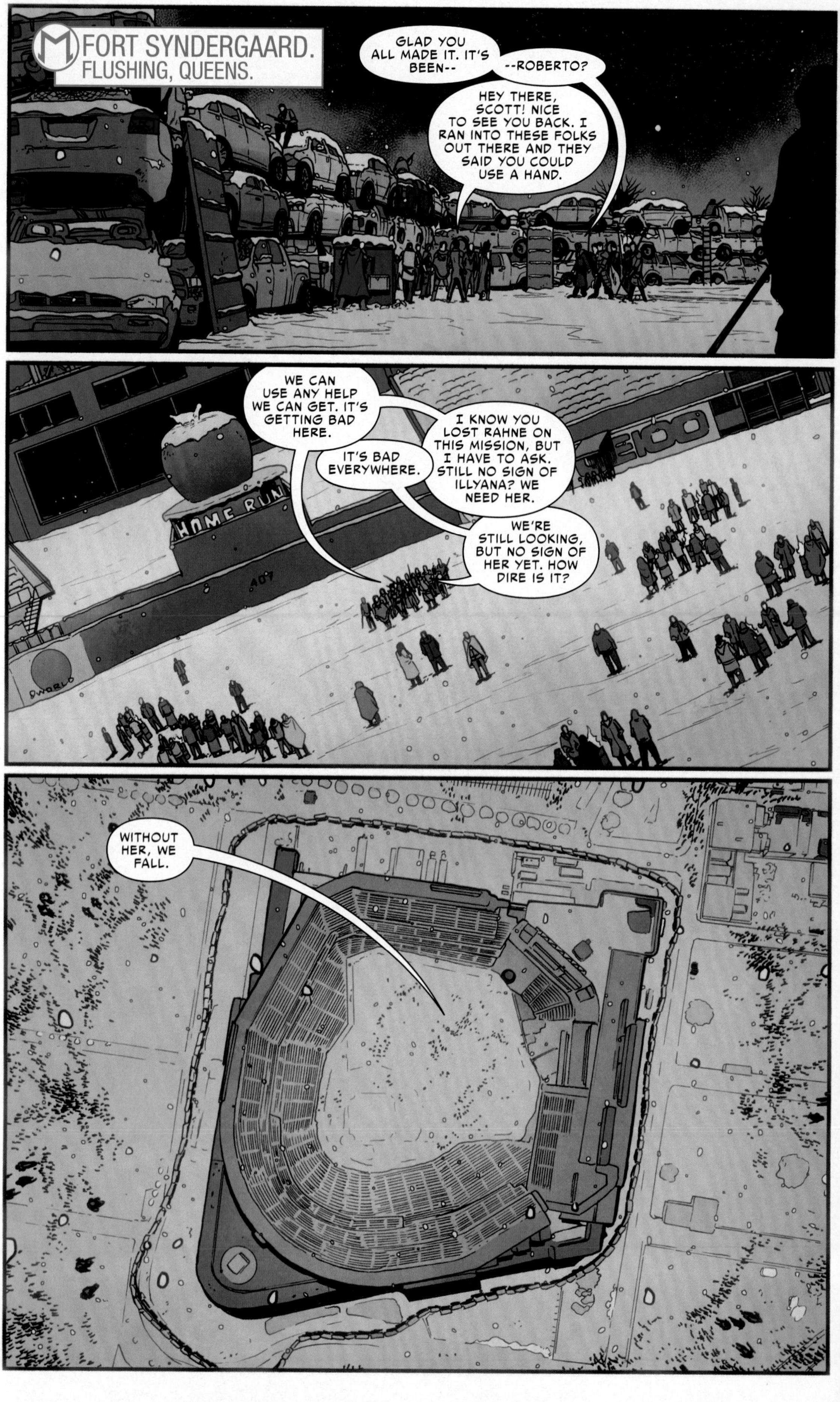
FORT SYNDERGAARD.
FLUSHING, QUEENS.
GLAD YOU ALL MADE IT. IT'S BEEN--
--ROBERTO?
HEY THERE, SCOTT! NICE TO SEE YOU BACK. I RAN INTO THESE FOLKS OUT THERE AND THEY SAID YOU COULD USE A HAND.
WE CAN USE ANY HELP WE CAN GET. IT'S GETTING BAD HERE.
I KNOW YOU LOST RAHNE ON THIS MISSION, BUT I HAVE TO ASK. STILL NO SIGN OF ILLYANA? WE NEED HER.
IT'S BAD EVERYWHERE.
WE'RE STILL LOOKING, BUT NO SIGN OF HER YET. HOW DIRE IS IT?
HOME RUN
WITHOUT HER, WE FALL.

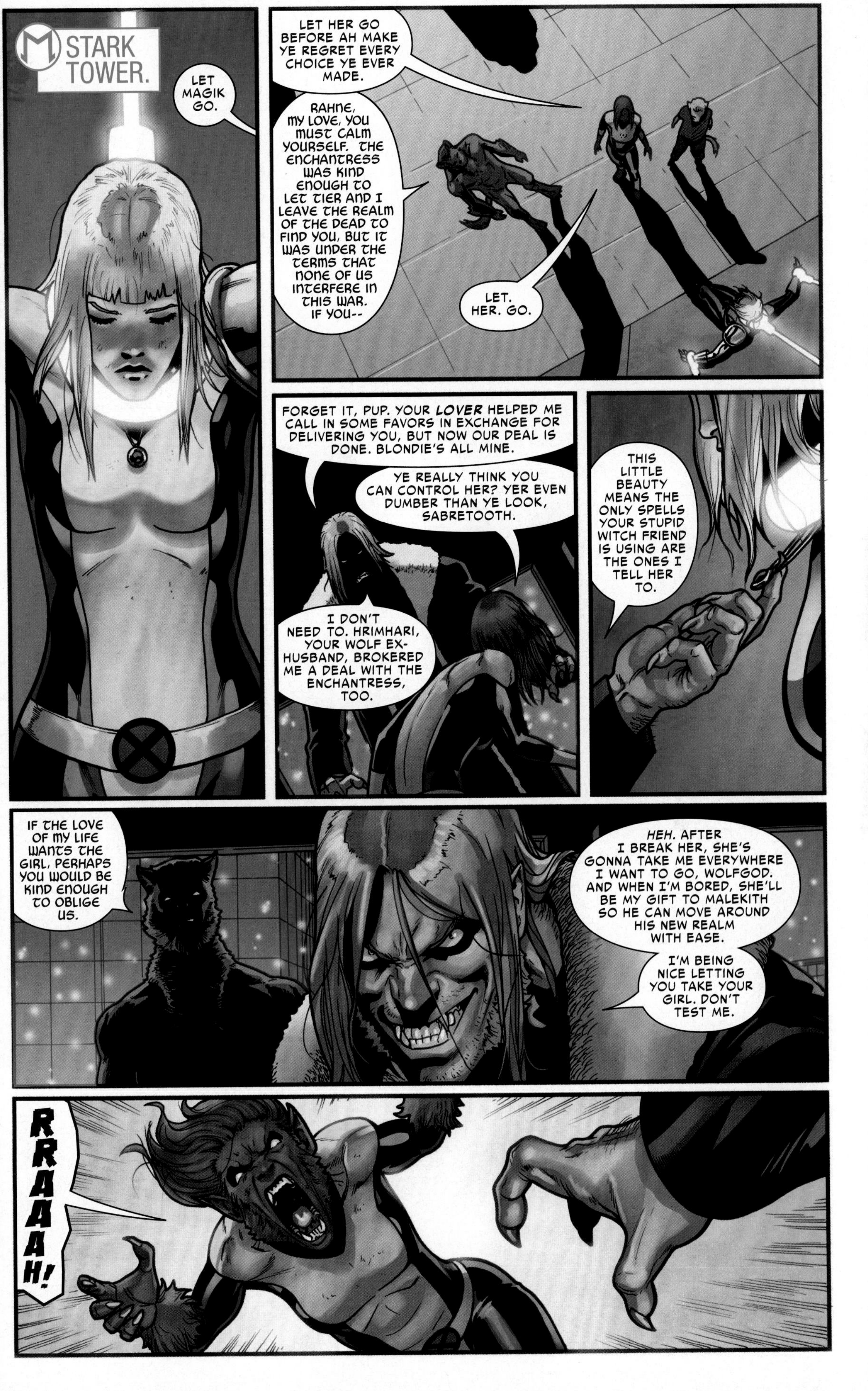
STARK TOWER.
LET MAGIK GO.
LET HER GO BEFORE AH MAKE YE REGRET EVERY CHOICE YE EVER MADE.
RAHNE, MY LOVE, YOU MUST CALM YOURSELF. THE ENCHANTRESS WAS KIND ENOUGH TO LET TIER AND I LEAVE THE REALM OF THE DEAD TO FIND YOU, BUT IT WAS UNDER THE TERMS THAT NONE OF US INTERFERE IN THIS WAR. IF YOU--
LET. HER. GO.
FORGET IT, PUP. YOUR LOVER HELPED ME CALL IN SOME FAVORS IN EXCHANGE FOR DELIVERING YOU, BUT NOW OUR DEAL IS DONE. BLONDIE'S ALL MINE.
YE REALLY THINK YOU CAN CONTROL HER? YER EVEN DUMBER THAN YE LOOK, SABRETOOTH.
I DON'T NEED TO. HRIMHARI, YOUR WOLF EX-HUSBAND, BROKERED ME A DEAL WITH THE ENCHANTRESS, TOO.
THIS LITTLE BEAUTY MEANS THE ONLY SPELLS YOUR STUPID WITCH FRIEND IS USING ARE THE ONES I TELL HER TO.
IF THE LOVE OF MY LIFE WANTS THE GIRL, PERHAPS YOU WOULD BE KIND ENOUGH TO OBLIGE US.
HEH. AFTER I BREAK HER, SHE'S GONNA TAKE ME EVERYWHERE I WANT TO GO, WOLFGOD. AND WHEN I'M BORED, SHE'LL BE MY GIFT TO MALEKITH SO HE CAN MOVE AROUND HIS NEW REALM WITH EASE.
I'M BEING NICE LETTING YOU TAKE YOUR GIRL. DON'T TEST ME.
RRAAAH!

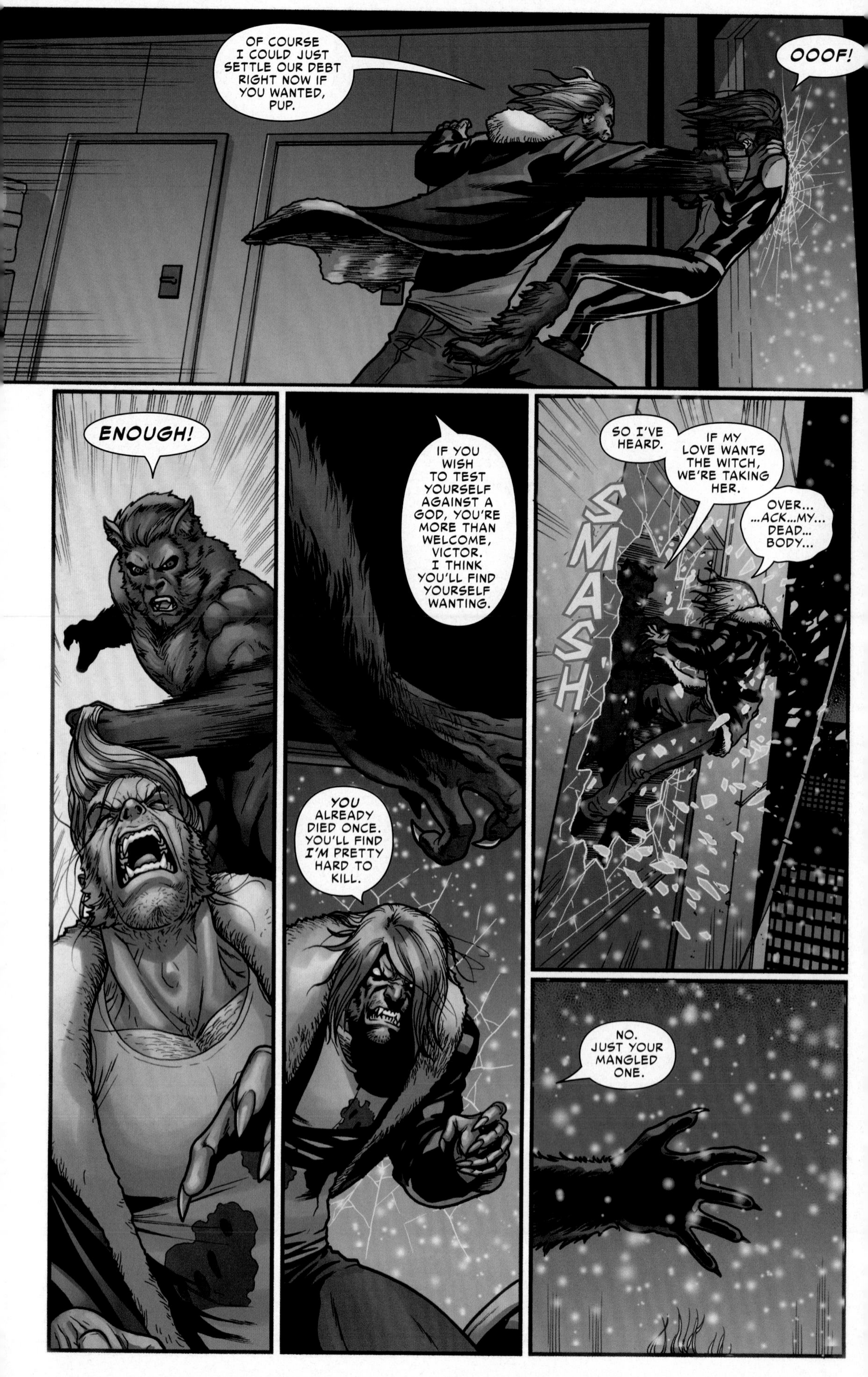
OF COURSE I COULD JUST SETTLE OUR DEBT RIGHT NOW IF YOU WANTED, PUP.
OOOF!
ENOUGH!
IF YOU WISH TO TEST YOURSELF AGAINST A GOD, YOU'RE MORE THAN WELCOME, VICTOR. I THINK YOU'LL FIND YOURSELF WANTING.
YOU ALREADY DIED ONCE. YOU'LL FIND I'M PRETTY HARD TO KILL.
SO I'VE HEARD.
IF MY LOVE WANTS THE WITCH, WE'RE TAKING HER.
OVER... ...ACK...MY... DEAD... BODY...
SMASH
NO. JUST YOUR MANGLED ONE.

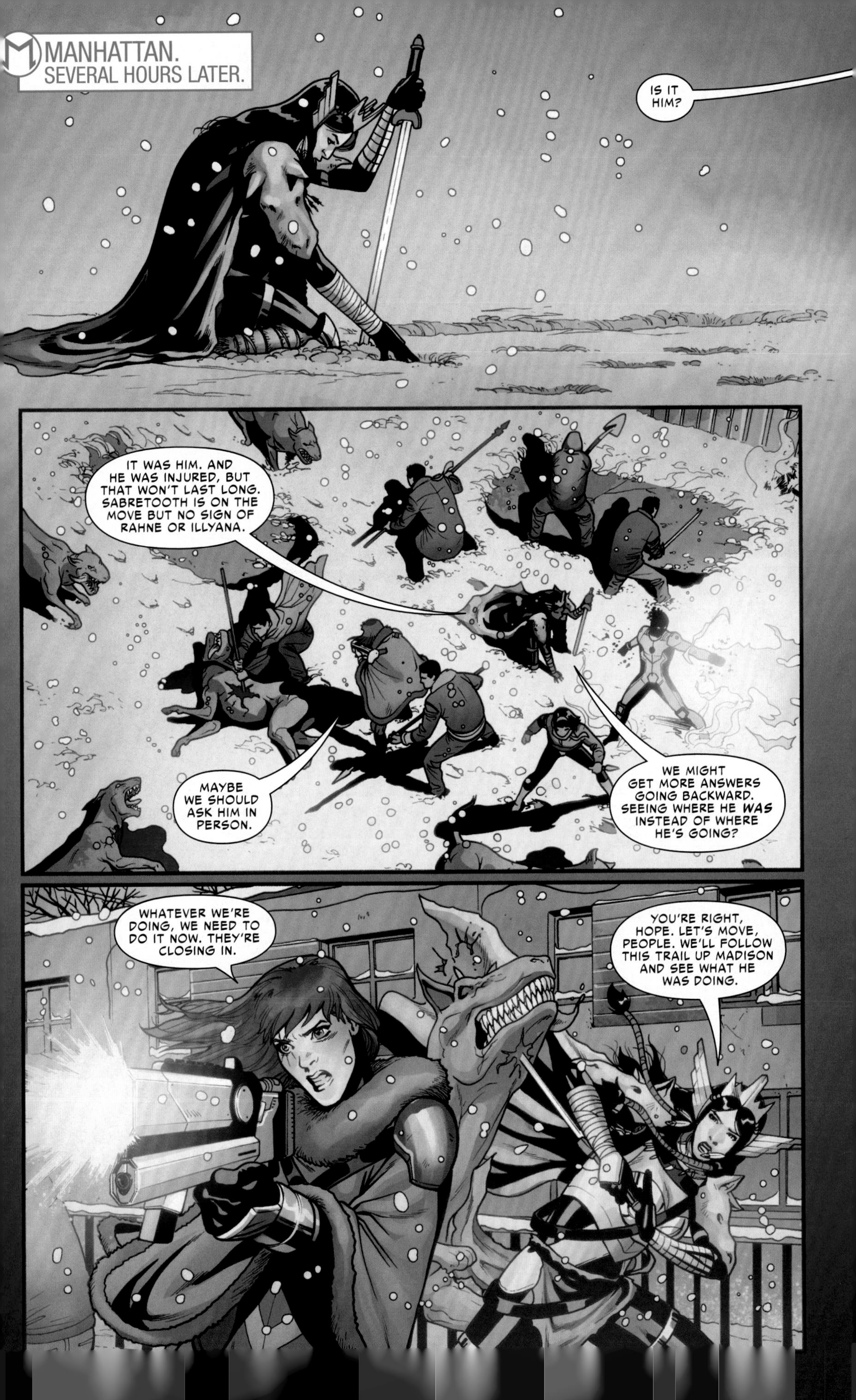
MANHATTAN.
SEVERAL HOURS LATER.
IS IT HIM?
IT WAS HIM. AND HE WAS INJURED, BUT THAT WON'T LAST LONG. SABRETOOTH IS ON THE MOVE BUT NO SIGN OF RAHNE OR ILLYANA.
MAYBE WE SHOULD ASK HIM IN PERSON.
WE MIGHT GET MORE ANSWERS GOING BACKWARD. SEEING WHERE HE WAS INSTEAD OF WHERE HE'S GOING?
WHATEVER WE'RE DOING, WE NEED TO DO IT NOW. THEY'RE CLOSING IN.
YOU'RE RIGHT, HOPE. LET'S MOVE, PEOPLE. WE'LL FOLLOW THIS TRAIL UP MADISON AND SEE WHAT HE WAS DOING.

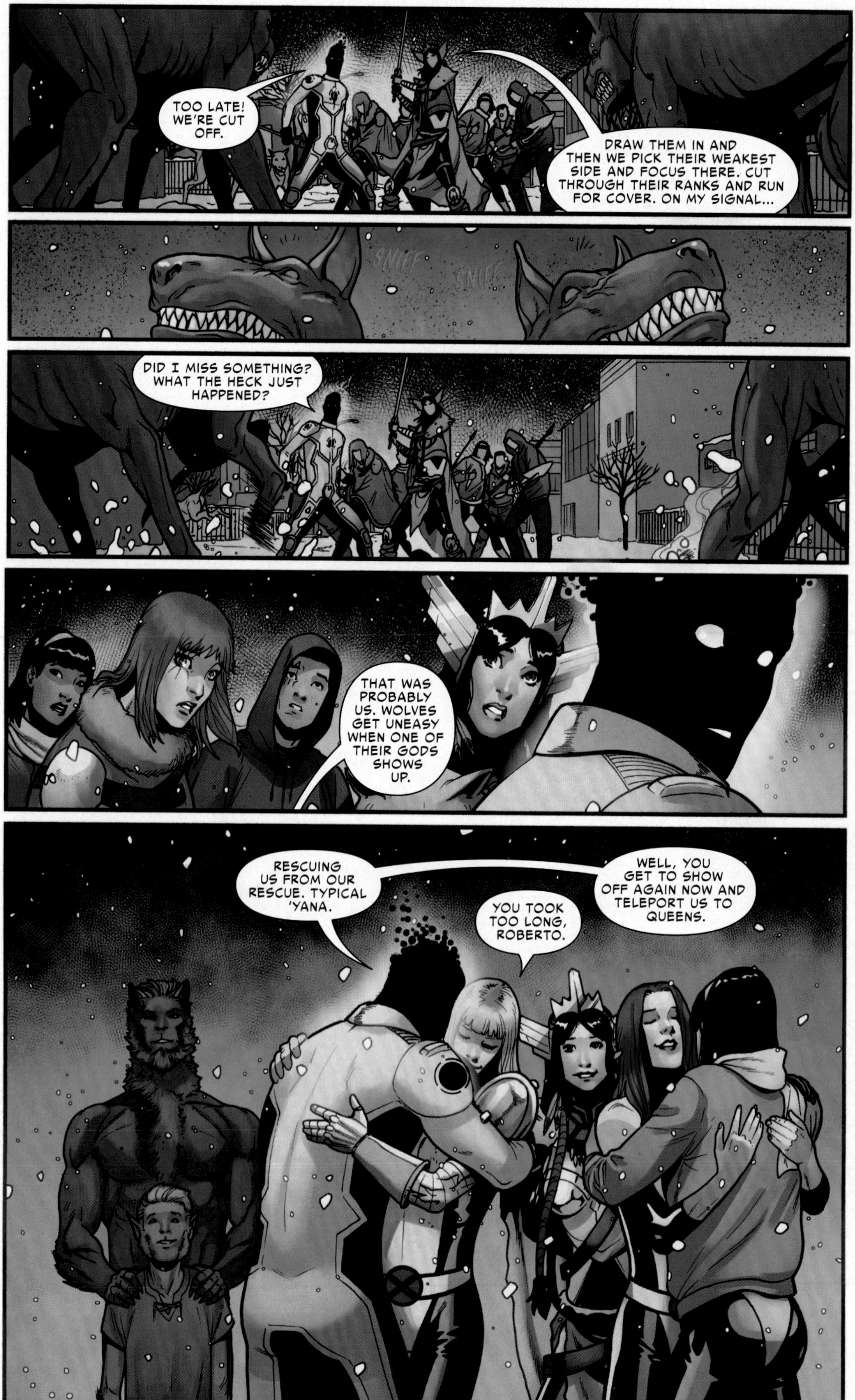

TOO LATE! WE'RE CUT OFF.
DRAW THEM IN AND THEN WE PICK THEIR WEAKEST SIDE AND FOCUS THERE. CUT THROUGH THEIR RANKS AND RUN FOR COVER. ON MY SIGNAL...
SNIFF
SNIFF
DID I MISS SOMETHING? WHAT THE HECK JUST HAPPENED?
THAT WAS PROBABLY US. WOLVES GET UNEASY WHEN ONE OF THEIR GODS SHOWS UP.
RESCUING US FROM OUR RESCUE. TYPICAL 'YANA.
WELL, YOU GET TO SHOW OFF AGAIN NOW AND TELEPORT US TO QUEENS.
YOU TOOK TOO LONG, ROBERTO.

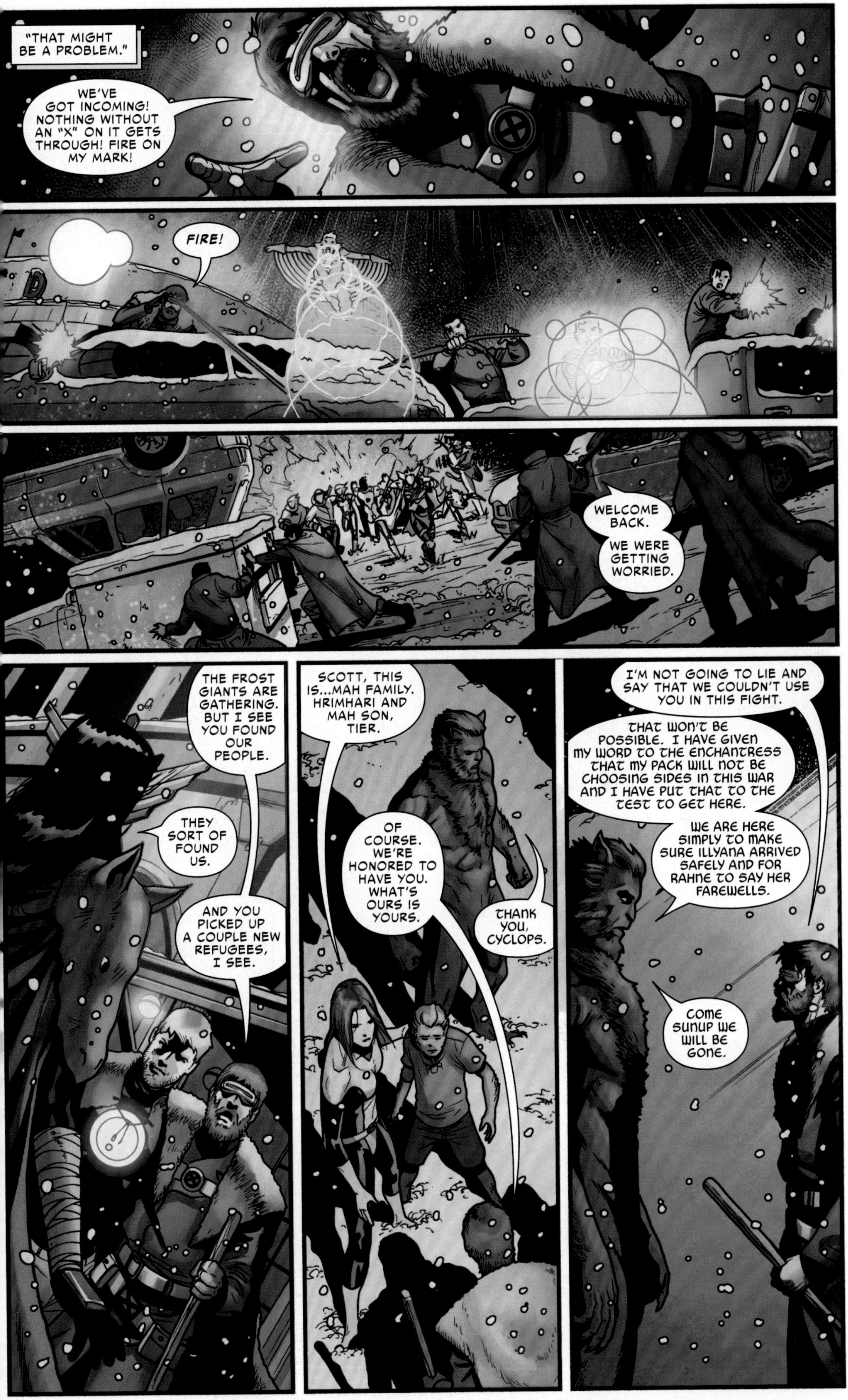
"THAT MIGHT BE A PROBLEM."
WE'VE GOT INCOMING! NOTHING WITHOUT AN "X" ON IT GETS THROUGH! FIRE ON MY MARK!
FIRE!
WELCOME BACK.
WE WERE GETTING WORRIED.
THE FROST GIANTS ARE GATHERING. BUT I SEE YOU FOUND OUR PEOPLE.
THEY SORT OF FOUND US.
AND YOU PICKED UP A COUPLE NEW REFUGEES, I SEE.
SCOTT, THIS IS...MAH FAMILY. HRIMHARI AND MAH SON, TIER.
OF COURSE. WE'RE HONORED TO HAVE YOU. WHAT'S OURS IS YOURS.
THANK YOU, CYCLOPS.
I'M NOT GOING TO LIE AND SAY THAT WE COULDN'T USE YOU IN THIS FIGHT.
THAT WON'T BE POSSIBLE. I HAVE GIVEN MY WORD TO THE ENCHANTRESS THAT MY PACK WILL NOT BE CHOOSING SIDES IN THIS WAR AND I HAVE PUT THAT TO THE TEST TO GET HERE.
WE ARE HERE SIMPLY TO MAKE SURE ILLYANA ARRIVED SAFELY AND FOR RAHNE TO SAY HER FAREWELLS.
COME SUNUP WE WILL BE GONE.

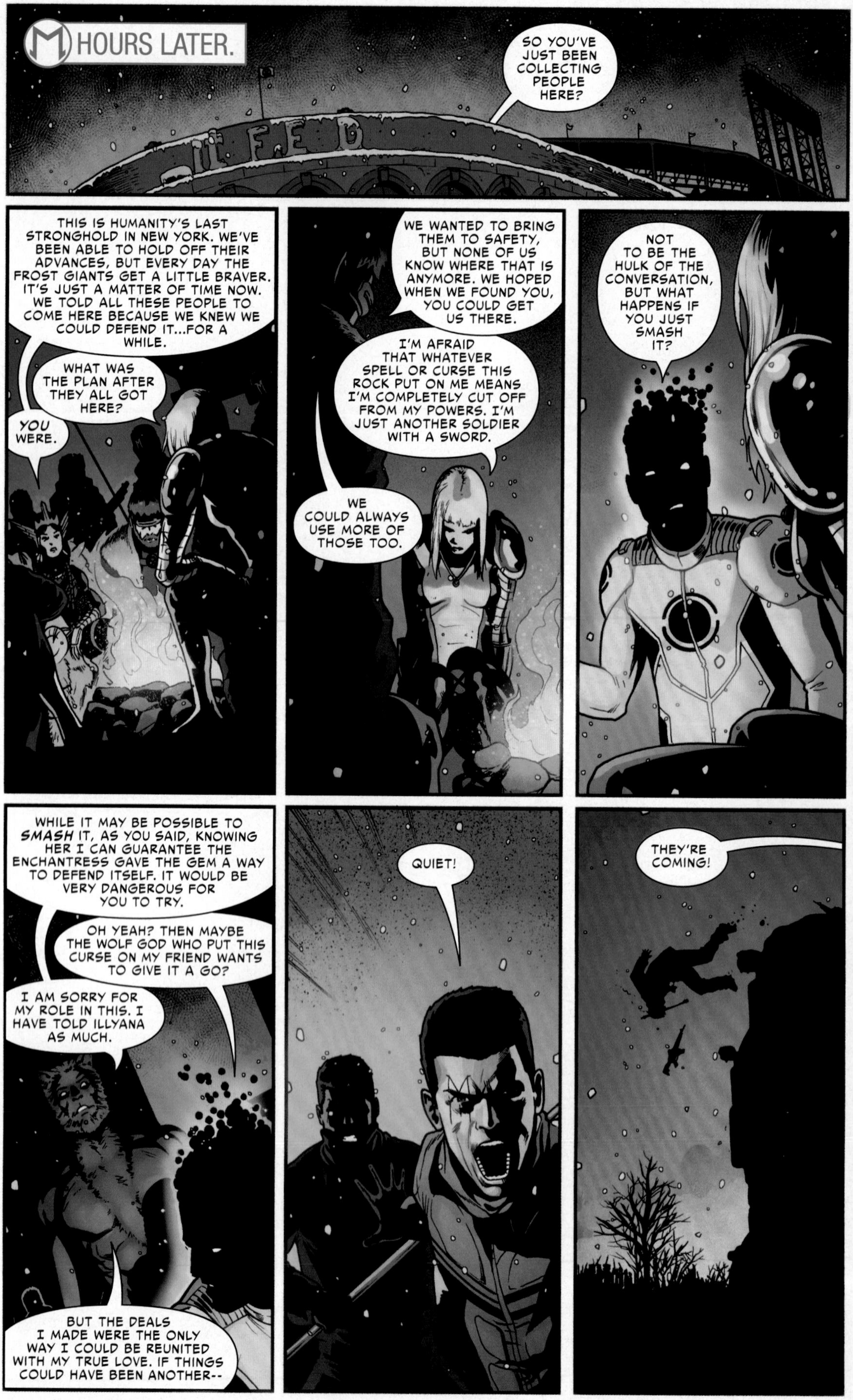
HOURS LATER.
SO YOU'VE JUST BEEN COLLECTING PEOPLE HERE?
THIS IS HUMANITY'S LAST STRONGHOLD IN NEW YORK. WE'VE BEEN ABLE TO HOLD OFF THEIR ADVANCES, BUT EVERY DAY THE FROST GIANTS GET A LITTLE BRAVER. IT'S JUST A MATTER OF TIME NOW. WE TOLD ALL THESE PEOPLE TO COME HERE BECAUSE WE KNEW WE COULD DEFEND IT...FOR A WHILE.
WHAT WAS THE PLAN AFTER THEY ALL GOT HERE?
YOU WERE.
WE WANTED TO BRING THEM TO SAFETY, BUT NONE OF US KNOW WHERE THAT IS ANYMORE. WE HOPED WHEN WE FOUND YOU, YOU COULD GET US THERE.
I'M AFRAID THAT WHATEVER SPELL OR CURSE THIS ROCK PUT ON ME MEANS I'M COMPLETELY CUT OFF FROM MY POWERS. I'M JUST ANOTHER SOLDIER WITH A SWORD.
WE COULD ALWAYS USE MORE OF THOSE TOO.
NOT TO BE THE HULK OF THE CONVERSATION, BUT WHAT HAPPENS IF YOU JUST SMASH IT?
WHILE IT MAY BE POSSIBLE TO SMASH IT, AS YOU SAID, KNOWING HER I CAN GUARANTEE THE ENCHANTRESS GAVE THE GEM A WAY TO DEFEND ITSELF. IT WOULD BE VERY DANGEROUS FOR YOU TO TRY.
OH YEAH? THEN MAYBE THE WOLF GOD WHO PUT THIS CURSE ON MY FRIEND WANTS TO GIVE IT A GO?
I AM SORRY FOR MY ROLE IN THIS. I HAVE TOLD ILLYANA AS MUCH.
BUT THE DEALS I MADE WERE THE ONLY WAY I COULD BE REUNITED WITH MY TRUE LOVE. IF THINGS COULD HAVE BEEN ANOTHER--
QUIET!
THEY'RE COMING!

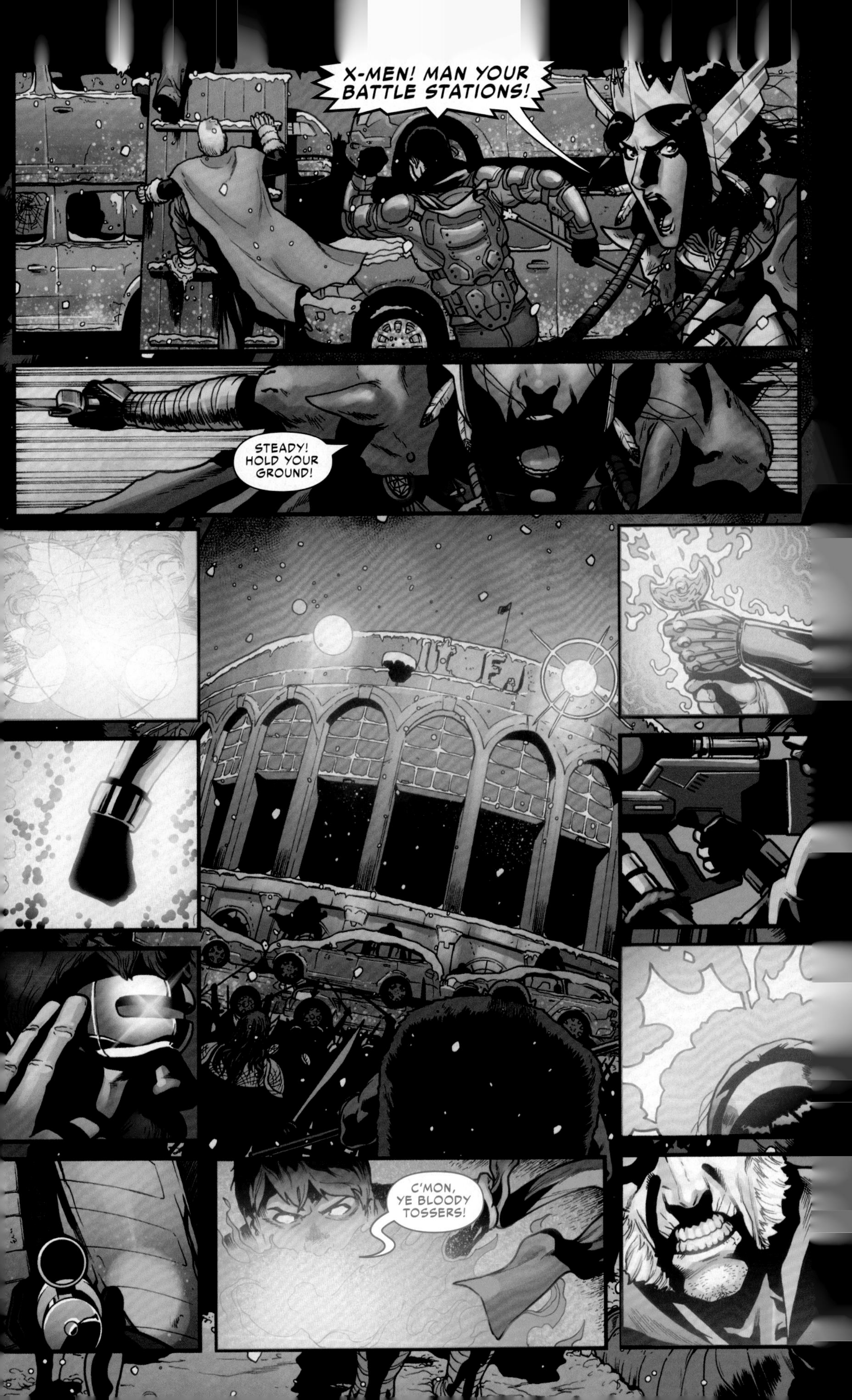

X-MEN! MAN YOUR BATTLE STATIONS!
STEADY! HOLD YOUR GROUND!
C'MON, YE BLOODY TOSSERS!

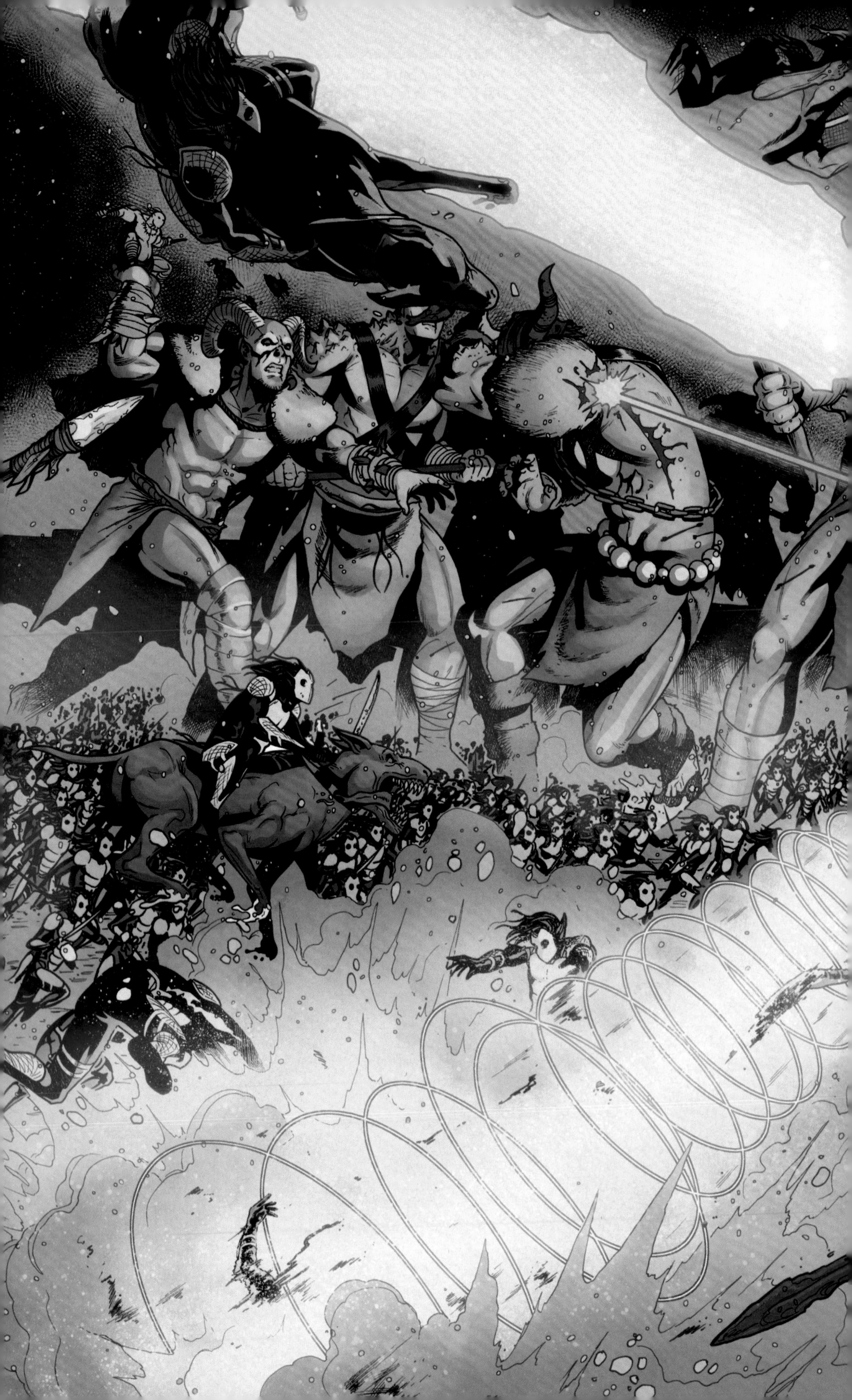

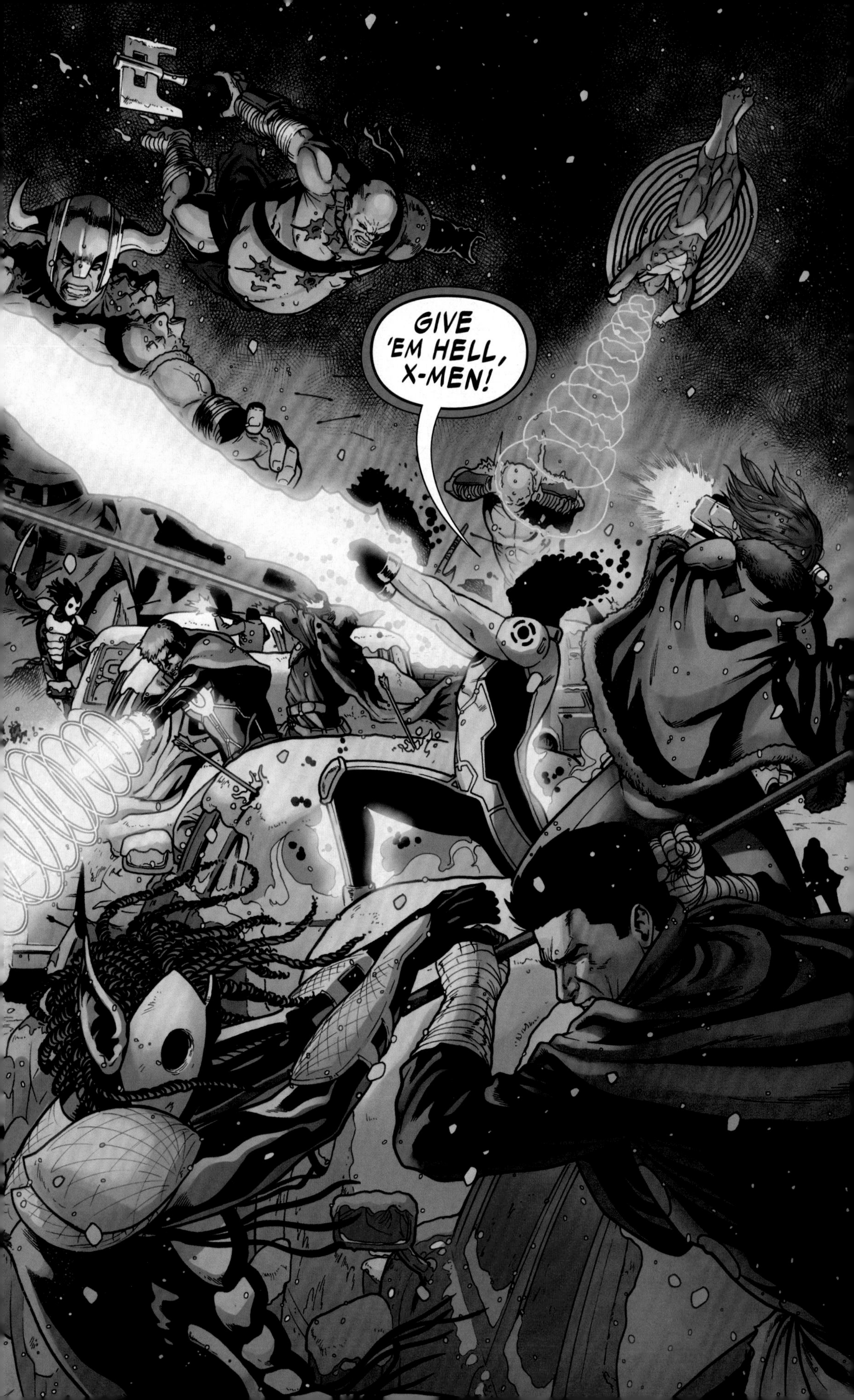
GIVE 'EM HELL, X-MEN!

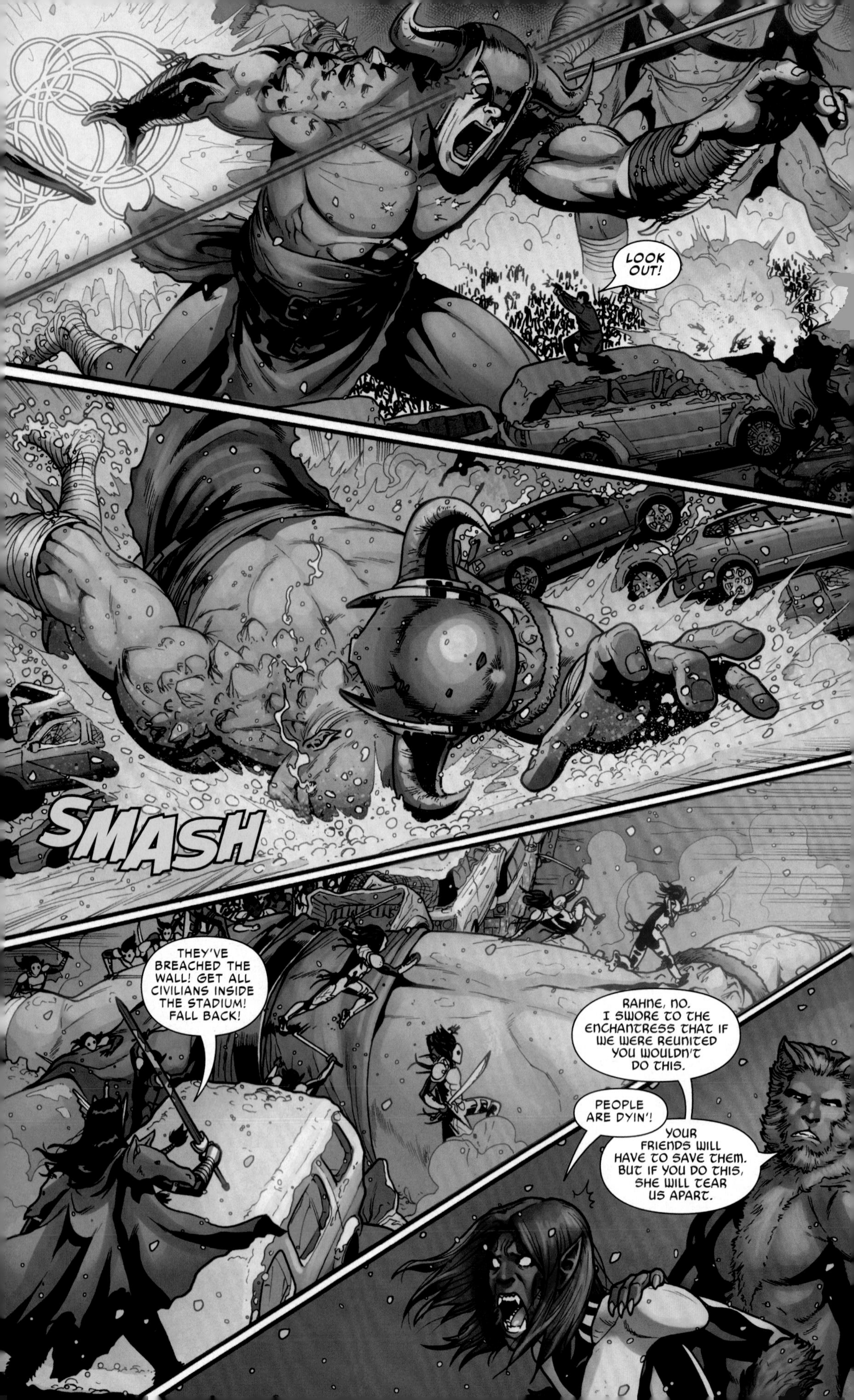
LOOK OUT!
SMASH
THEY'VE BREACHED THE WALL! GET ALL CIVILIANS INSIDE THE STADIUM! FALL BACK!
RAHNE, NO. I SWORE TO THE ENCHANTRESS THAT IF WE WERE REUNITED YOU WOULDN'T DO THIS.
PEOPLE ARE DYIN'!
YOUR FRIENDS WILL HAVE TO SAVE THEM. BUT IF YOU DO THIS, SHE WILL TEAR US APART.

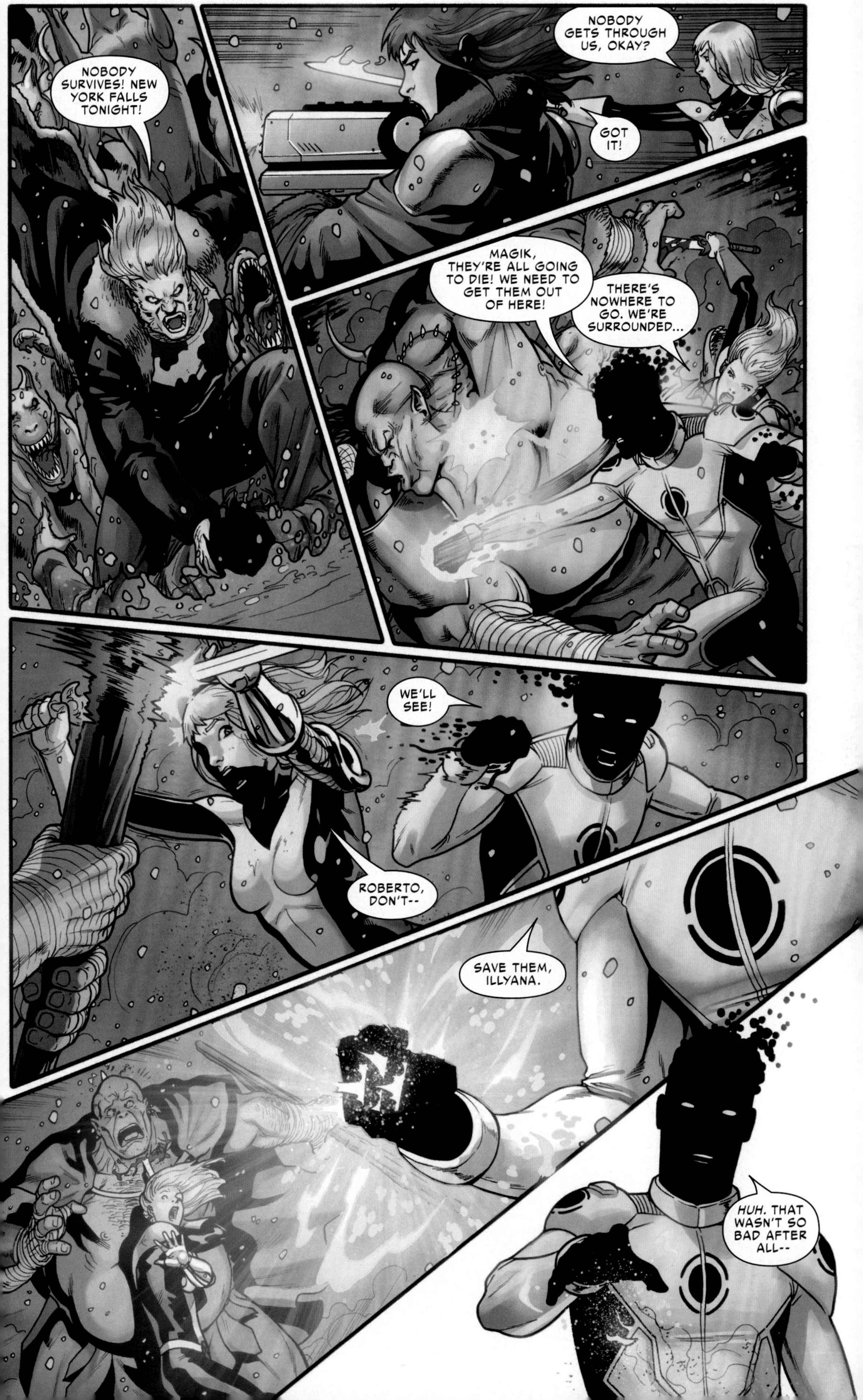
NOBODY SURVIVES! NEW YORK FALLS TONIGHT!
NOBODY GETS THROUGH US, OKAY?
GOT IT!
MAGIK, THEY'RE ALL GOING TO DIE! WE NEED TO GET THEM OUT OF HERE!
THERE'S NOWHERE TO GO. WE'RE SURROUNDED...
WE'LL SEE!
ROBERTO, DON'T--
SAVE THEM, ILLYANA.
HUH. THAT WASN'T SO BAD AFTER ALL--

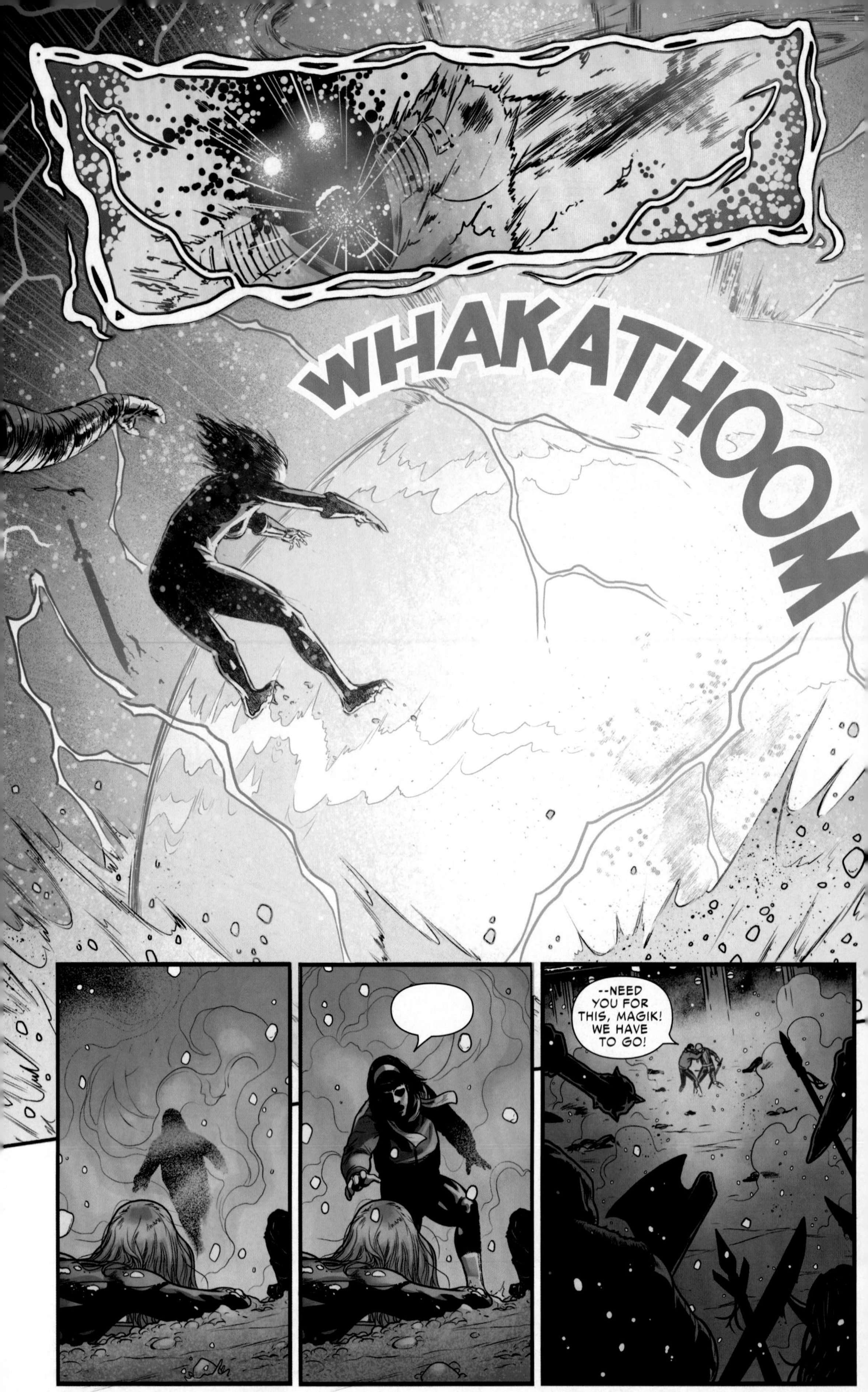
WHAKATHOOM
--NEED YOU FOR THIS, MAGIK! WE HAVE TO GO!

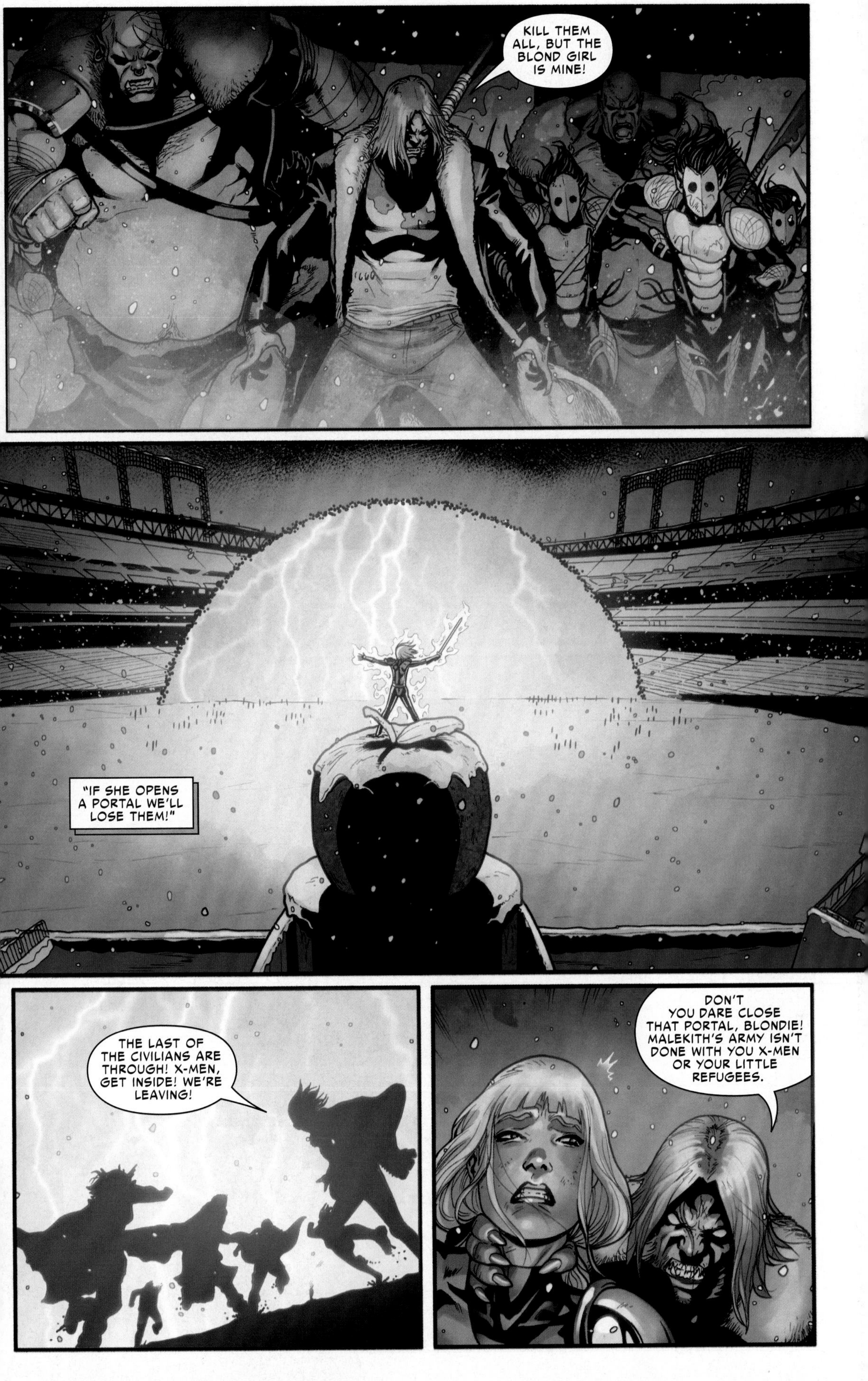
KILL THEM ALL, BUT THE BLOND GIRL IS MINE!
"IF SHE OPENS A PORTAL WE'LL LOSE THEM!"
THE LAST OF THE CIVILIANS ARE THROUGH! X-MEN, GET INSIDE! WE'RE LEAVING!
DON'T YOU DARE CLOSE THAT PORTAL, BLONDIE! MALEKITH'S ARMY ISN'T DONE WITH YOU X-MEN OR YOUR LITTLE REFUGEES.

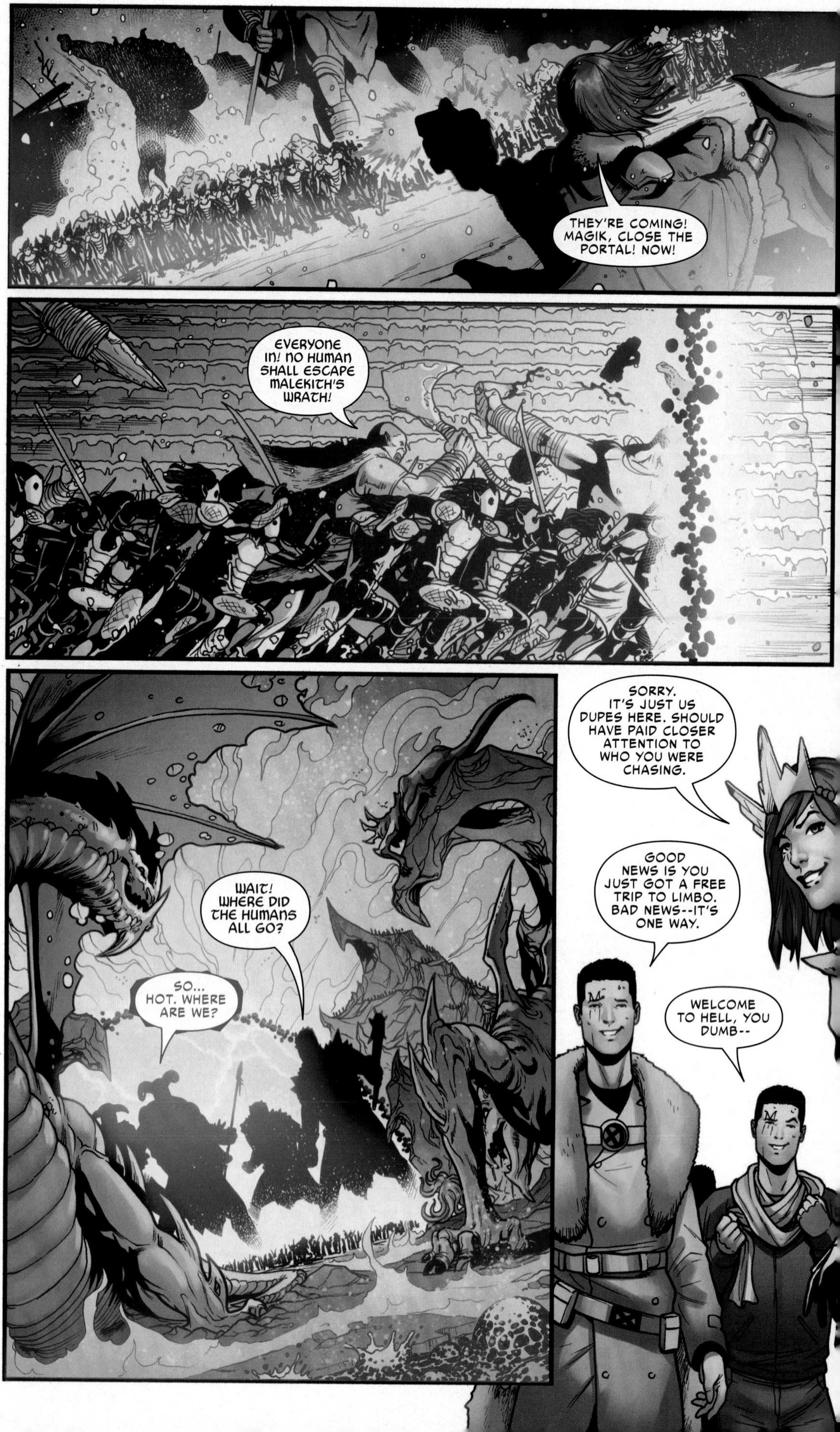
THEY'RE COMING! MAGIK, CLOSE THE PORTAL! NOW!
EVERYONE IN! NO HUMAN SHALL ESCAPE MALEKITH'S WRATH!
WAIT! WHERE DID THE HUMANS ALL GO?
SO... HOT. WHERE ARE WE?
SORRY. IT'S JUST US DUPES HERE. SHOULD HAVE PAID CLOSER ATTENTION TO WHO YOU WERE CHASING.
GOOD NEWS IS YOU JUST GOT A FREE TRIP TO LIMBO. BAD NEWS--IT'S ONE WAY.
WELCOME TO HELL, YOU DUMB--

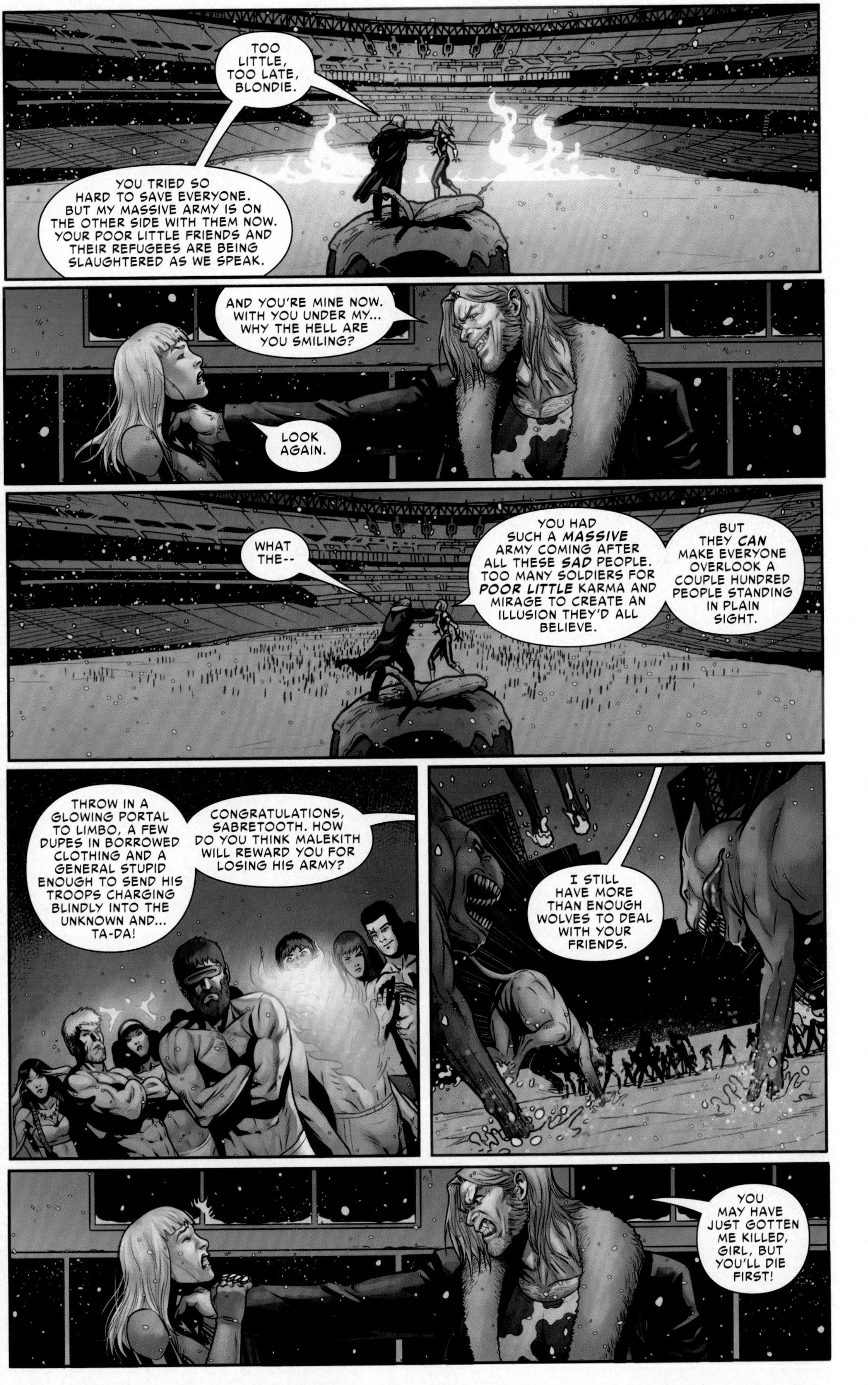

TOO LITTLE, TOO LATE, BLONDIE.
YOU TRIED SO HARD TO SAVE EVERYONE. BUT MY MASSIVE ARMY IS ON THE OTHER SIDE WITH THEM NOW. YOUR POOR LITTLE FRIENDS AND THEIR REFUGEES ARE BEING SLAUGHTERED AS WE SPEAK.
AND YOU'RE MINE NOW. WITH YOU UNDER MY... WHY THE HELL ARE YOU SMILING?
LOOK AGAIN.
WHAT THE--
YOU HAD SUCH A MASSIVE ARMY COMING AFTER ALL THESE SAD PEOPLE. TOO MANY SOLDIERS FOR POOR LITTLE KARMA AND MIRAGE TO CREATE AN ILLUSION THEY'D ALL BELIEVE.
BUT THEY CAN MAKE EVERYONE OVERLOOK A COUPLE HUNDRED PEOPLE STANDING IN PLAIN SIGHT.
THROW IN A GLOWING PORTAL TO LIMBO, A FEW DUPES IN BORROWED CLOTHING AND A GENERAL STUPID ENOUGH TO SEND HIS TROOPS CHARGING BLINDLY INTO THE UNKNOWN AND... TA-DA!
CONGRATULATIONS, SABRETOOTH. HOW DO YOU THINK MALEKITH WILL REWARD YOU FOR LOSING HIS ARMY?
I STILL HAVE MORE THAN ENOUGH WOLVES TO DEAL WITH YOUR FRIENDS.
YOU MAY HAVE JUST GOTTEN ME KILLED, GIRL, BUT YOU'LL DIE FIRST!

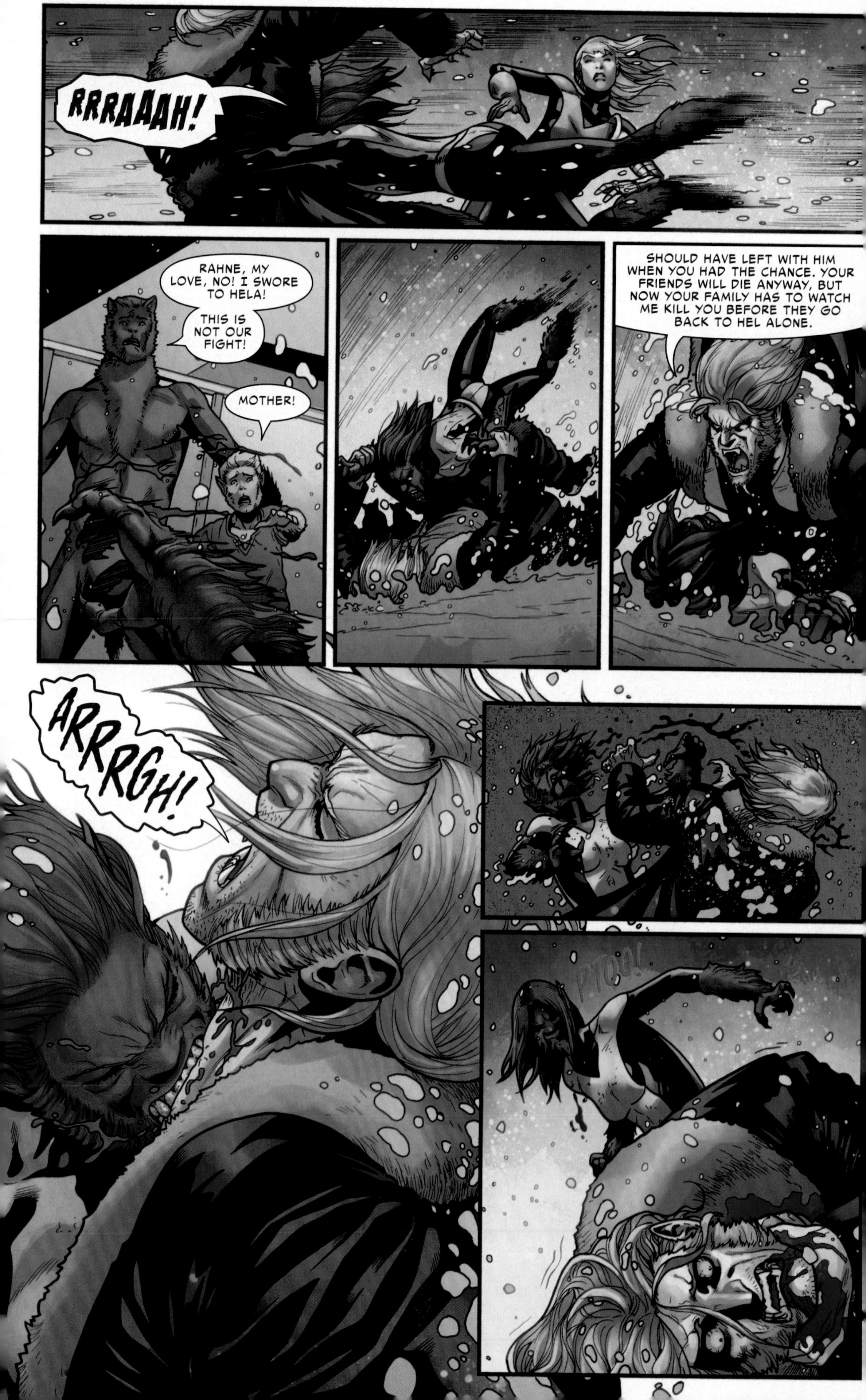
RRRAAAH!
RAHNE, MY LOVE, NO! I SWORE TO HELA!
THIS IS NOT OUR FIGHT!
MOTHER!
SHOULD HAVE LEFT WITH HIM WHEN YOU HAD THE CHANCE. YOUR FRIENDS WILL DIE ANYWAY, BUT NOW YOUR FAMILY HAS TO WATCH ME KILL YOU BEFORE THEY GO BACK TO HEL ALONE.
ARRRGH!
PTOO!

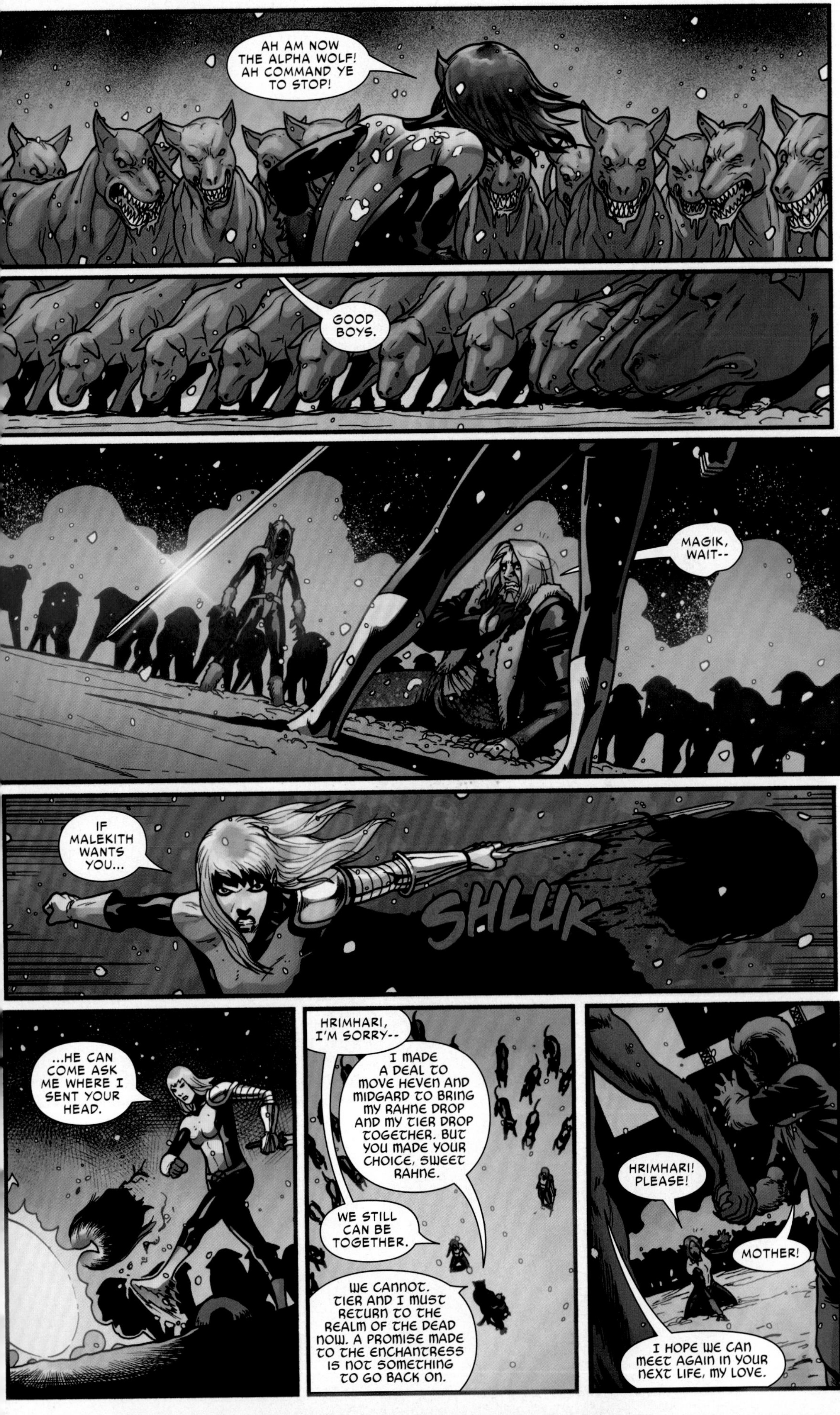
AH AM NOW THE ALPHA WOLF! AH COMMAND YE TO STOP!
GOOD BOYS.
MAGIK, WAIT--
IF MALEKITH WANTS YOU...
SHLUK
...HE CAN COME ASK ME WHERE I SENT YOUR HEAD.
HRIMHARI, I'M SORRY--
I MADE A DEAL TO MOVE HEVEN AND MIDGARD TO BRING MY RAHNE DROP AND MY TIER DROP TOGETHER. BUT YOU MADE YOUR CHOICE, SWEET RAHNE.
WE STILL CAN BE TOGETHER.
WE CANNOT. TIER AND I MUST RETURN TO THE REALM OF THE DEAD NOW. A PROMISE MADE TO THE ENCHANTRESS IS NOT SOMETHING TO GO BACK ON.
HRIMHARI! PLEASE!
MOTHER!
I HOPE WE CAN MEET AGAIN IN YOUR NEXT LIFE, MY LOVE.

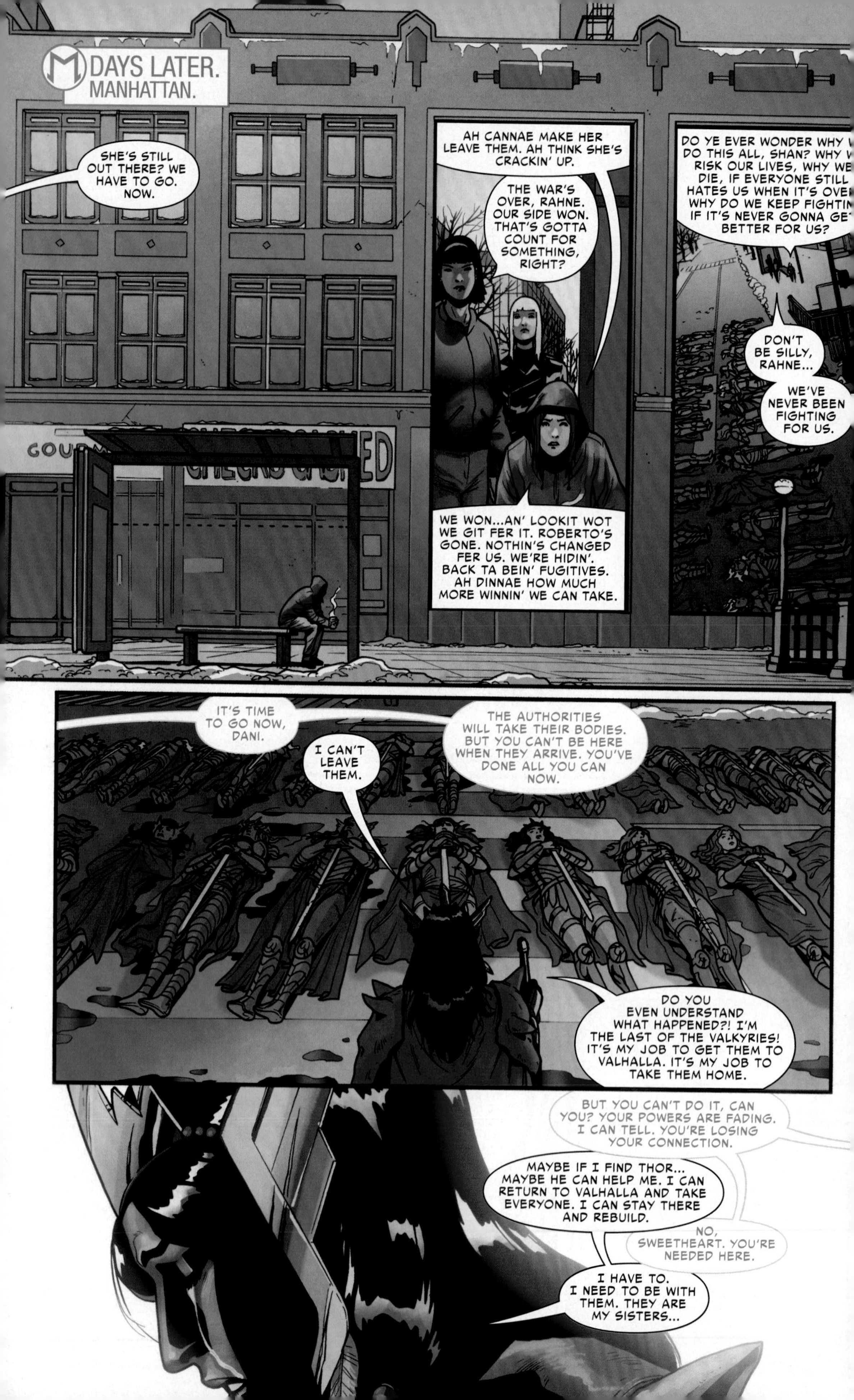
DAYS LATER. MANHATTAN.
SHE'S STILL OUT THERE? WE HAVE TO GO. NOW.
AH CANNAE MAKE HER LEAVE THEM. AH THINK SHE'S CRACKIN' UP.
THE WAR'S OVER, RAHNE. OUR SIDE WON. THAT'S GOTTA COUNT FOR SOMETHING, RIGHT?
WE WON...AN' LOOKIT WOT WE GIT FER IT. ROBERTO'S GONE. NOTHIN'S CHANGED FER US. WE'RE HIDIN'. BACK TA BEIN' FUGITIVES. AH DINNAE HOW MUCH MORE WINNIN' WE CAN TAKE.
DO YE EVER WONDER WHY DO THIS ALL, SHAN? WHY RISK OUR LIVES, WHY WE DIE, IF EVERYONE STILL HATES US WHEN IT'S OVE WHY DO WE KEEP FIGHTI IF IT'S NEVER GONNA GE BETTER FOR US?
DON'T BE SILLY, RAHNE...
WE'VE NEVER BEEN FIGHTING FOR US.
IT'S TIME TO GO NOW, DANI.
I CAN'T LEAVE THEM.
THE AUTHORITIES WILL TAKE THEIR BODIES. BUT YOU CAN'T BE HERE WHEN THEY ARRIVE. YOU'VE DONE ALL YOU CAN NOW.
DO YOU EVEN UNDERSTAND WHAT HAPPENED?! I'M THE LAST OF THE VALKYRIES! IT'S MY JOB TO GET THEM TO VALHALLA. IT'S MY JOB TO TAKE THEM HOME.
BUT YOU CAN'T DO IT, CAN YOU? YOUR POWERS ARE FADING. I CAN TELL. YOU'RE LOSING YOUR CONNECTION.
MAYBE IF I FIND THOR... MAYBE HE CAN HELP ME. I CAN RETURN TO VALHALLA AND TAKE EVERYONE. I CAN STAY THERE AND REBUILD.
NO, SWEETHEART. YOU'RE NEEDED HERE.
I HAVE TO. I NEED TO BE WITH THEM. THEY ARE MY SISTERS...

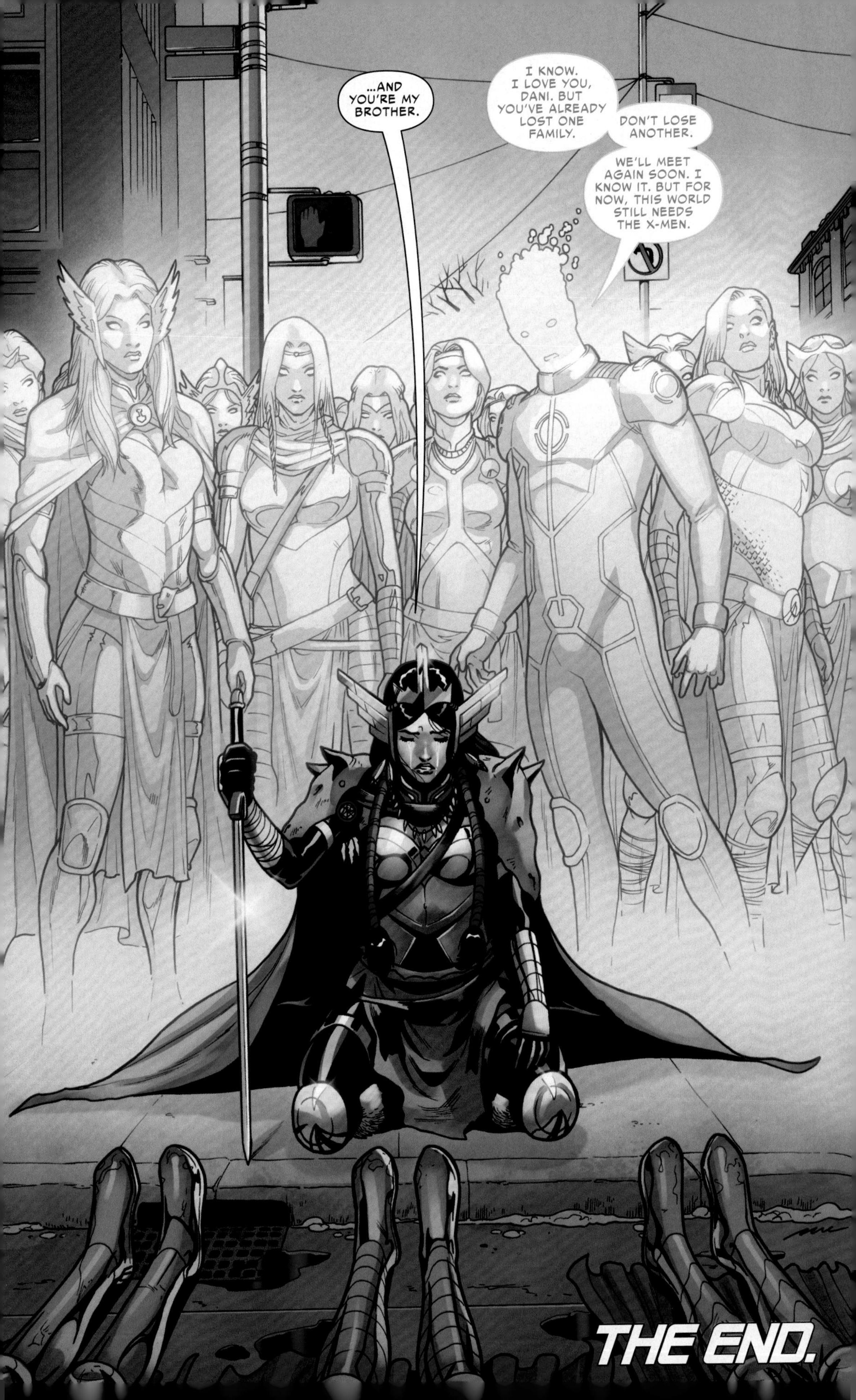

...AND YOU'RE MY BROTHER.
I KNOW. I LOVE YOU, DANI. BUT YOU'VE ALREADY LOST ONE FAMILY.
DON'T LOSE ANOTHER.
WE'LL MEET AGAIN SOON. I KNOW IT. BUT FOR NOW, THIS WORLD STILL NEEDS THE X-MEN.
THE END.

Joseph, Magneto's younger clone, gathered former Brotherhood of Evil Mutants members Pyro, Avalanche, Toad, Random and Juggernaut to attack a U.S. Air Force base in Transia. The X-Men intervened and were ready to take Joseph into custody when Kwannon, a telekinetic ninja with tenuous ties to the X-Men, executed him. Before the X-Men could deal with their newest addition, Mirage suffered a massive psychic shock caused by the death of their former teammate Wolfsbane!

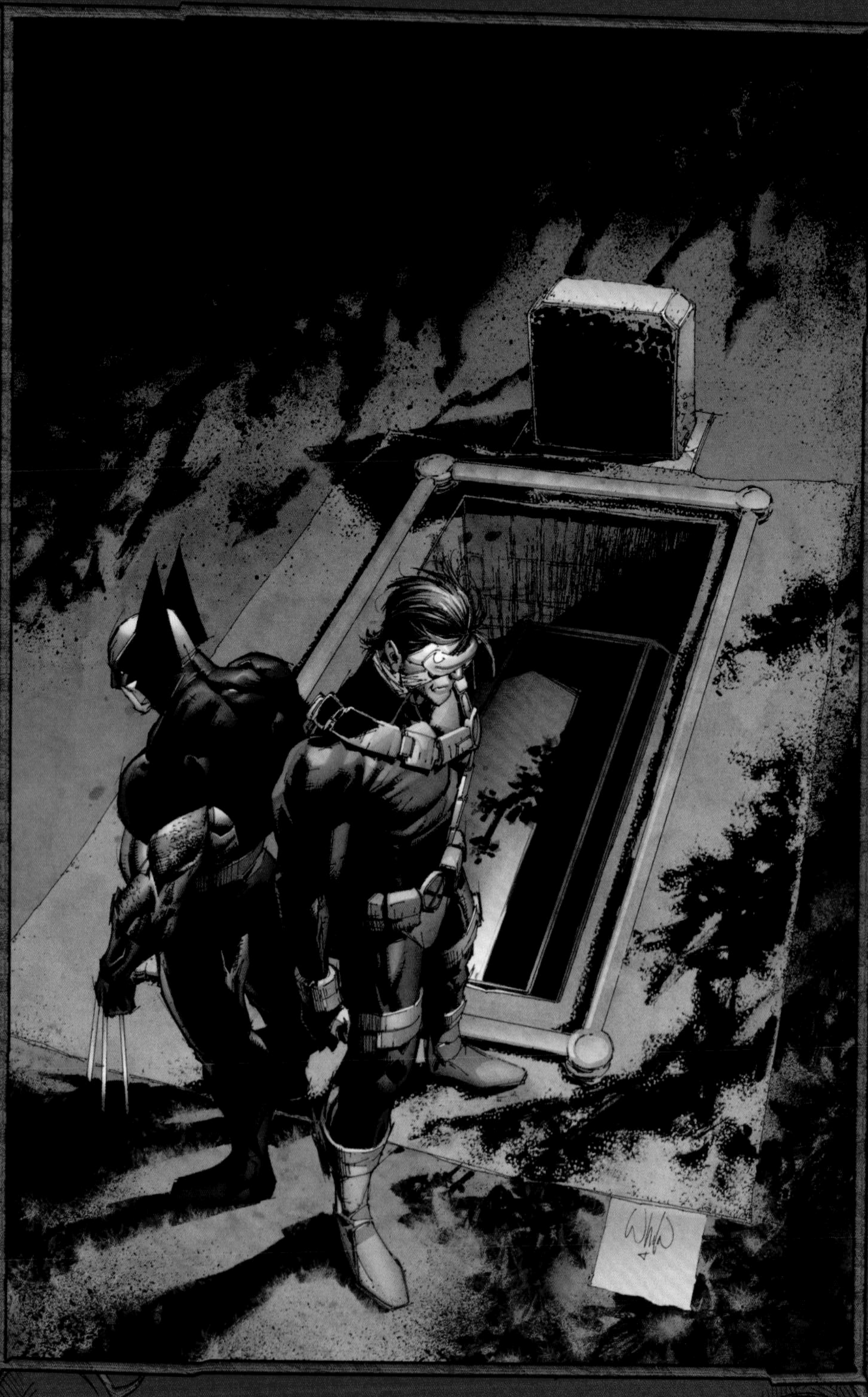

UNCANNY X-MEN #17

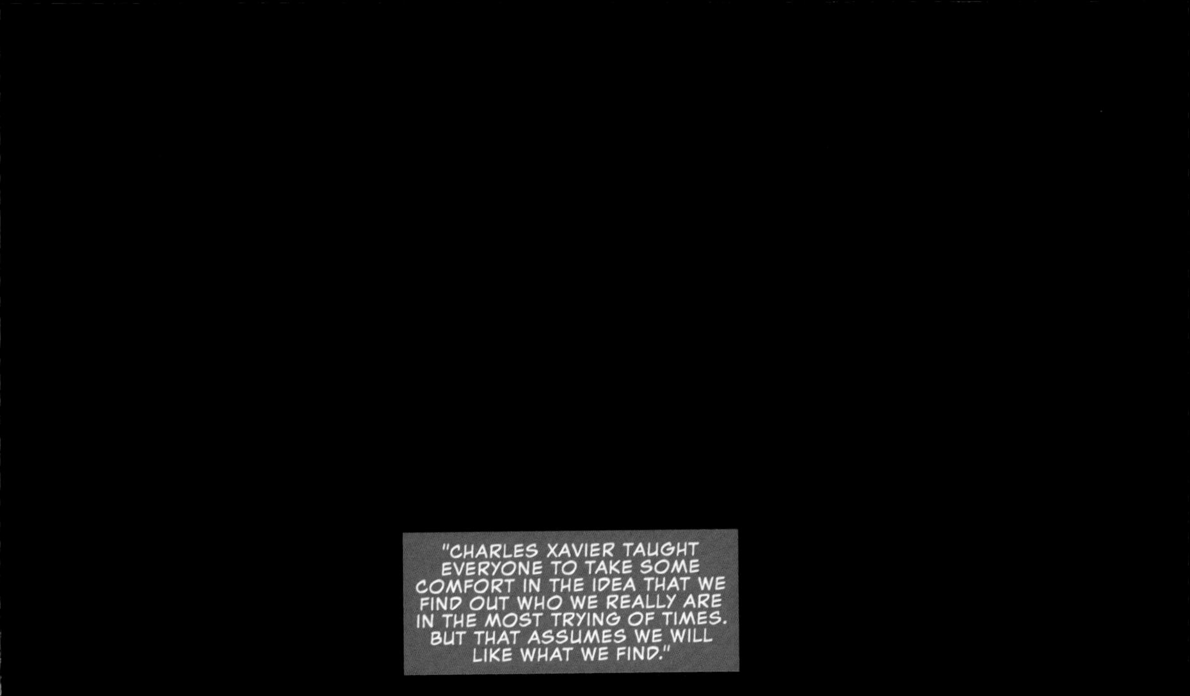
"CHARLES XAVIER TAUGHT EVERYONE TO TAKE SOME COMFORT IN THE IDEA THAT WE FIND OUT WHO WE REALLY ARE IN THE MOST TRYING OF TIMES. BUT THAT ASSUMES WE WILL LIKE WHAT WE FIND."

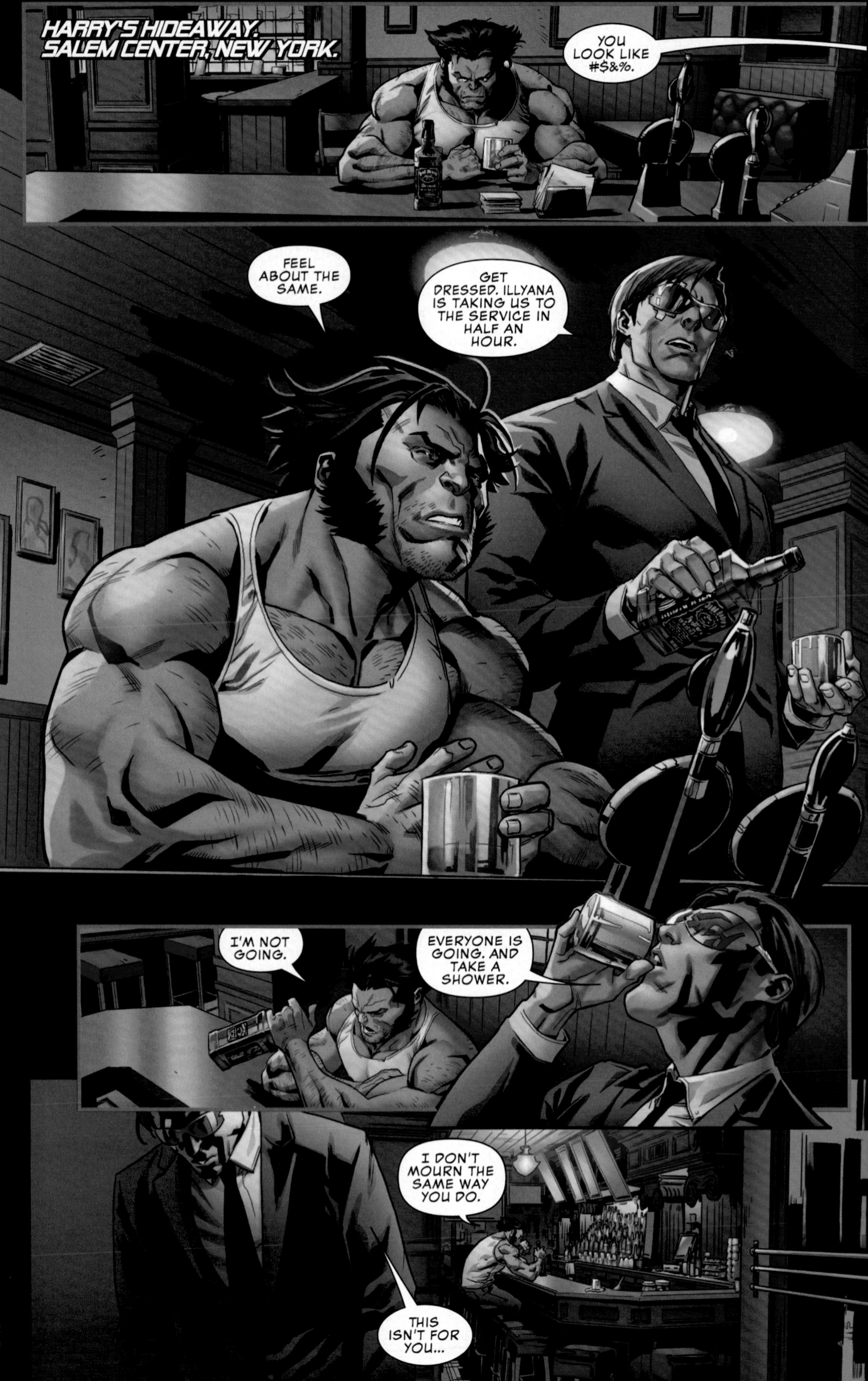
HARRY'S HIDEAWAY. SALEM CENTER, NEW YORK.
YOU LOOK LIKE #$&%.
FEEL ABOUT THE SAME.
GET DRESSED. ILLYANA IS TAKING US TO THE SERVICE IN HALF AN HOUR.
I'M NOT GOING.
EVERYONE IS GOING. AND TAKE A SHOWER.
I DON'T MOURN THE SAME WAY YOU DO.
THIS ISN'T FOR YOU...

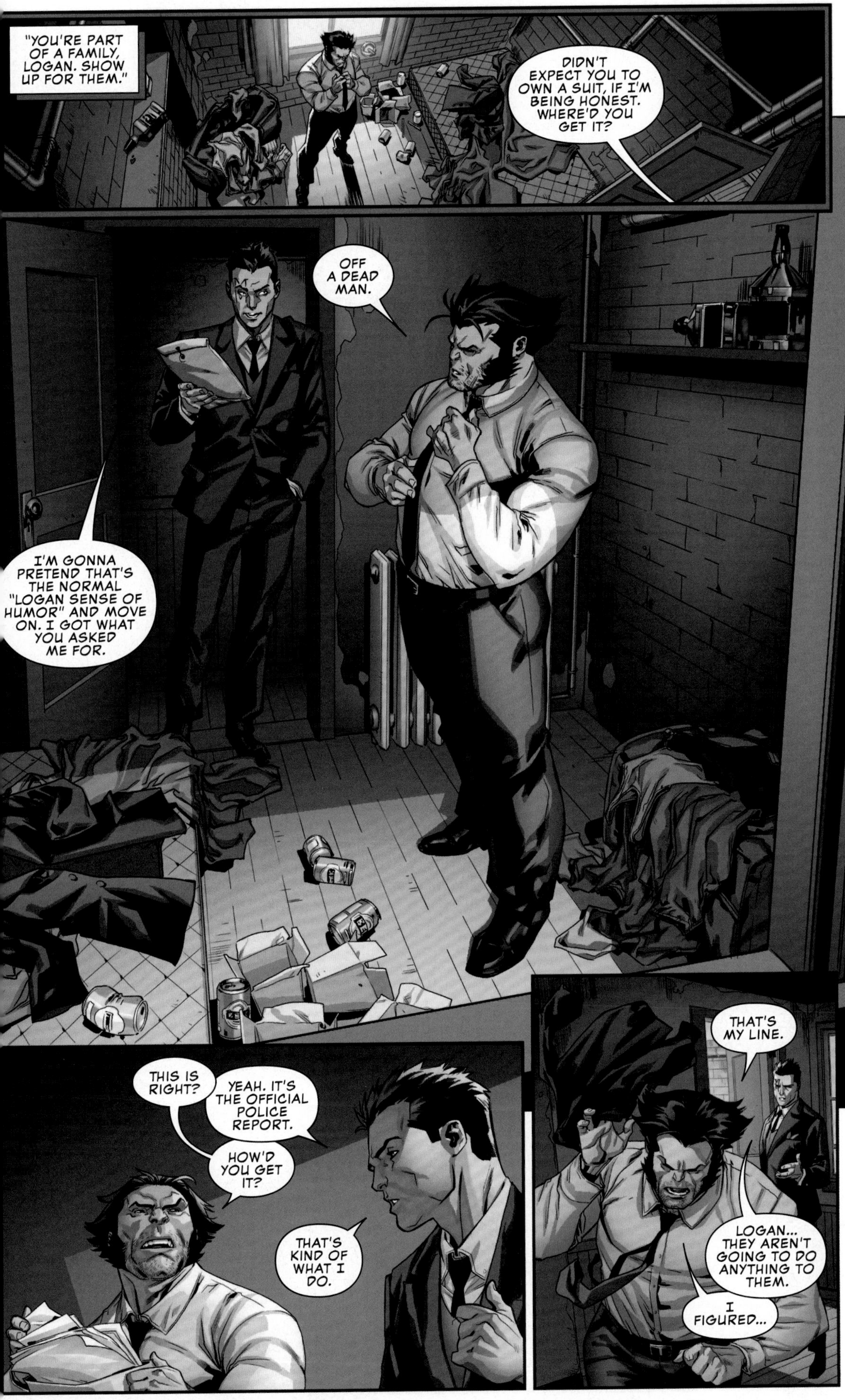

"YOU'RE PART OF A FAMILY, LOGAN. SHOW UP FOR THEM."
DIDN'T EXPECT YOU TO OWN A SUIT, IF I'M BEING HONEST. WHERE'D YOU GET IT?
OFF A DEAD MAN.
I'M GONNA PRETEND THAT'S THE NORMAL "LOGAN SENSE OF HUMOR" AND MOVE ON. I GOT WHAT YOU ASKED ME FOR.
THIS IS RIGHT?
YEAH. IT'S THE OFFICIAL POLICE REPORT.
HOW'D YOU GET IT?
THAT'S KIND OF WHAT I DO.
THAT'S MY LINE.
LOGAN... THEY AREN'T GOING TO DO ANYTHING TO THEM.
I FIGURED...

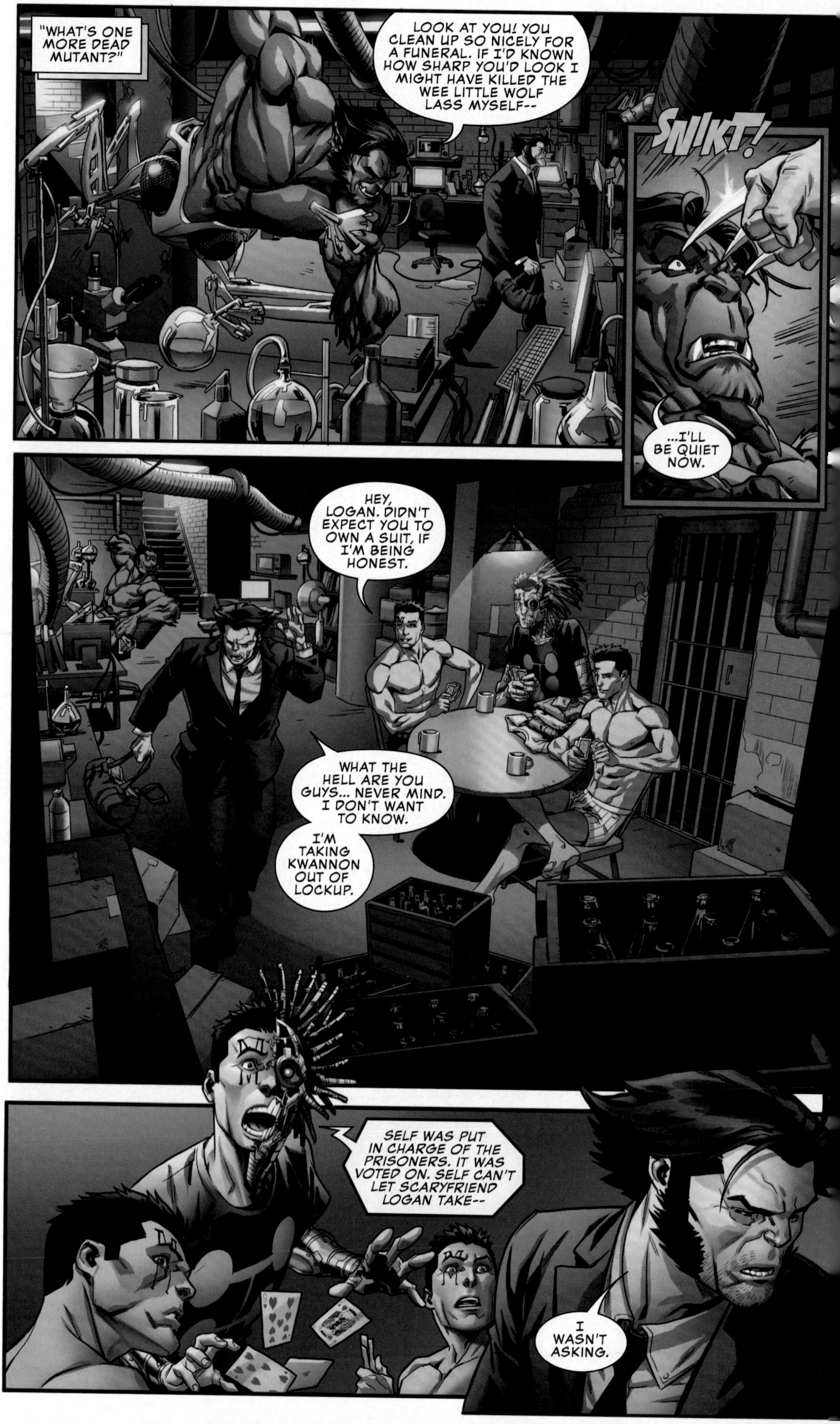

"WHAT'S ONE MORE DEAD MUTANT?"
LOOK AT YOU! YOU CLEAN UP SO NICELY FOR A FUNERAL. IF I'D KNOWN HOW SHARP YOU'D LOOK I MIGHT HAVE KILLED THE WEE LITTLE WOLF LASS MYSELF--
SNIKT!
...I'LL BE QUIET NOW.
HEY, LOGAN. DIDN'T EXPECT YOU TO OWN A SUIT, IF I'M BEING HONEST.
WHAT THE HELL ARE YOU GUYS... NEVER MIND. I DON'T WANT TO KNOW.
I'M TAKING KWANNON OUT OF LOCKUP.
SELF WAS PUT IN CHARGE OF THE PRISONERS. IT WAS VOTED ON. SELF CAN'T LET SCARYFRIEND LOGAN TAKE--
I WASN'T ASKING.

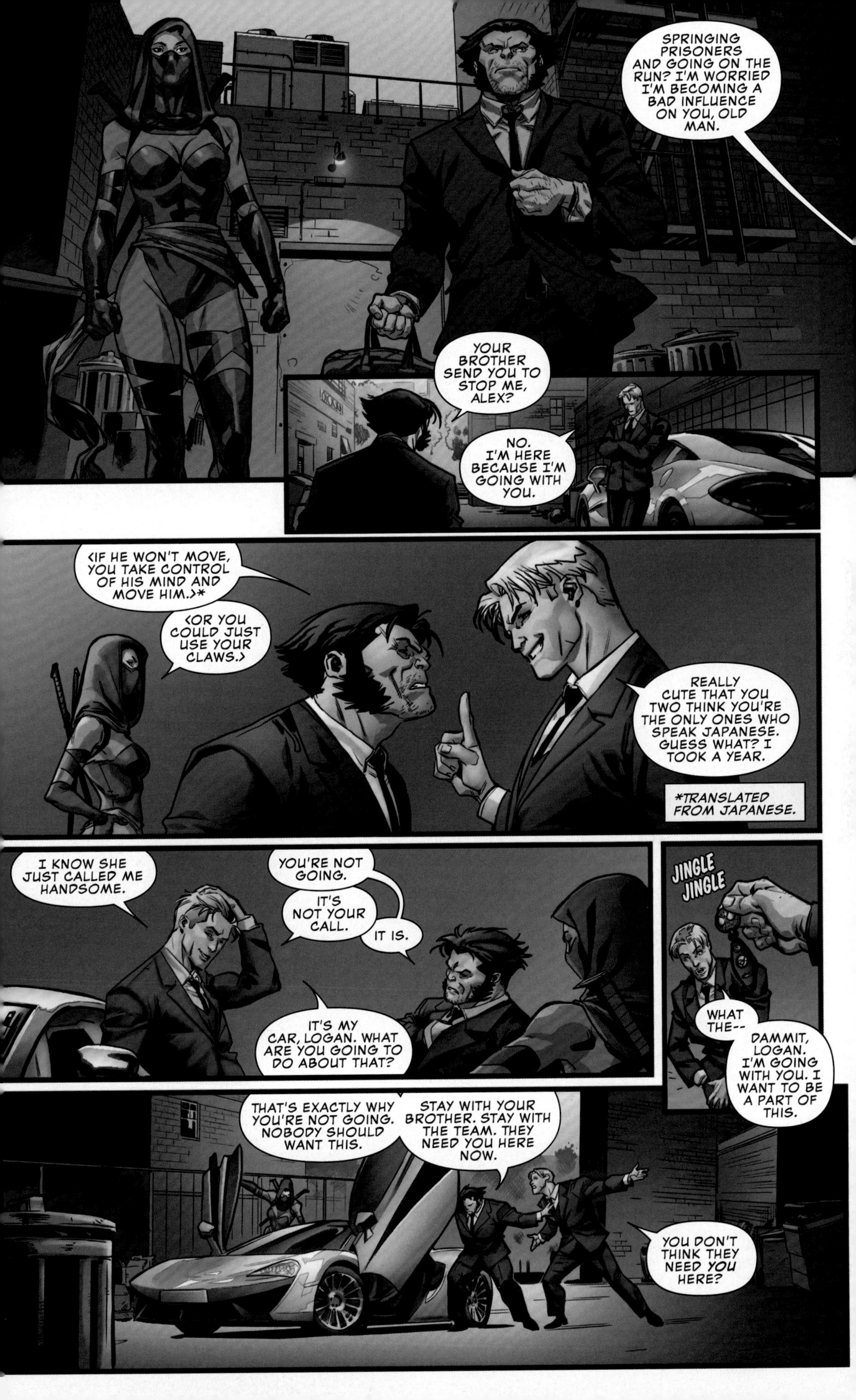
SPRINGING PRISONERS AND GOING ON THE RUN? I'M WORRIED I'M BECOMING A BAD INFLUENCE ON YOU, OLD MAN.
YOUR BROTHER SEND YOU TO STOP ME, ALEX?
NO. I'M HERE BECAUSE I'M GOING WITH YOU.
<IF HE WON'T MOVE, YOU TAKE CONTROL OF HIS MIND AND MOVE HIM.>*
<OR YOU COULD JUST USE YOUR CLAWS.>
REALLY CUTE THAT YOU TWO THINK YOU'RE THE ONLY ONES WHO SPEAK JAPANESE. GUESS WHAT? I TOOK A YEAR.
*TRANSLATED FROM JAPANESE.
I KNOW SHE JUST CALLED ME HANDSOME.
YOU'RE NOT GOING.
IT'S NOT YOUR CALL.
IT IS.
IT'S MY CAR, LOGAN. WHAT ARE YOU GOING TO DO ABOUT THAT?
JINGLE JINGLE
WHAT THE--
DAMMIT, LOGAN. I'M GOING WITH YOU. I WANT TO BE A PART OF THIS.
THAT'S EXACTLY WHY YOU'RE NOT GOING. NOBODY SHOULD WANT THIS.
STAY WITH YOUR BROTHER. STAY WITH THE TEAM. THEY NEED YOU HERE NOW.
YOU DON'T THINK THEY NEED *YOU* HERE?

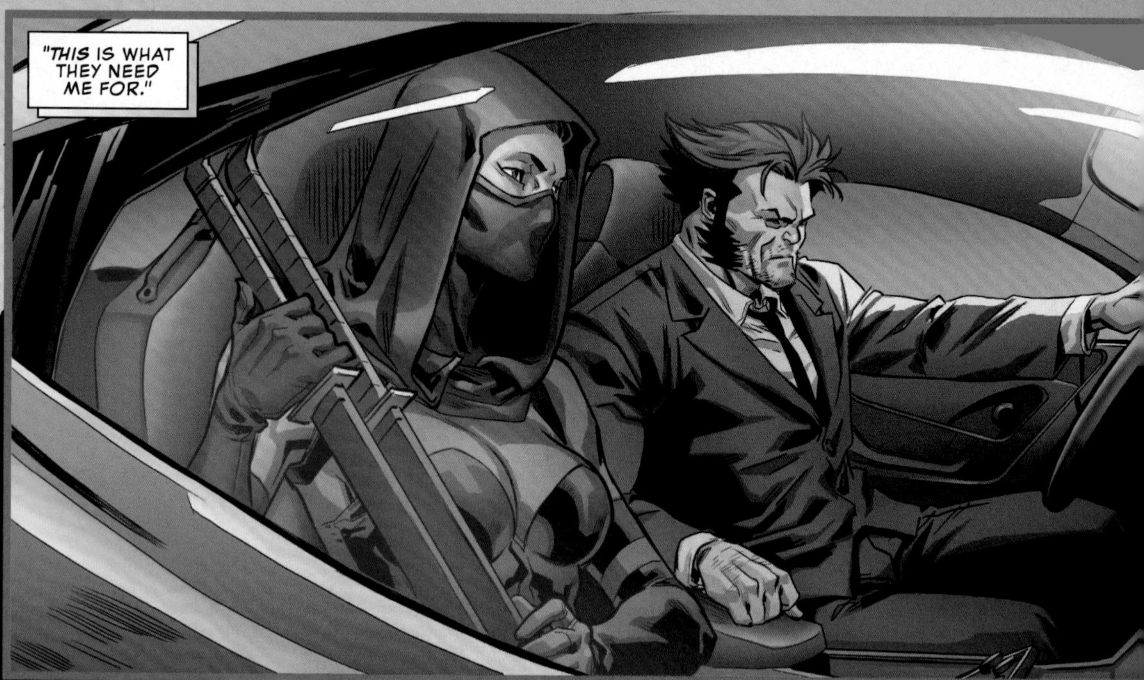
"THIS IS WHAT THEY NEED ME FOR."

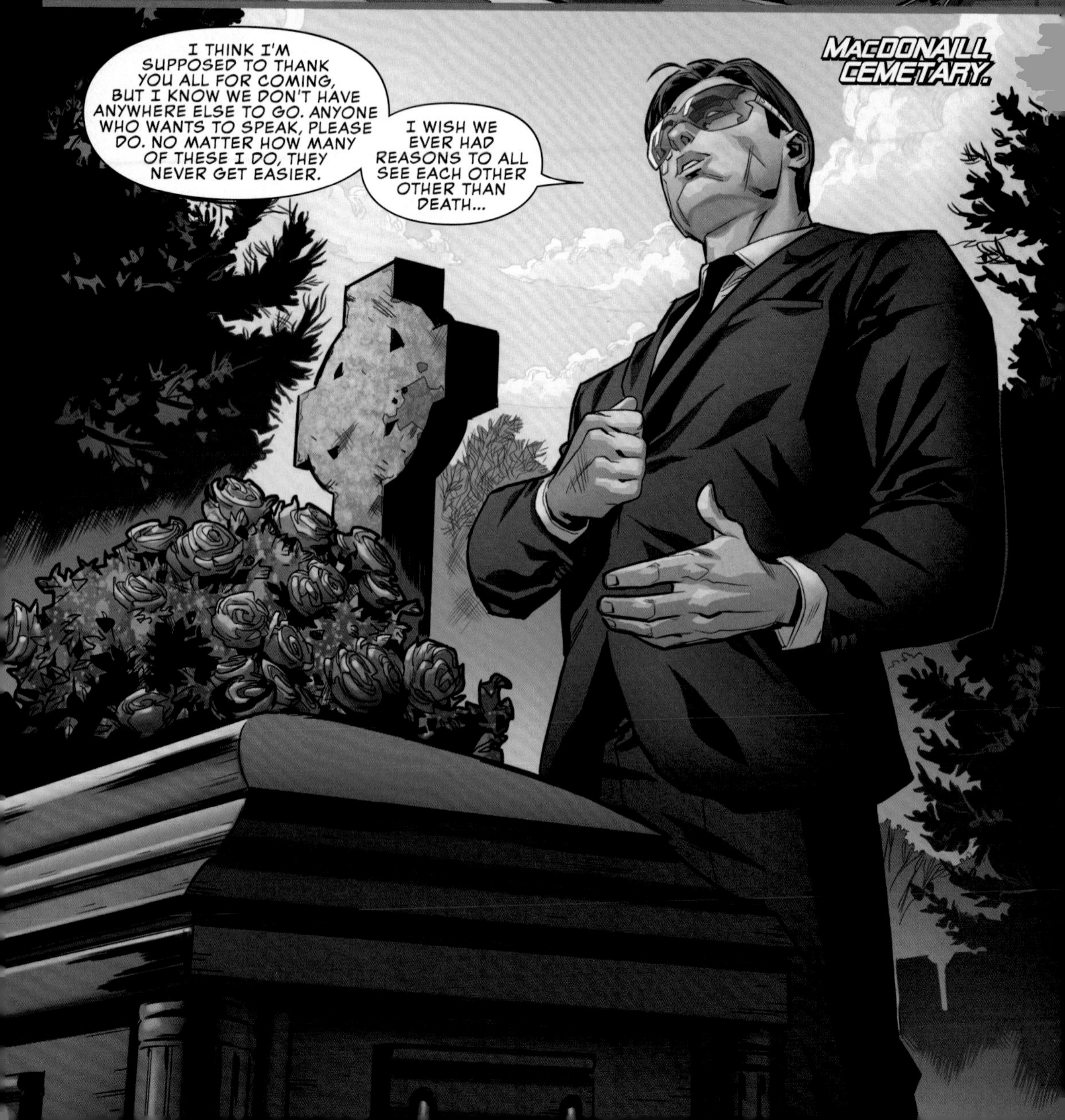
MacDONAILL CEMETARY.
I THINK I'M SUPPOSED TO THANK YOU ALL FOR COMING, BUT I KNOW WE DON'T HAVE ANYWHERE ELSE TO GO. ANYONE WHO WANTS TO SPEAK, PLEASE DO. NO MATTER HOW MANY OF THESE I DO, THEY NEVER GET EASIER.
I WISH WE EVER HAD REASONS TO ALL SEE EACH OTHER OTHER THAN DEATH...

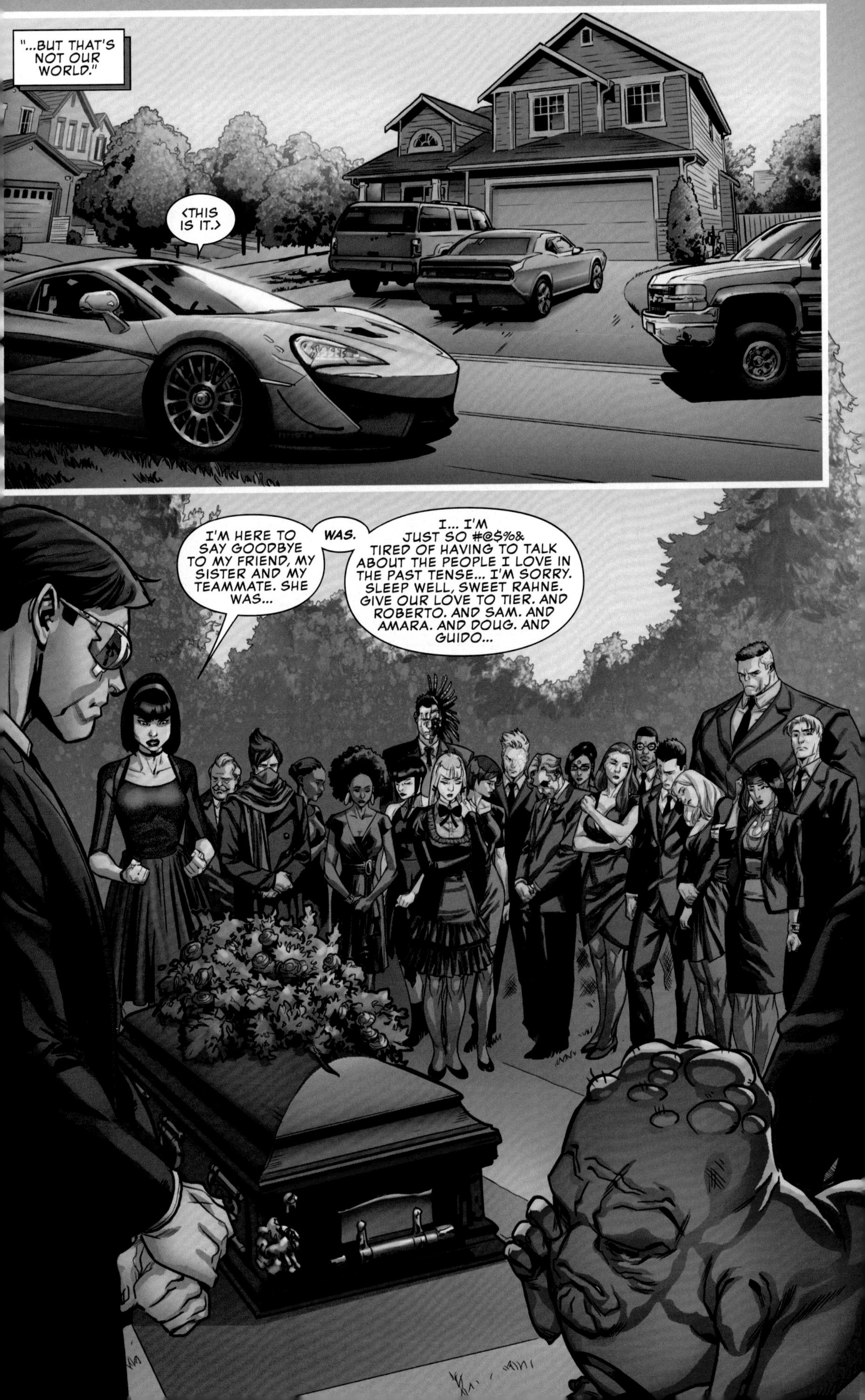
"...BUT THAT'S NOT OUR WORLD."
<THIS IS IT.>
I'M HERE TO SAY GOODBYE TO MY FRIEND, MY SISTER AND MY TEAMMATE. SHE WAS...
WAS.
I... I'M JUST SO #@$%& TIRED OF HAVING TO TALK ABOUT THE PEOPLE I LOVE IN THE PAST TENSE... I'M SORRY. SLEEP WELL, SWEET RAHNE. GIVE OUR LOVE TO TIER. AND ROBERTO. AND SAM. AND AMARA. AND DOUG. AND GUIDO...

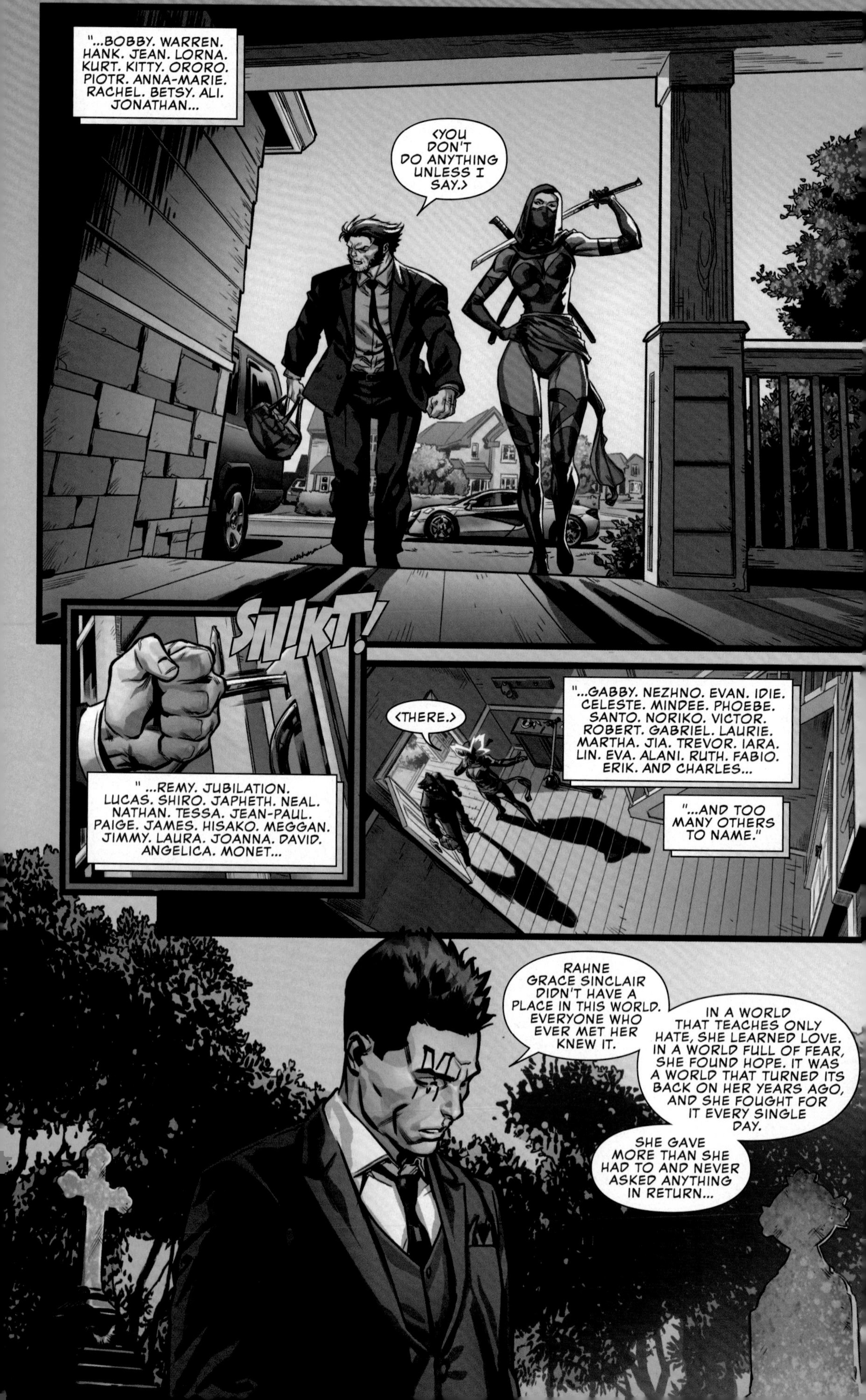
"...BOBBY. WARREN. HANK. JEAN. LORNA. KURT. KITTY. ORORO. PIOTR. ANNA-MARIE. RACHEL. BETSY. ALI. JONATHAN...
<YOU DON'T DO ANYTHING UNLESS I SAY.>
SNIKT!
" ...REMY. JUBILATION. LUCAS. SHIRO. JAPHETH. NEAL. NATHAN. TESSA. JEAN-PAUL. PAIGE. JAMES. HISAKO. MEGGAN. JIMMY. LAURA. JOANNA. DAVID. ANGELICA. MONET...
<THERE.>
"...GABBY. NEZHNO. EVAN. IDIE. CELESTE. MINDEE. PHOEBE. SANTO. NORIKO. VICTOR. ROBERT. GABRIEL. LAURIE. MARTHA. JIA. TREVOR. IARA. LIN. EVA. ALANI. RUTH. FABIO. ERIK. AND CHARLES...
"...AND TOO MANY OTHERS TO NAME."
RAHNE GRACE SINCLAIR DIDN'T HAVE A PLACE IN THIS WORLD. EVERYONE WHO EVER MET HER KNEW IT.
IN A WORLD THAT TEACHES ONLY HATE, SHE LEARNED LOVE. IN A WORLD FULL OF FEAR, SHE FOUND HOPE. IT WAS A WORLD THAT TURNED ITS BACK ON HER YEARS AGO, AND SHE FOUGHT FOR IT EVERY SINGLE DAY.
SHE GAVE MORE THAN SHE HAD TO AND NEVER ASKED ANYTHING IN RETURN...

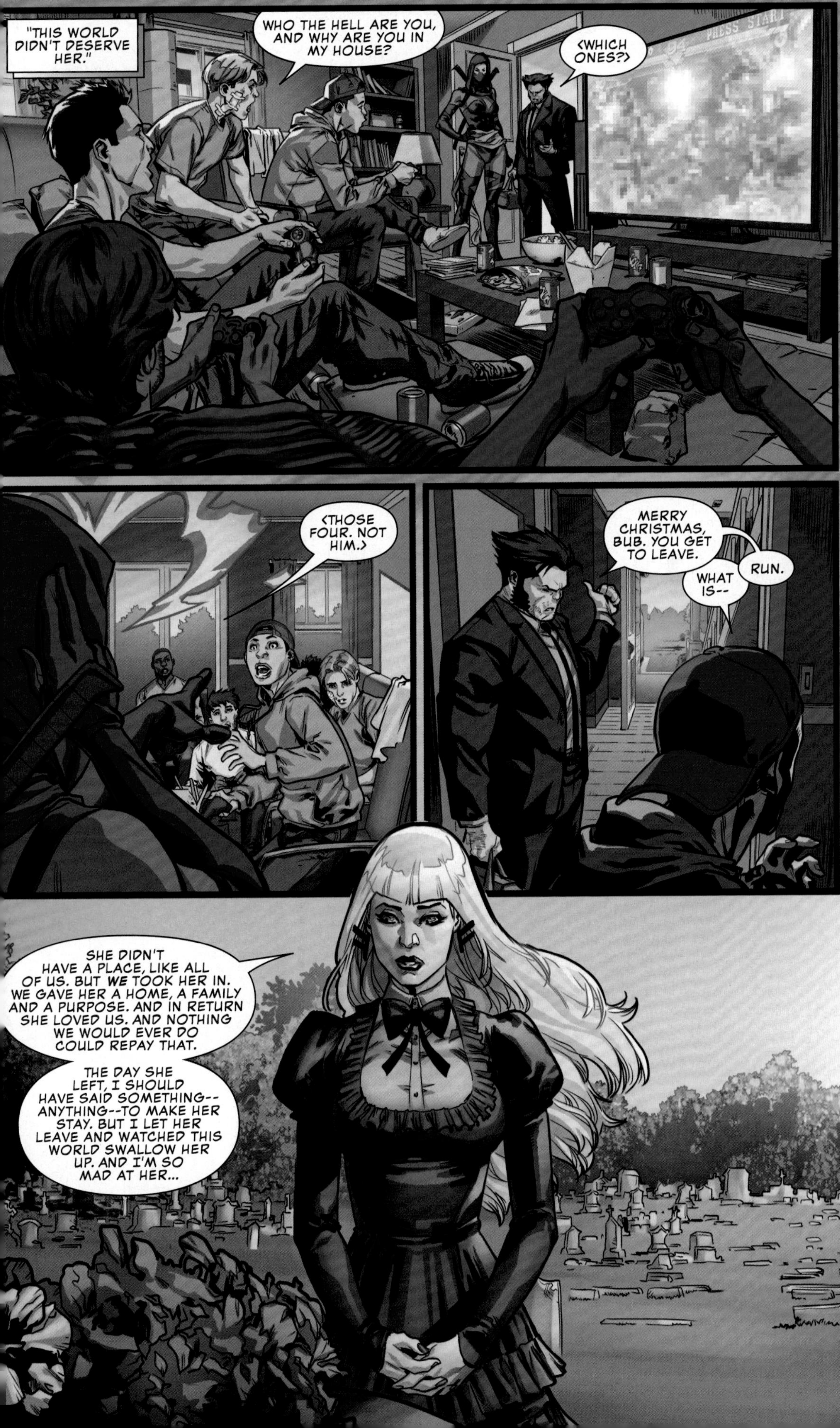
"THIS WORLD DIDN'T DESERVE HER."
WHO THE HELL ARE YOU, AND WHY ARE YOU IN MY HOUSE?
<WHICH ONES?>
PRESS START
<THOSE FOUR. NOT HIM.>
MERRY CHRISTMAS, BUB. YOU GET TO LEAVE.
WHAT IS--
RUN.
SHE DIDN'T HAVE A PLACE, LIKE ALL OF US. BUT *WE* TOOK HER IN. WE GAVE HER A HOME, A FAMILY AND A PURPOSE. AND IN RETURN SHE LOVED US. AND NOTHING WE WOULD EVER DO COULD REPAY THAT.
THE DAY SHE LEFT, I SHOULD HAVE SAID SOMETHING-- ANYTHING--TO MAKE HER STAY. BUT I LET HER LEAVE AND WATCHED THIS WORLD SWALLOW HER UP. AND I'M SO MAD AT HER...

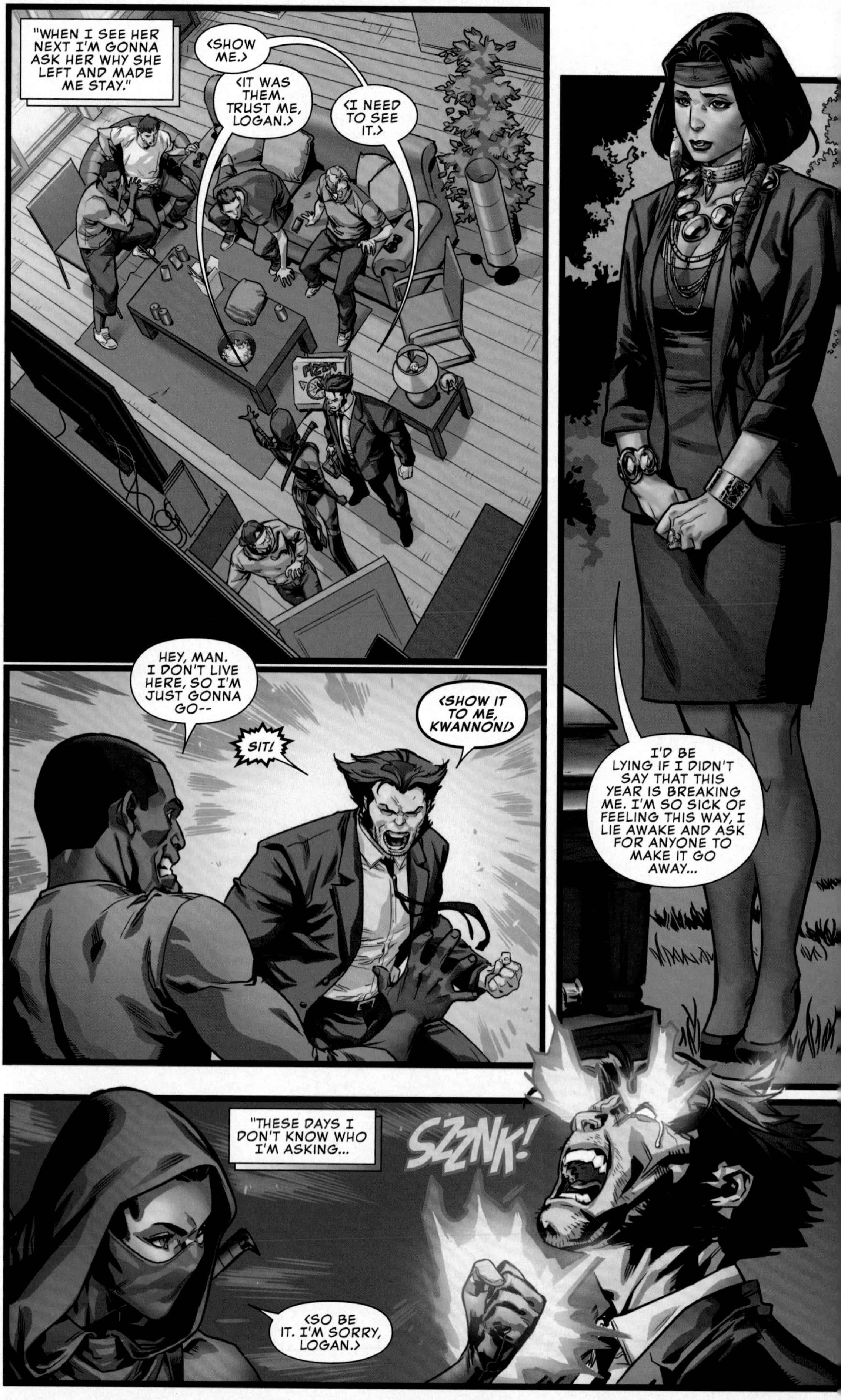
"WHEN I SEE HER NEXT I'M GONNA ASK HER WHY SHE LEFT AND MADE ME STAY."
<SHOW ME.>
<IT WAS THEM. TRUST ME, LOGAN.>
<I NEED TO SEE IT.>
I'D BE LYING IF I DIDN'T SAY THAT THIS YEAR IS BREAKING ME. I'M SO SICK OF FEELING THIS WAY, I LIE AWAKE AND ASK FOR ANYONE TO MAKE IT GO AWAY...
HEY, MAN. I DON'T LIVE HERE, SO I'M JUST GONNA GO--
SIT!
<SHOW IT TO ME, KWANNON!>
"THESE DAYS I DON'T KNOW WHO I'M ASKING...
SZZNK!
<SO BE IT. I'M SORRY, LOGAN.>

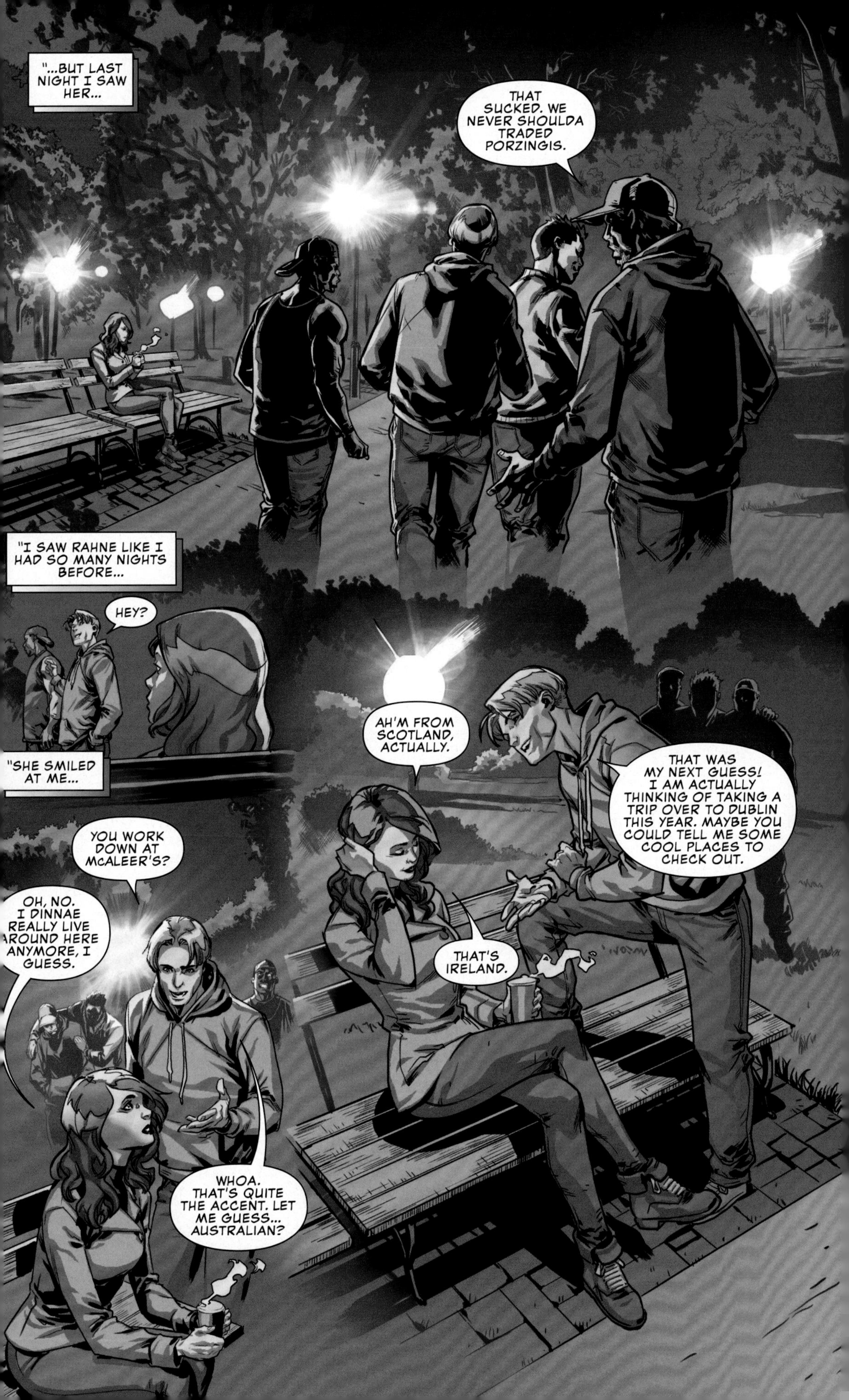
"...BUT LAST NIGHT I SAW HER...
THAT SUCKED. WE NEVER SHOULDA TRADED PORZINGIS.
"I SAW RAHNE LIKE I HAD SO MANY NIGHTS BEFORE...
HEY?
"SHE SMILED AT ME...
YOU WORK DOWN AT McALEER'S?
OH, NO. I DINNAE REALLY LIVE AROUND HERE ANYMORE, I GUESS.
WHOA. THAT'S QUITE THE ACCENT. LET ME GUESS... AUSTRALIAN?
AH'M FROM SCOTLAND, ACTUALLY.
THAT'S IRELAND.
THAT WAS MY NEXT GUESS! I AM ACTUALLY THINKING OF TAKING A TRIP OVER TO DUBLIN THIS YEAR. MAYBE YOU COULD TELL ME SOME COOL PLACES TO CHECK OUT.

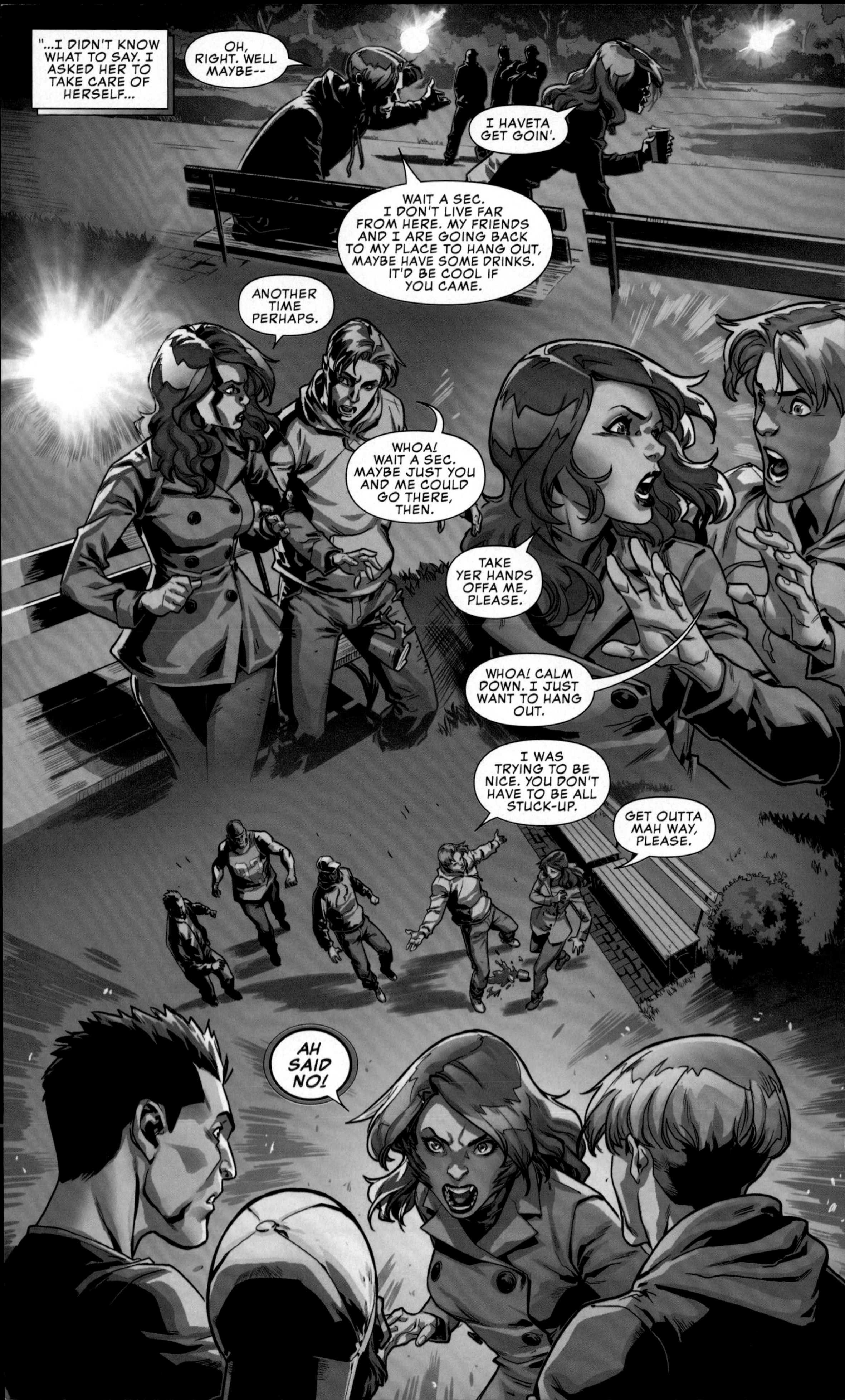
"...I DIDN'T KNOW WHAT TO SAY. I ASKED HER TO TAKE CARE OF HERSELF...
OH, RIGHT. WELL MAYBE--
I HAVETA GET GOIN'.
WAIT A SEC. I DON'T LIVE FAR FROM HERE. MY FRIENDS AND I ARE GOING BACK TO MY PLACE TO HANG OUT, MAYBE HAVE SOME DRINKS. IT'D BE COOL IF YOU CAME.
ANOTHER TIME PERHAPS.
WHOA! WAIT A SEC. MAYBE JUST YOU AND ME COULD GO THERE, THEN.
TAKE YER HANDS OFFA ME, PLEASE.
WHOA! CALM DOWN. I JUST WANT TO HANG OUT.
I WAS TRYING TO BE NICE. YOU DON'T HAVE TO BE ALL STUCK-UP.
GET OUTTA MAH WAY, PLEASE.
AH SAID NO!

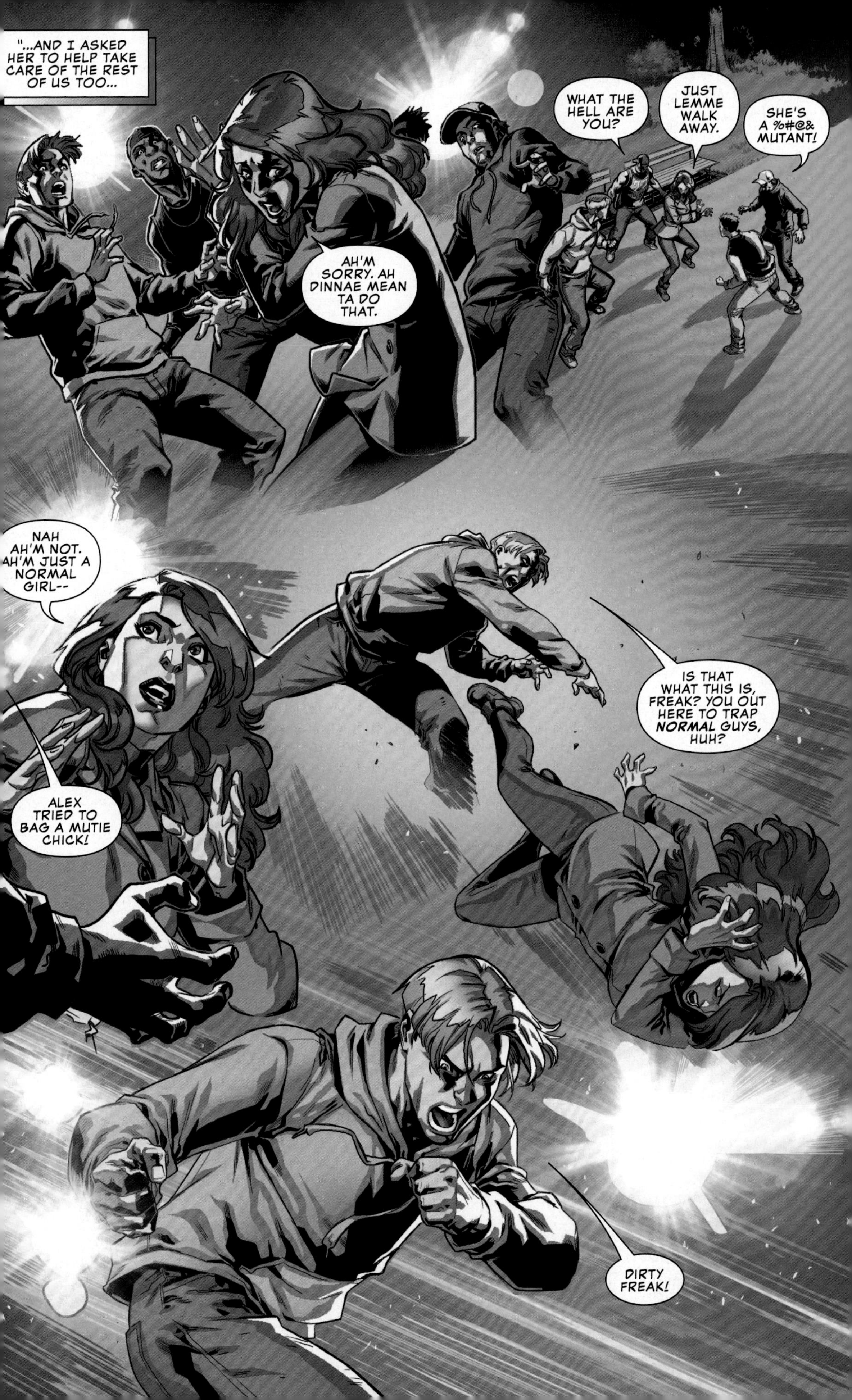
"...AND I ASKED HER TO HELP TAKE CARE OF THE REST OF US TOO...
WHAT THE HELL ARE YOU?
JUST LEMME WALK AWAY.
SHE'S A %#@& MUTANT!
AH'M SORRY. AH DINNAE MEAN TA DO THAT.
NAH AH'M NOT. AH'M JUST A NORMAL GIRL--
IS THAT WHAT THIS IS, FREAK? YOU OUT HERE TO TRAP NORMAL GUYS, HUH?
ALEX TRIED TO BAG A MUTIE CHICK!
DIRTY FREAK!

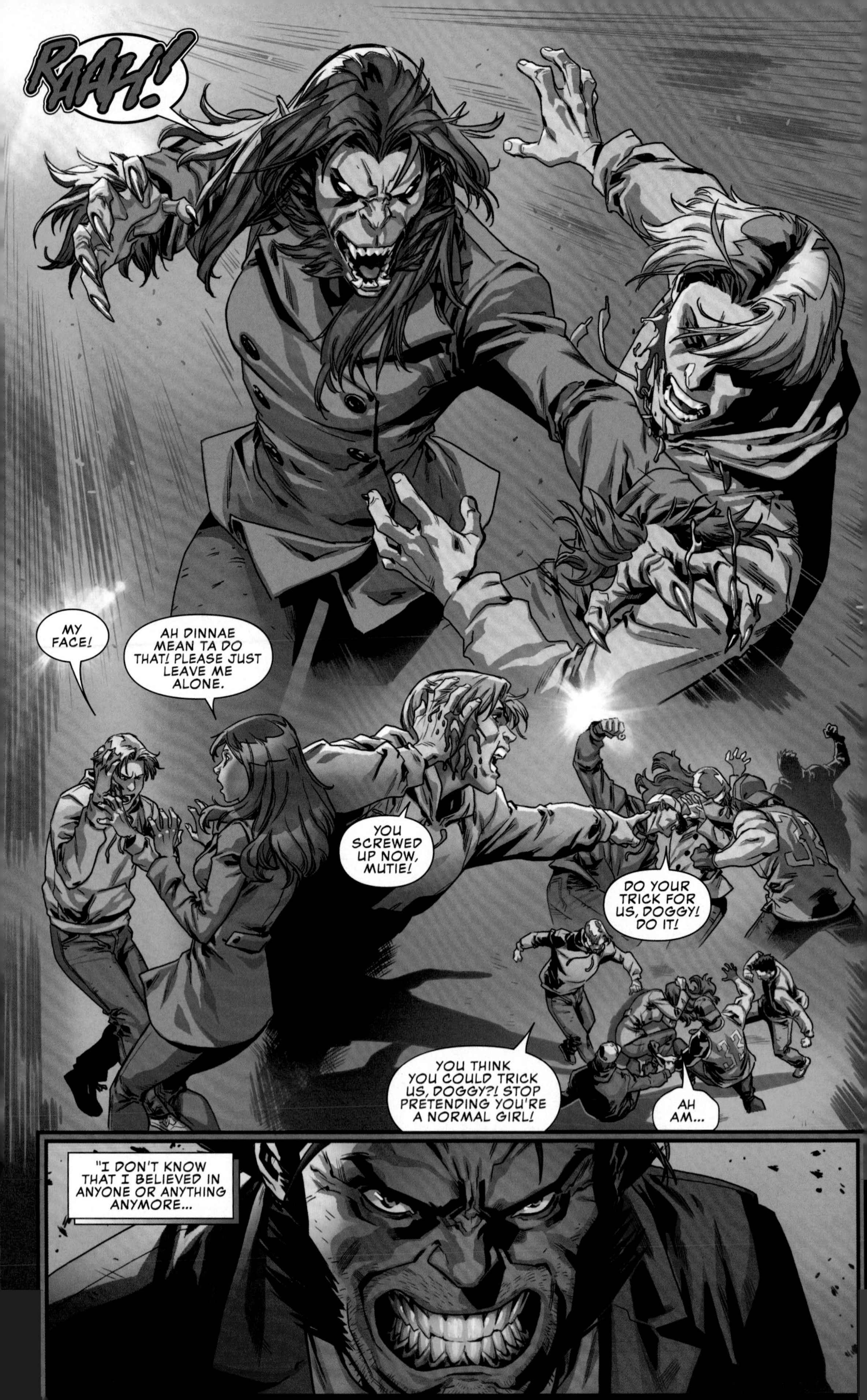
RAAH!
MY FACE!
AH DINNAE MEAN TA DO THAT! PLEASE JUST LEAVE ME ALONE.
YOU SCREWED UP NOW, MUTIE!
DO YOUR TRICK FOR US, DOGGY! DO IT!
YOU THINK YOU COULD TRICK US, DOGGY?! STOP PRETENDING YOU'RE A NORMAL GIRL!
AH AM...
"I DON'T KNOW THAT I BELIEVED IN ANYONE OR ANYTHING ANYMORE...

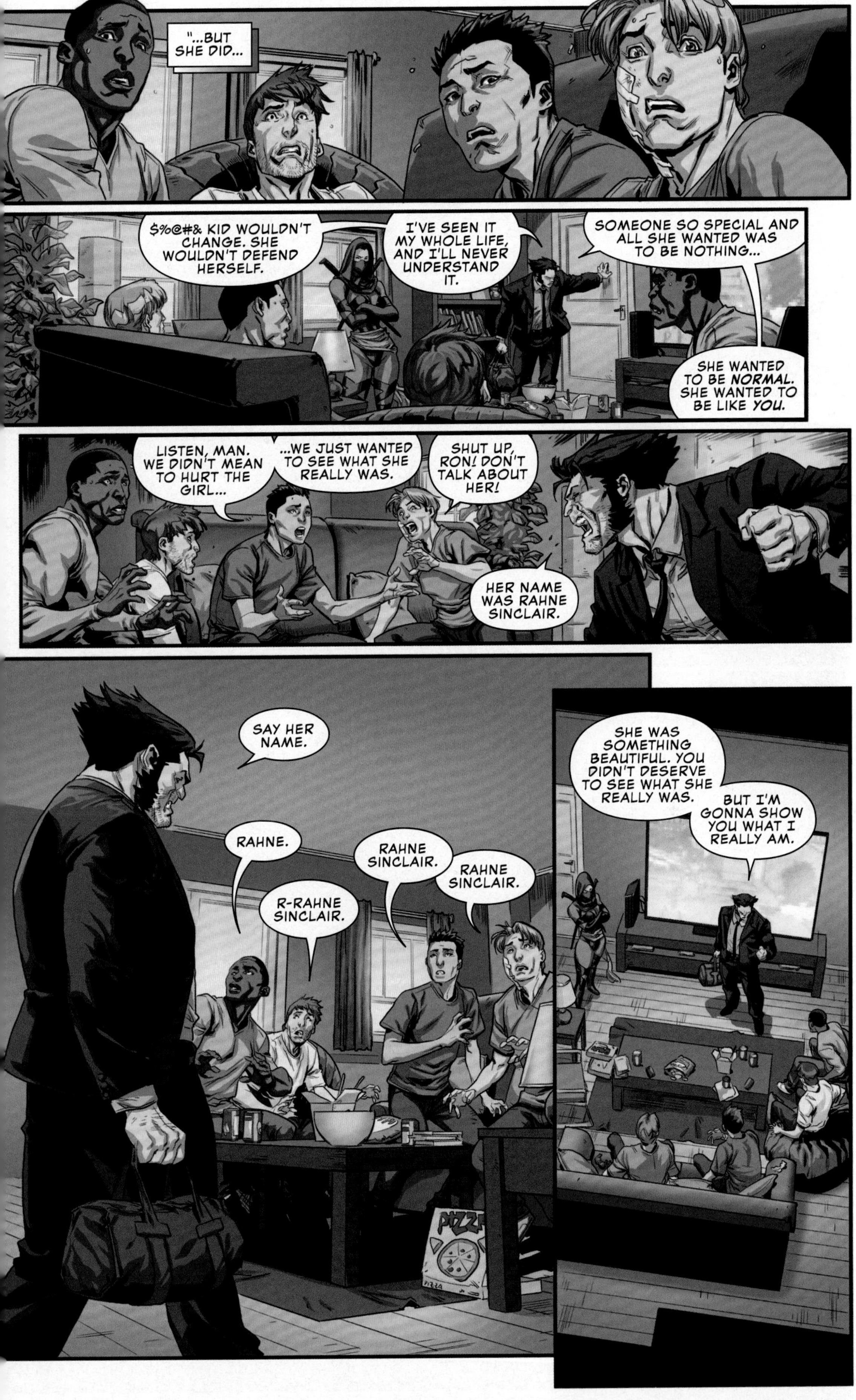
"...BUT SHE DID...
$%@#& KID WOULDN'T CHANGE. SHE WOULDN'T DEFEND HERSELF.
I'VE SEEN IT MY WHOLE LIFE, AND I'LL NEVER UNDERSTAND IT.
SOMEONE SO SPECIAL AND ALL SHE WANTED WAS TO BE NOTHING...
SHE WANTED TO BE NORMAL. SHE WANTED TO BE LIKE YOU.
LISTEN, MAN. WE DIDN'T MEAN TO HURT THE GIRL...
...WE JUST WANTED TO SEE WHAT SHE REALLY WAS.
SHUT UP, RON! DON'T TALK ABOUT HER!
HER NAME WAS RAHNE SINCLAIR.
SAY HER NAME.
RAHNE.
R-RAHNE SINCLAIR.
RAHNE SINCLAIR.
RAHNE SINCLAIR.
SHE WAS SOMETHING BEAUTIFUL. YOU DIDN'T DESERVE TO SEE WHAT SHE REALLY WAS.
BUT I'M GONNA SHOW YOU WHAT I REALLY AM.
PIZZA

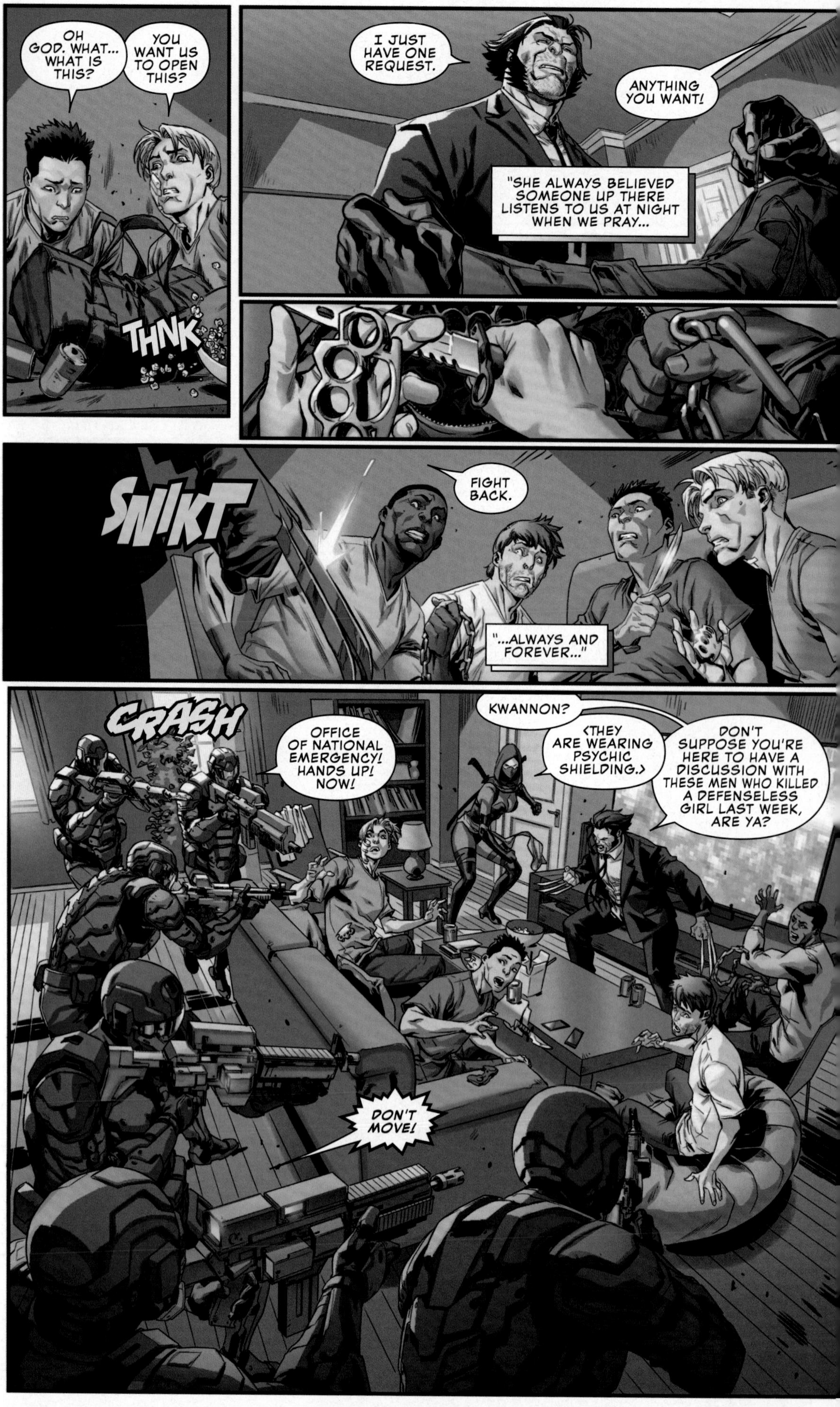
OH GOD. WHAT... WHAT IS THIS?
YOU WANT US TO OPEN THIS?
THNK
I JUST HAVE ONE REQUEST.
ANYTHING YOU WANT!
"SHE ALWAYS BELIEVED SOMEONE UP THERE LISTENS TO US AT NIGHT WHEN WE PRAY...
SNIKT
FIGHT BACK.
"...ALWAYS AND FOREVER..."
CRASH
OFFICE OF NATIONAL EMERGENCY! HANDS UP! NOW!
KWANNON?
<THEY ARE WEARING PSYCHIC SHIELDING.>
DON'T SUPPOSE YOU'RE HERE TO HAVE A DISCUSSION WITH THESE MEN WHO KILLED A DEFENSELESS GIRL LAST WEEK, ARE YA?
DON'T MOVE!

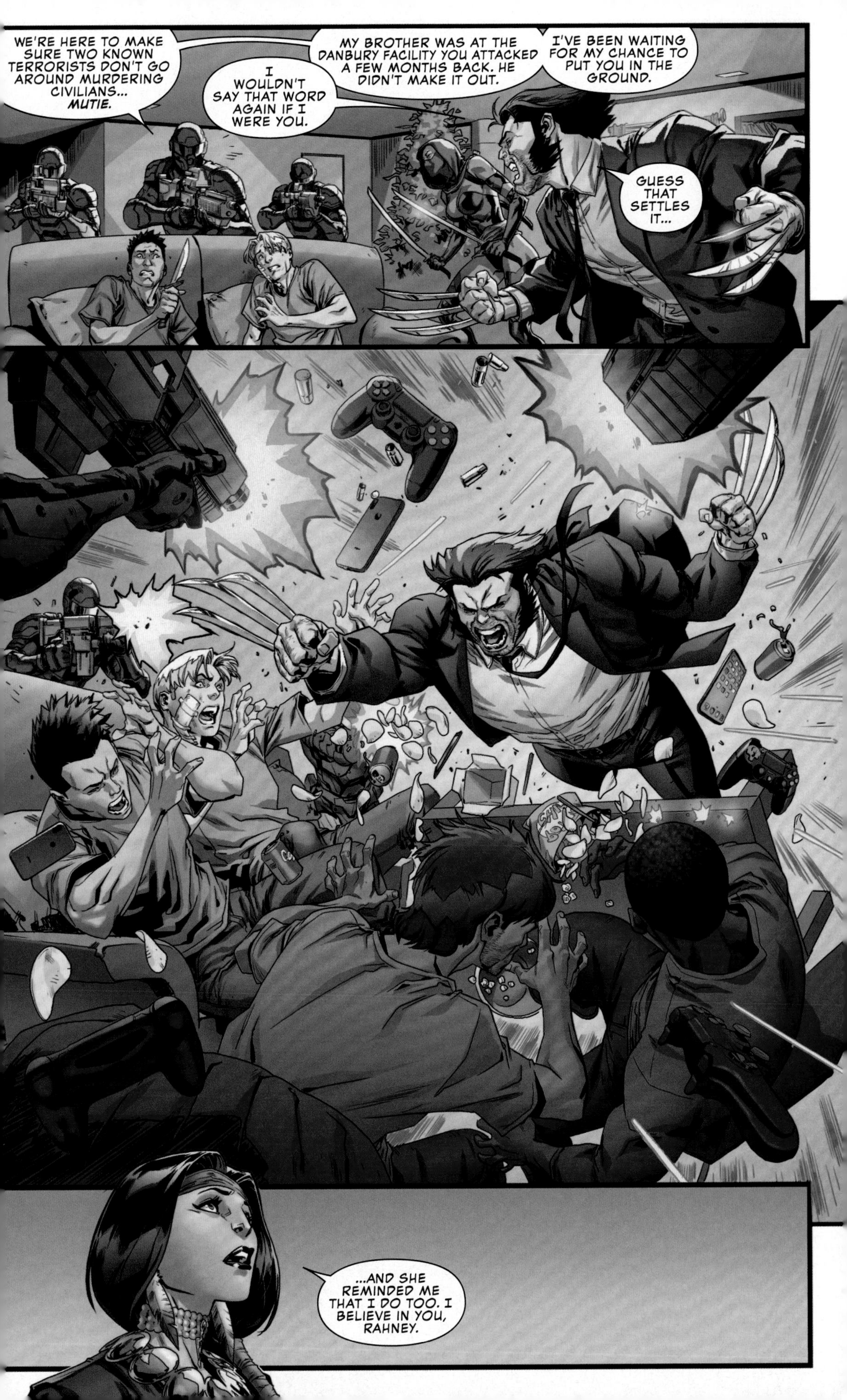
WE'RE HERE TO MAKE SURE TWO KNOWN TERRORISTS DON'T GO AROUND MURDERING CIVILIANS... MUTIE.
I WOULDN'T SAY THAT WORD AGAIN IF I WERE YOU.
MY BROTHER WAS AT THE DANBURY FACILITY YOU ATTACKED A FEW MONTHS BACK. HE DIDN'T MAKE IT OUT.
I'VE BEEN WAITING FOR MY CHANCE TO PUT YOU IN THE GROUND.
GUESS THAT SETTLES IT...
...AND SHE REMINDED ME THAT I DO TOO. I BELIEVE IN YOU, RAHNEY.

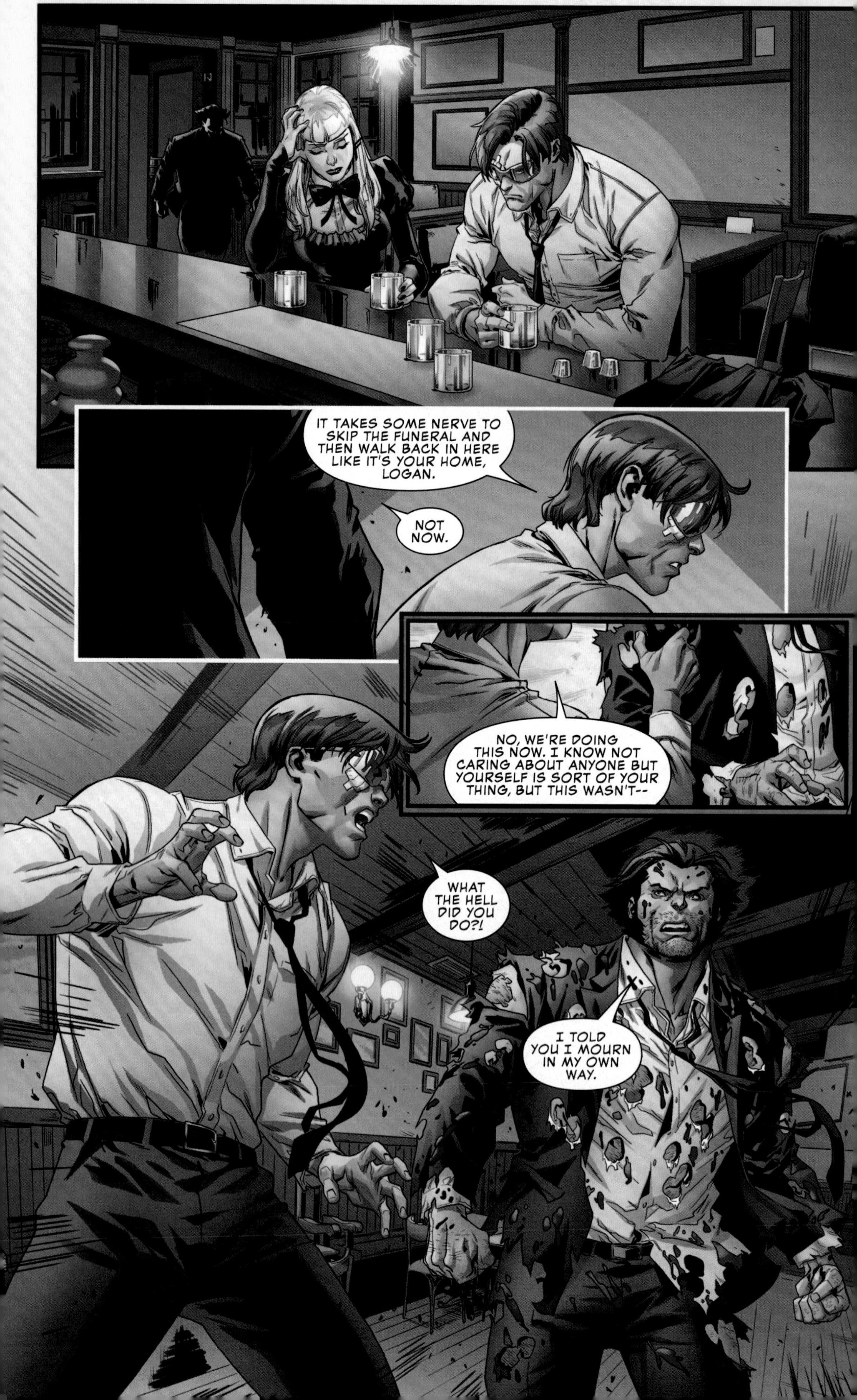
IT TAKES SOME NERVE TO SKIP THE FUNERAL AND THEN WALK BACK IN HERE LIKE IT'S YOUR HOME, LOGAN.
NOT NOW.
NO, WE'RE DOING THIS NOW. I KNOW NOT CARING ABOUT ANYONE BUT YOURSELF IS SORT OF YOUR THING, BUT THIS WASN'T--
WHAT THE HELL DID YOU DO?!
I TOLD YOU I MOURN IN MY OWN WAY.

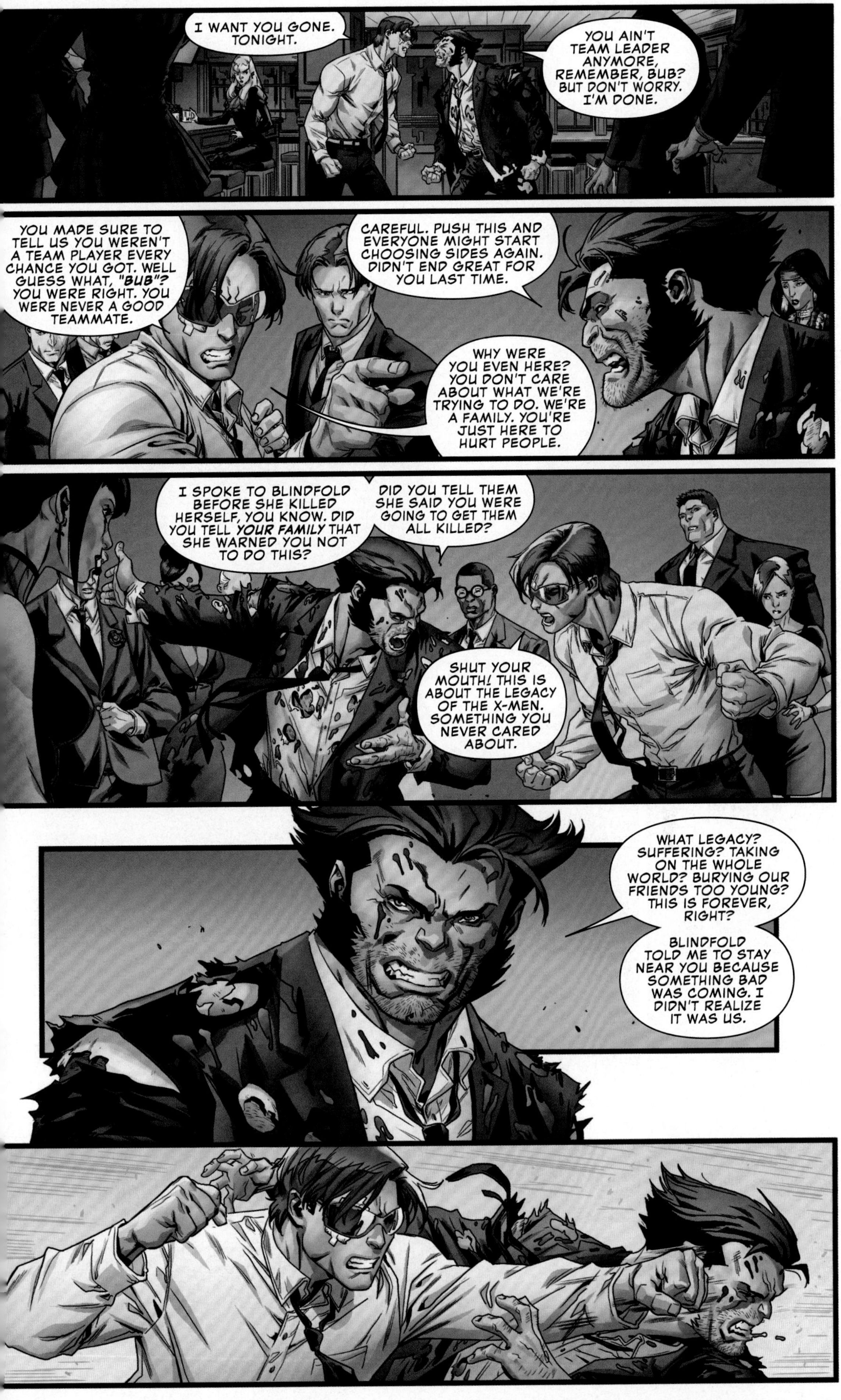
I WANT YOU GONE. TONIGHT.
YOU AIN'T TEAM LEADER ANYMORE, REMEMBER, BUB? BUT DON'T WORRY. I'M DONE.
YOU MADE SURE TO TELL US YOU WEREN'T A TEAM PLAYER EVERY CHANCE YOU GOT. WELL GUESS WHAT, "BUB"? YOU WERE RIGHT. YOU WERE NEVER A GOOD TEAMMATE.
CAREFUL. PUSH THIS AND EVERYONE MIGHT START CHOOSING SIDES AGAIN. DIDN'T END GREAT FOR YOU LAST TIME.
WHY WERE YOU EVEN HERE? YOU DON'T CARE ABOUT WHAT WE'RE TRYING TO DO. WE'RE A FAMILY. YOU'RE JUST HERE TO HURT PEOPLE.
I SPOKE TO BLINDFOLD BEFORE SHE KILLED HERSELF, YOU KNOW. DID YOU TELL YOUR FAMILY THAT SHE WARNED YOU NOT TO DO THIS?
DID YOU TELL THEM SHE SAID YOU WERE GOING TO GET THEM ALL KILLED?
SHUT YOUR MOUTH! THIS IS ABOUT THE LEGACY OF THE X-MEN. SOMETHING YOU NEVER CARED ABOUT.
WHAT LEGACY? SUFFERING? TAKING ON THE WHOLE WORLD? BURYING OUR FRIENDS TOO YOUNG? THIS IS FOREVER, RIGHT?
BLINDFOLD TOLD ME TO STAY NEAR YOU BECAUSE SOMETHING BAD WAS COMING. I DIDN'T REALIZE IT WAS US.

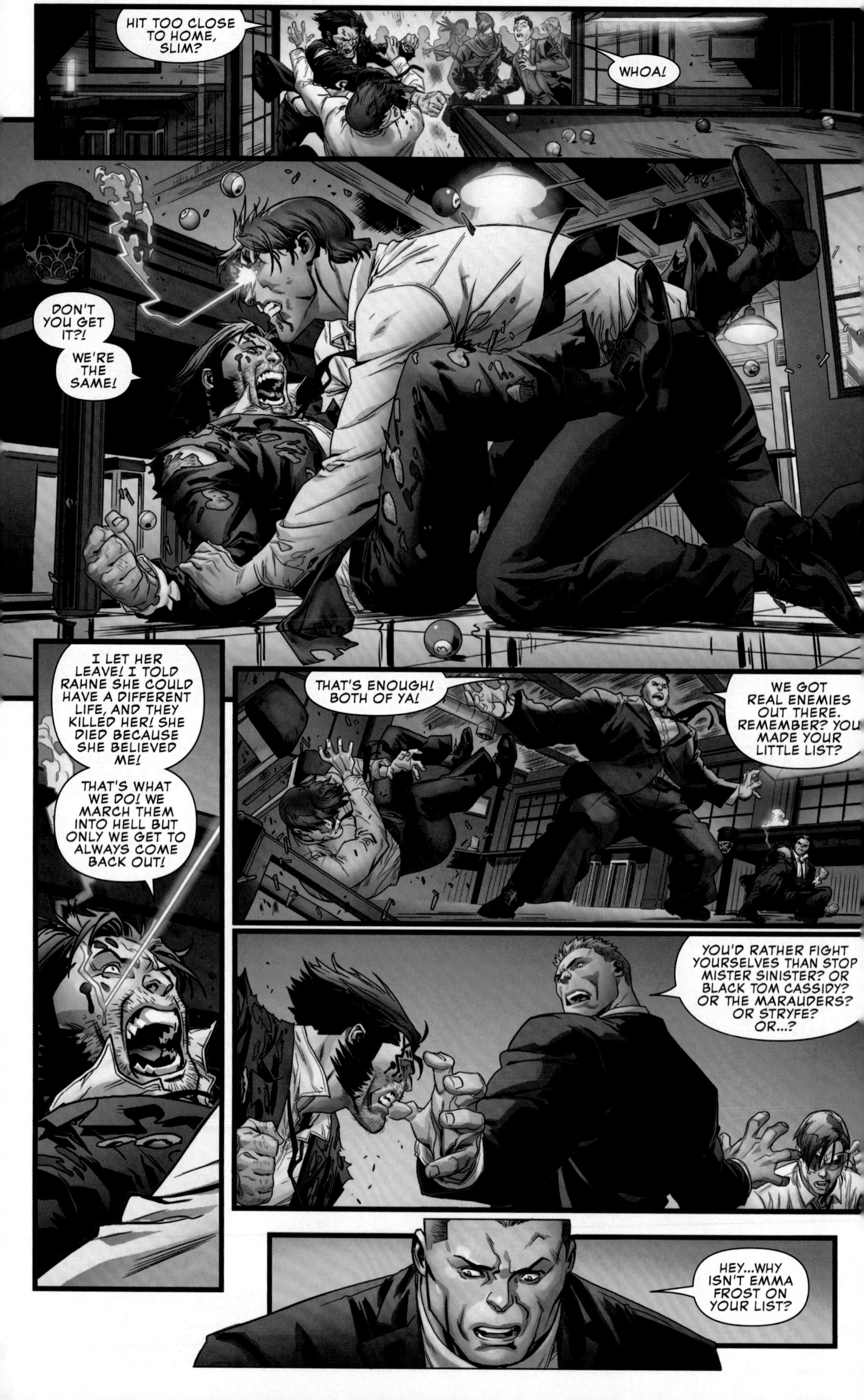
HIT TOO CLOSE TO HOME, SLIM?
WHOA!
DON'T YOU GET IT?!
WE'RE THE SAME!
I LET HER LEAVE! I TOLD RAHNE SHE COULD HAVE A DIFFERENT LIFE, AND THEY KILLED HER! SHE DIED BECAUSE SHE BELIEVED ME!
THAT'S WHAT WE DO! WE MARCH THEM INTO HELL BUT ONLY WE GET TO ALWAYS COME BACK OUT!
THAT'S ENOUGH! BOTH OF YA!
WE GOT REAL ENEMIES OUT THERE. REMEMBER? YOU MADE YOUR LITTLE LIST?
YOU'D RATHER FIGHT YOURSELVES THAN STOP MISTER SINISTER? OR BLACK TOM CASSIDY? OR THE MARAUDERS? OR STRYFE? OR...?
HEY...WHY ISN'T EMMA FROST ON YOUR LIST?

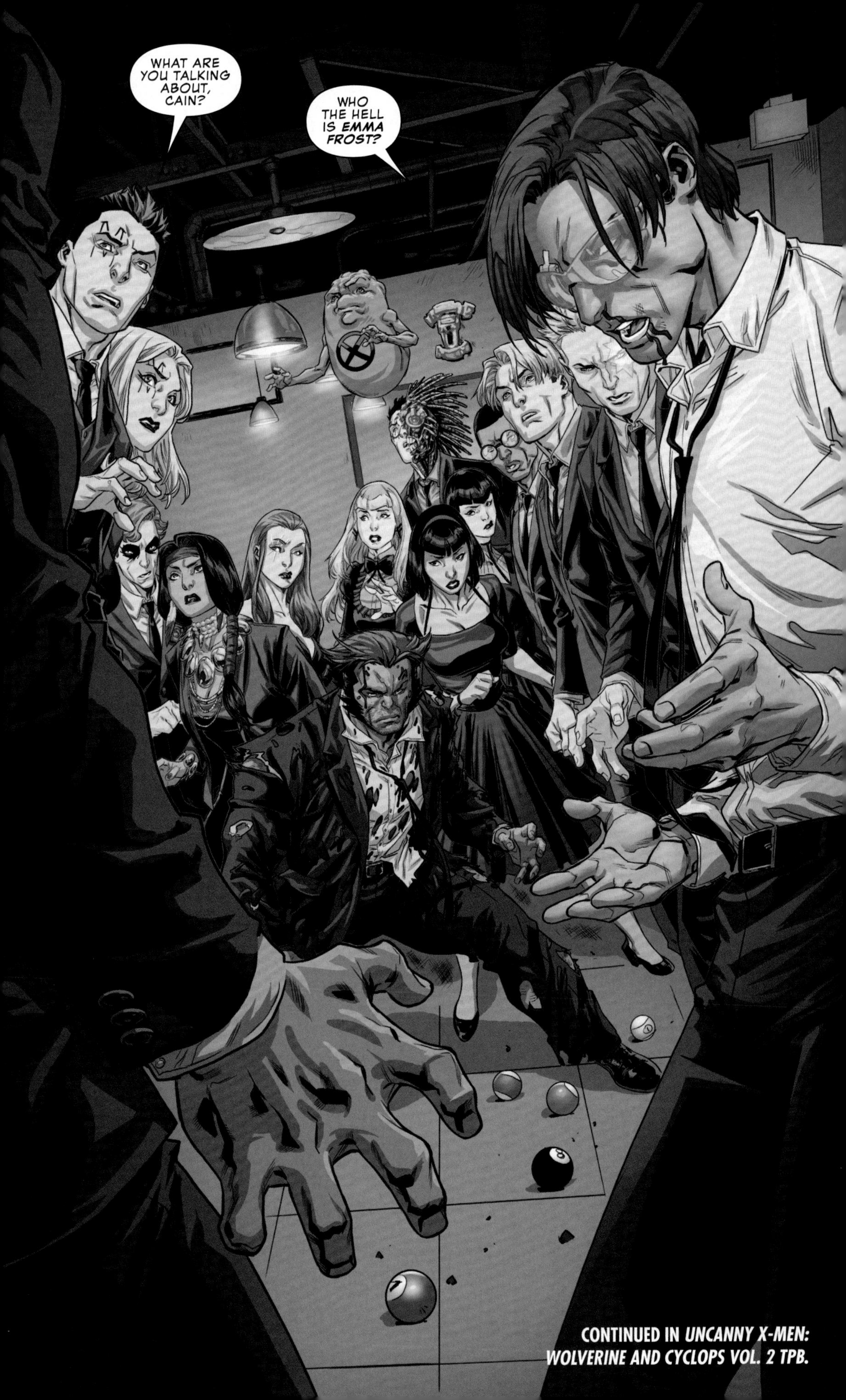
WHAT ARE YOU TALKING ABOUT, CAIN?
WHO THE HELL IS *EMMA FROST*?

CONTINUED IN *UNCANNY X-MEN: WOLVERINE AND CYCLOPS VOL. 2 TPB.*

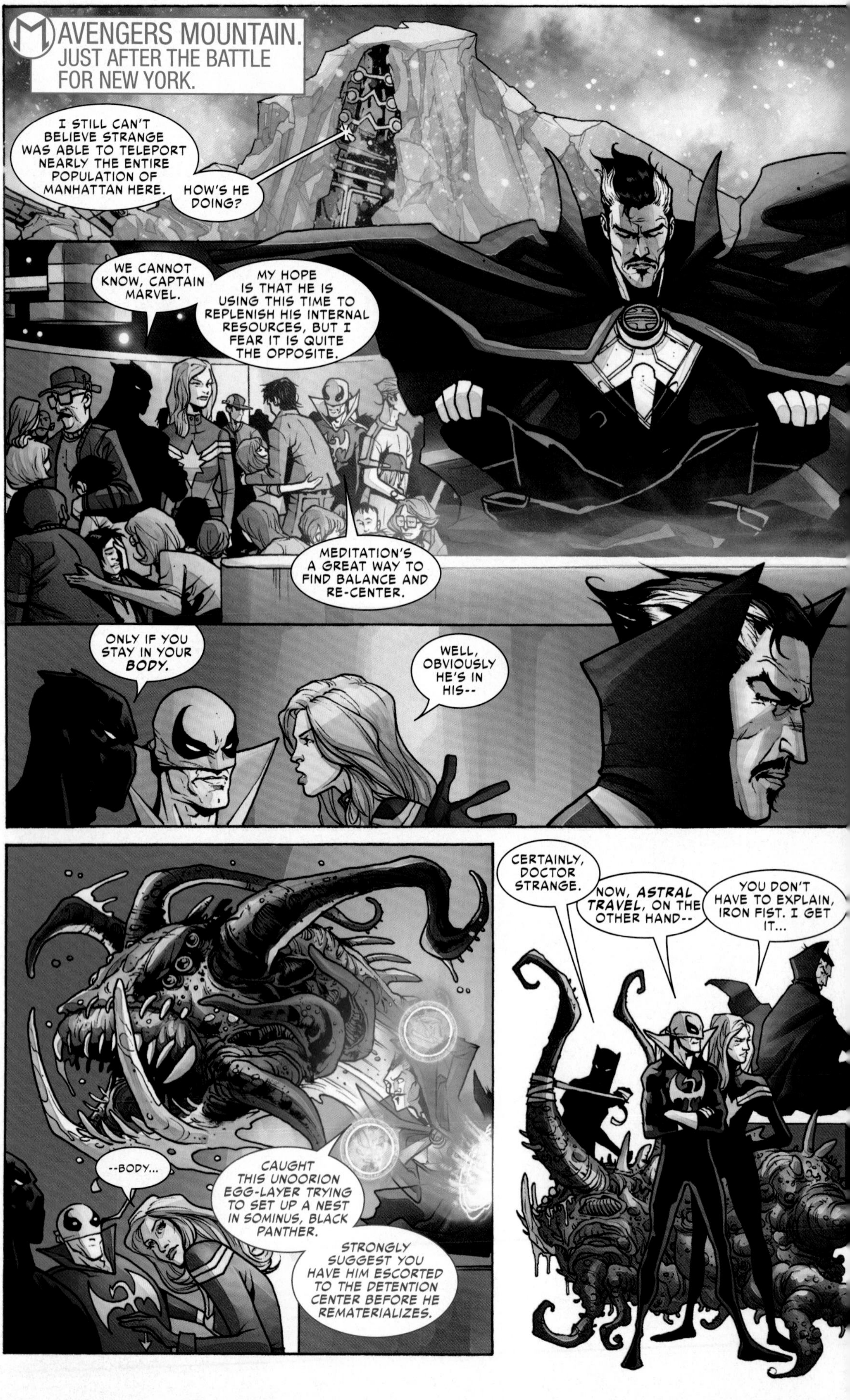
AVENGERS MOUNTAIN. JUST AFTER THE BATTLE FOR NEW YORK.
I STILL CAN'T BELIEVE STRANGE WAS ABLE TO TELEPORT NEARLY THE ENTIRE POPULATION OF MANHATTAN HERE.
HOW'S HE DOING?
WE CANNOT KNOW, CAPTAIN MARVEL.
MY HOPE IS THAT HE IS USING THIS TIME TO REPLENISH HIS INTERNAL RESOURCES, BUT I FEAR IT IS QUITE THE OPPOSITE.
MEDITATION'S A GREAT WAY TO FIND BALANCE AND RE-CENTER.
ONLY IF YOU STAY IN YOUR *BODY.*
WELL, OBVIOUSLY HE'S IN HIS--
--BODY...
CAUGHT THIS UNOORION EGG-LAYER TRYING TO SET UP A NEST IN SOMINUS, BLACK PANTHER.
STRONGLY SUGGEST YOU HAVE HIM ESCORTED TO THE DETENTION CENTER BEFORE HE REMATERIALIZES.
CERTAINLY, DOCTOR STRANGE.
NOW, *ASTRAL TRAVEL,* ON THE OTHER HAND--
YOU DON'T HAVE TO EXPLAIN, IRON FIST. I GET IT...

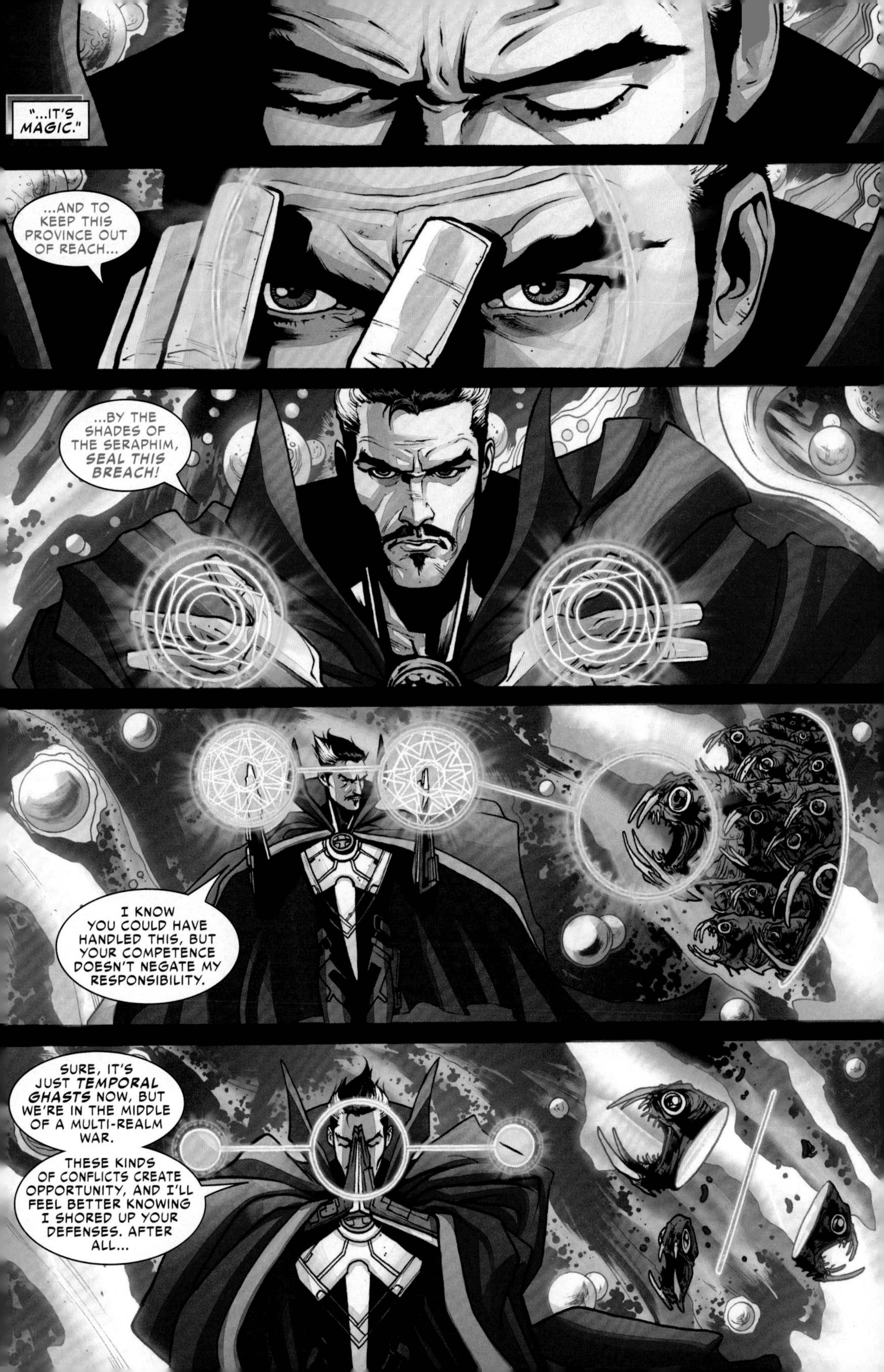
"...IT'S MAGIC."
...AND TO KEEP THIS PROVINCE OUT OF REACH...
...BY THE SHADES OF THE SERAPHIM, SEAL THIS BREACH!
I KNOW YOU COULD HAVE HANDLED THIS, BUT YOUR COMPETENCE DOESN'T NEGATE MY RESPONSIBILITY.
SURE, IT'S JUST TEMPORAL GHASTS NOW, BUT WE'RE IN THE MIDDLE OF A MULTI-REALM WAR.
THESE KINDS OF CONFLICTS CREATE OPPORTUNITY, AND I'LL FEEL BETTER KNOWING I SHORED UP YOUR DEFENSES. AFTER ALL...

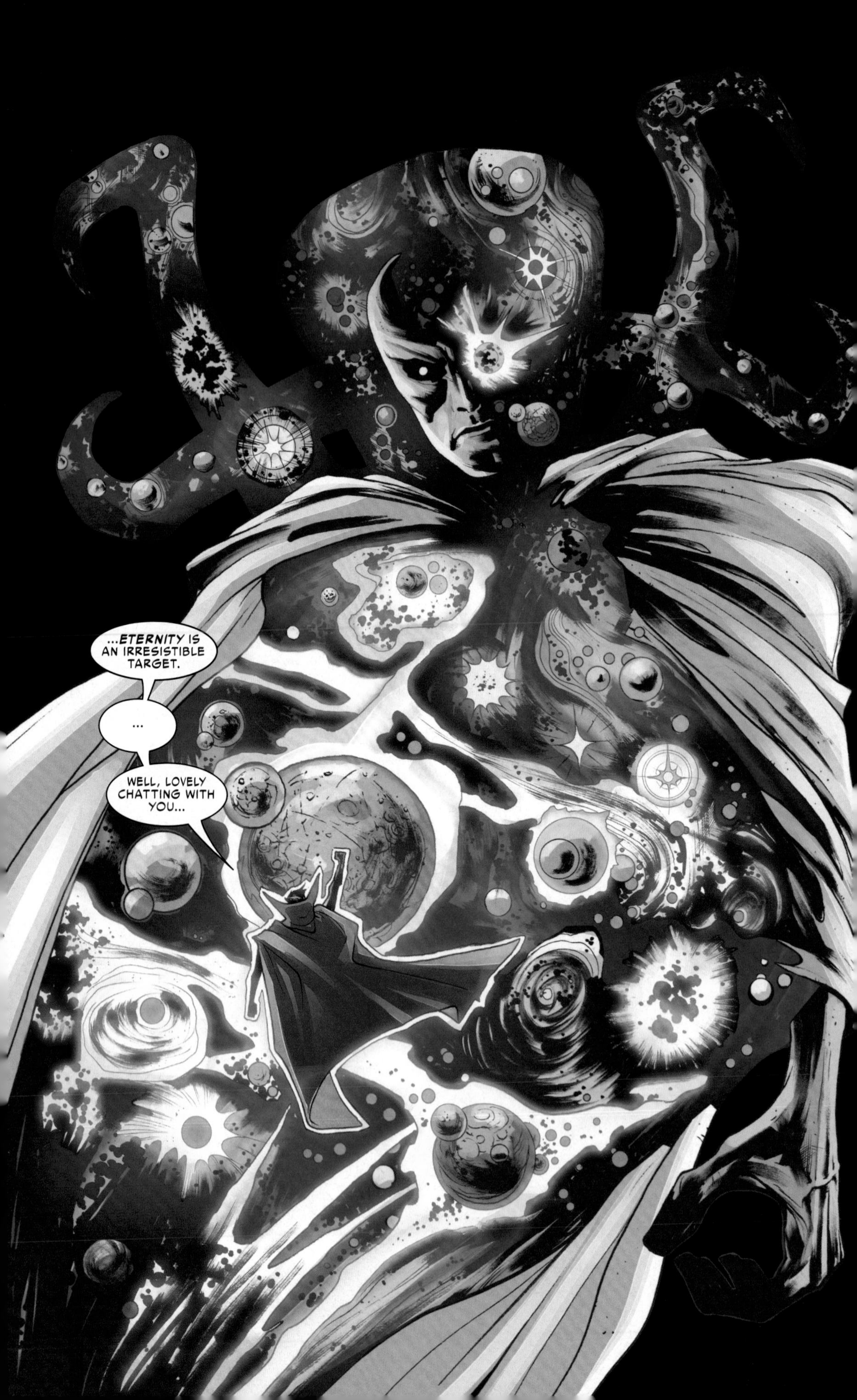
...ETERNITY IS AN IRRESISTIBLE TARGET.
...
WELL, LOVELY CHATTING WITH YOU...

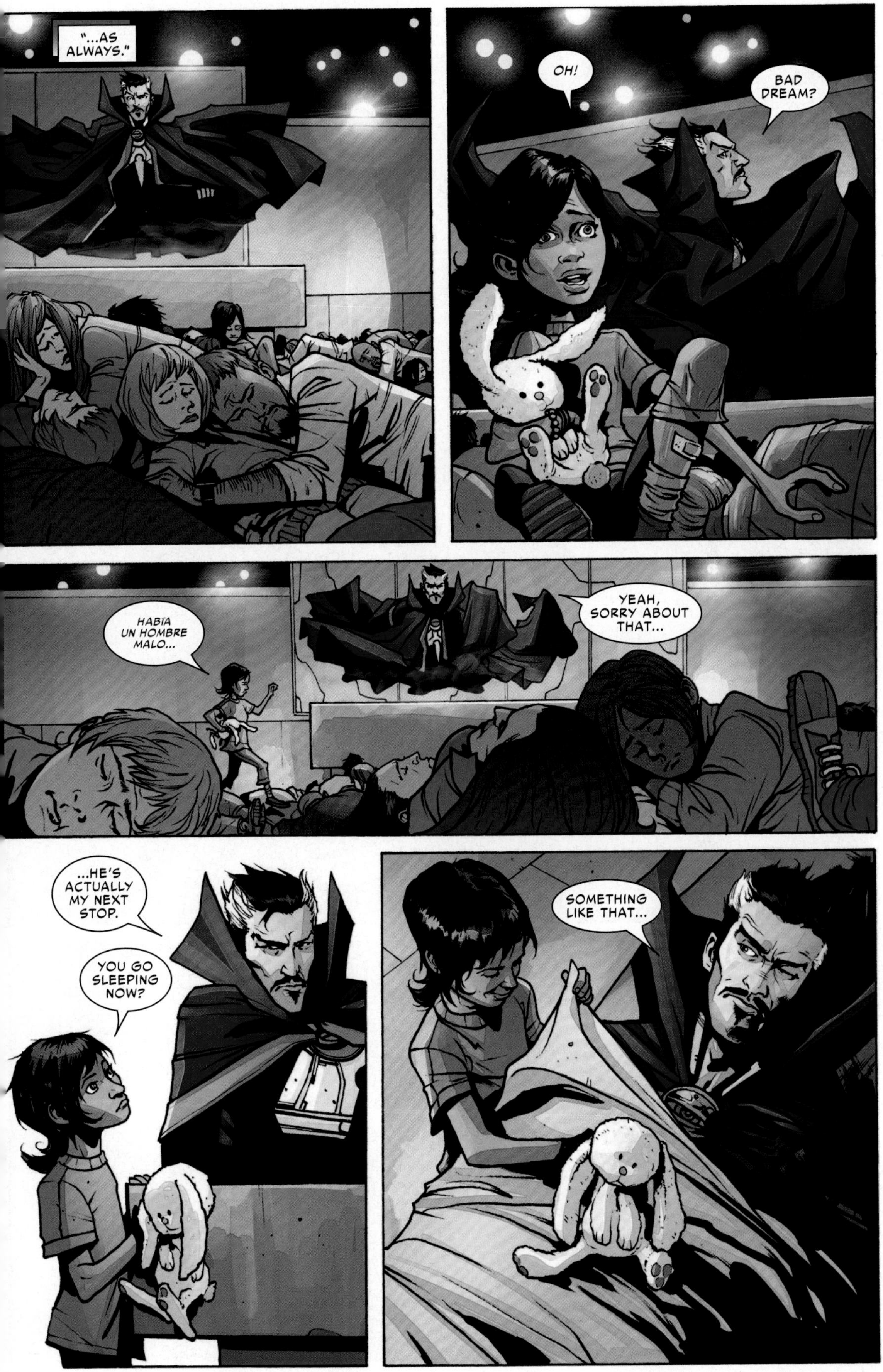
"...AS ALWAYS."
OH!
BAD DREAM?
HABÍA UN HOMBRE MALO...
YEAH, SORRY ABOUT THAT...
...HE'S ACTUALLY MY NEXT STOP.
YOU GO SLEEPING NOW?
SOMETHING LIKE THAT...

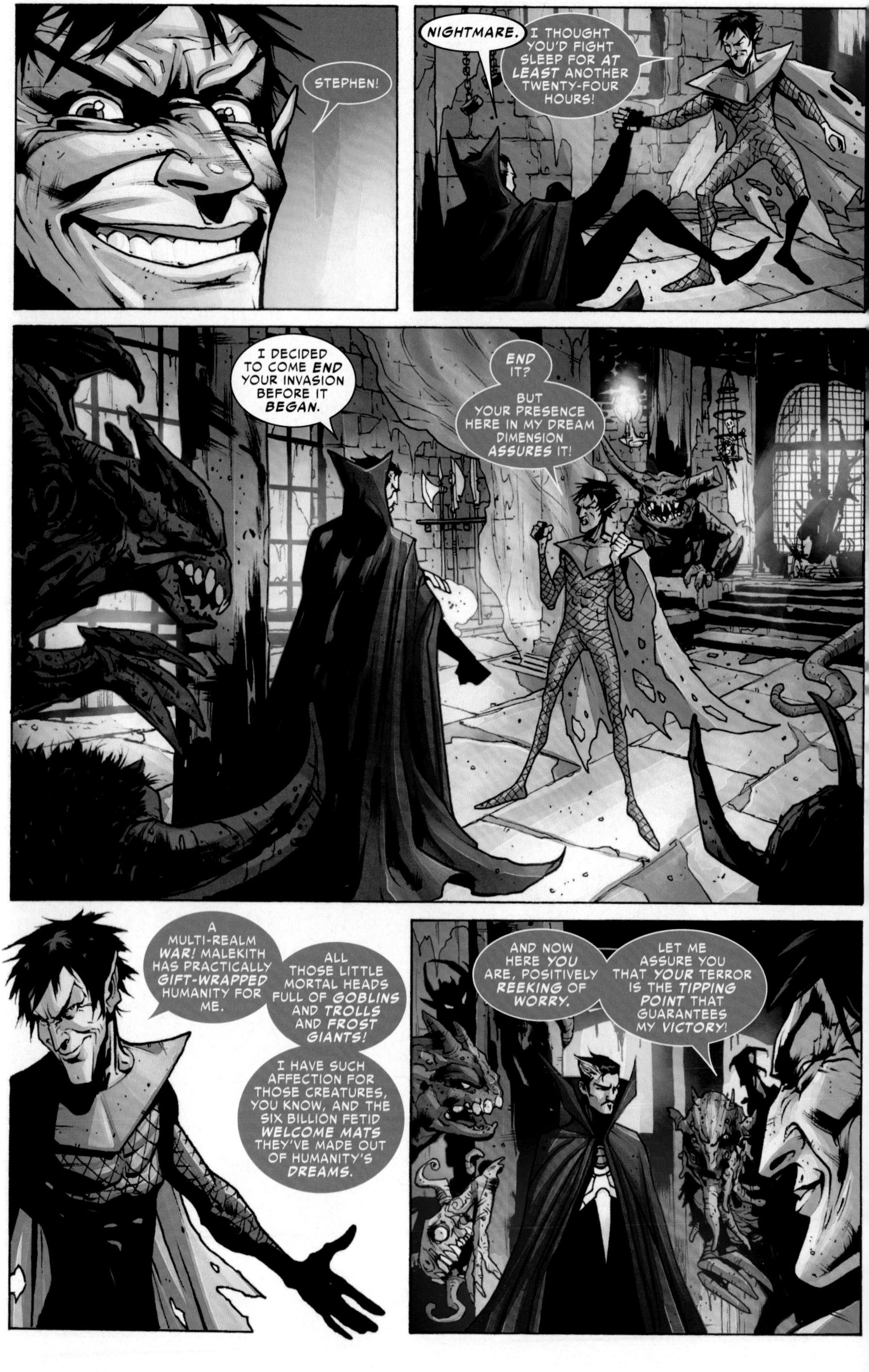
STEPHEN!
NIGHTMARE.
I THOUGHT YOU'D FIGHT SLEEP FOR AT LEAST ANOTHER TWENTY-FOUR HOURS!
I DECIDED TO COME END YOUR INVASION BEFORE IT BEGAN.
END IT?
BUT YOUR PRESENCE HERE IN MY DREAM DIMENSION ASSURES IT!
A MULTI-REALM WAR! MALEKITH HAS PRACTICALLY GIFT-WRAPPED HUMANITY FOR ME.
ALL THOSE LITTLE MORTAL HEADS FULL OF GOBLINS AND TROLLS AND FROST GIANTS!
I HAVE SUCH AFFECTION FOR THOSE CREATURES, YOU KNOW, AND THE SIX BILLION FETID WELCOME MATS THEY'VE MADE OUT OF HUMANITY'S DREAMS.
AND NOW HERE YOU ARE, POSITIVELY REEKING OF WORRY.
LET ME ASSURE YOU THAT YOUR TERROR IS THE TIPPING POINT THAT GUARANTEES MY VICTORY!

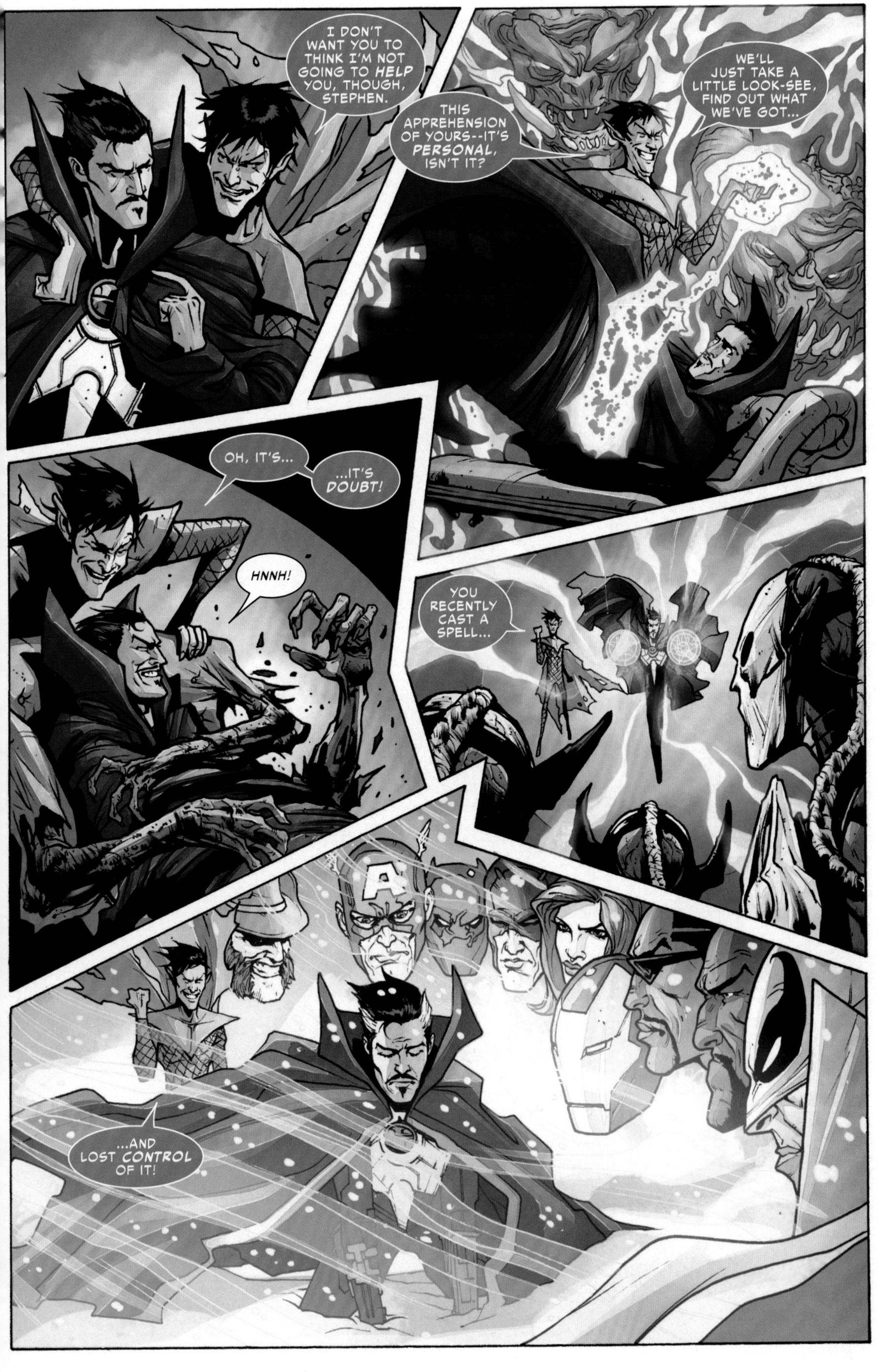
I DON'T WANT YOU TO THINK I'M NOT GOING TO *HELP* YOU, THOUGH, STEPHEN.
THIS APPREHENSION OF YOURS--IT'S *PERSONAL*, ISN'T IT?
WE'LL JUST TAKE A LITTLE LOOK-SEE, FIND OUT WHAT WE'VE GOT...
OH, IT'S...
...IT'S *DOUBT!*
HNNH!
YOU RECENTLY CAST A SPELL...
...AND LOST *CONTROL* OF IT!

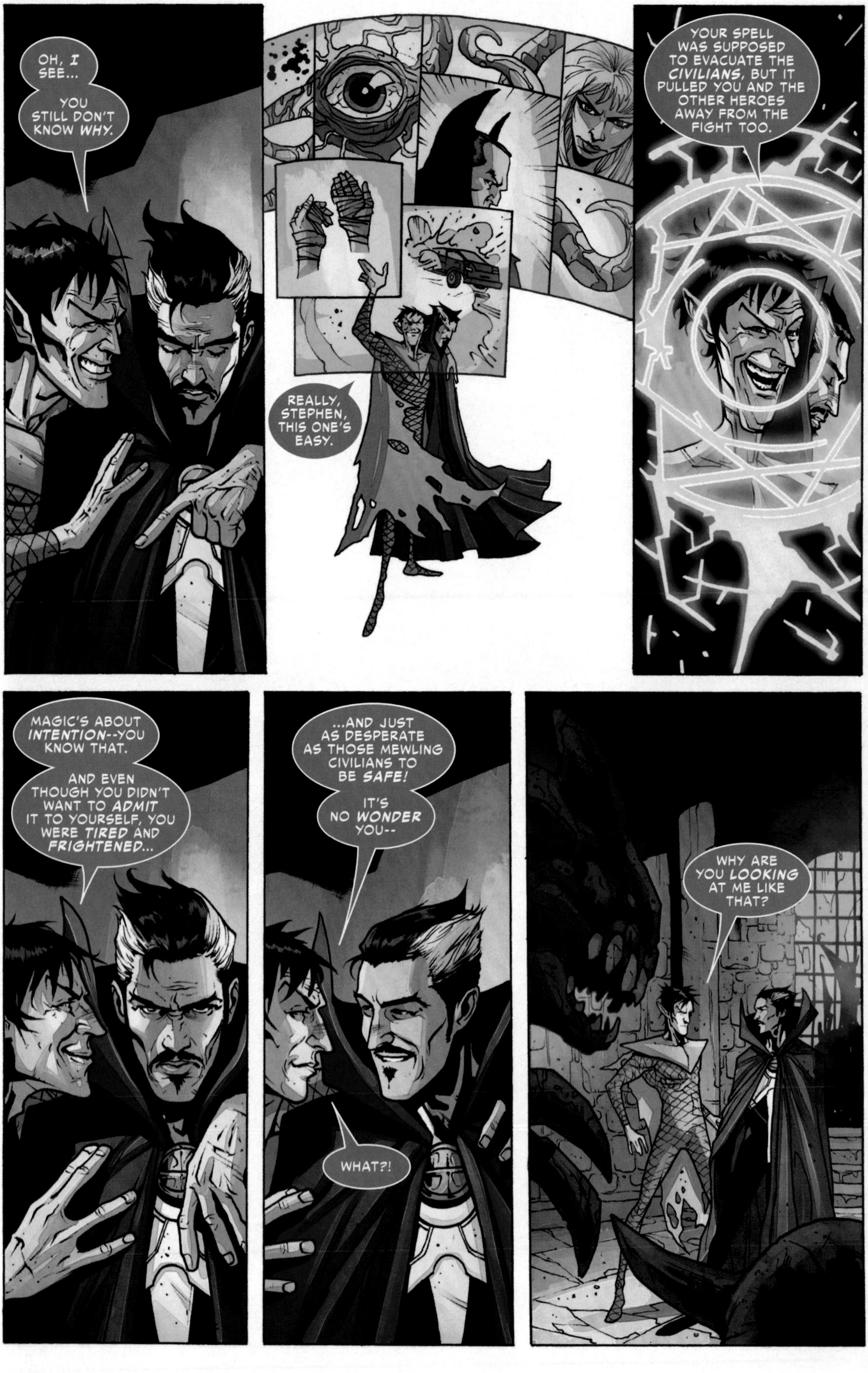
OH, I SEE...
YOU STILL DON'T KNOW WHY.
REALLY, STEPHEN, THIS ONE'S EASY.
YOUR SPELL WAS SUPPOSED TO EVACUATE THE CIVILIANS, BUT IT PULLED YOU AND THE OTHER HEROES AWAY FROM THE FIGHT TOO.
MAGIC'S ABOUT INTENTION--YOU KNOW THAT.
AND EVEN THOUGH YOU DIDN'T WANT TO ADMIT IT TO YOURSELF, YOU WERE TIRED AND FRIGHTENED...
...AND JUST AS DESPERATE AS THOSE MEWLING CIVILIANS TO BE SAFE!
IT'S NO WONDER YOU--
WHAT?!
WHY ARE YOU LOOKING AT ME LIKE THAT?

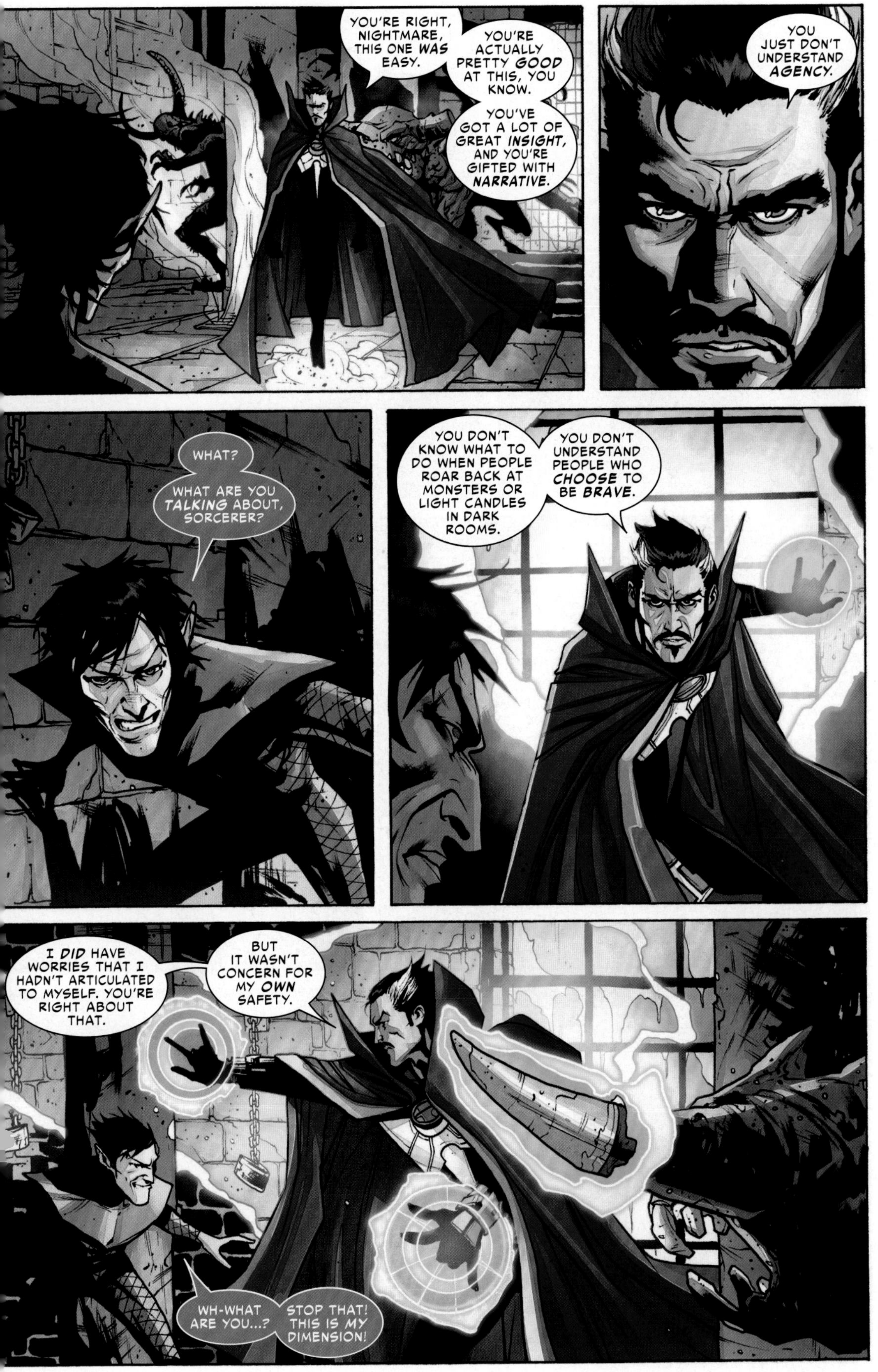
YOU'RE RIGHT, NIGHTMARE, THIS ONE WAS EASY.
YOU'RE ACTUALLY PRETTY GOOD AT THIS, YOU KNOW.
YOU'VE GOT A LOT OF GREAT INSIGHT, AND YOU'RE GIFTED WITH NARRATIVE.
YOU JUST DON'T UNDERSTAND AGENCY.
WHAT?
WHAT ARE YOU TALKING ABOUT, SORCERER?
YOU DON'T KNOW WHAT TO DO WHEN PEOPLE ROAR BACK AT MONSTERS OR LIGHT CANDLES IN DARK ROOMS.
YOU DON'T UNDERSTAND PEOPLE WHO CHOOSE TO BE BRAVE.
I DID HAVE WORRIES THAT I HADN'T ARTICULATED TO MYSELF. YOU'RE RIGHT ABOUT THAT.
BUT IT WASN'T CONCERN FOR MY OWN SAFETY.
WH-WHAT ARE YOU...?
STOP THAT! THIS IS MY DIMENSION!

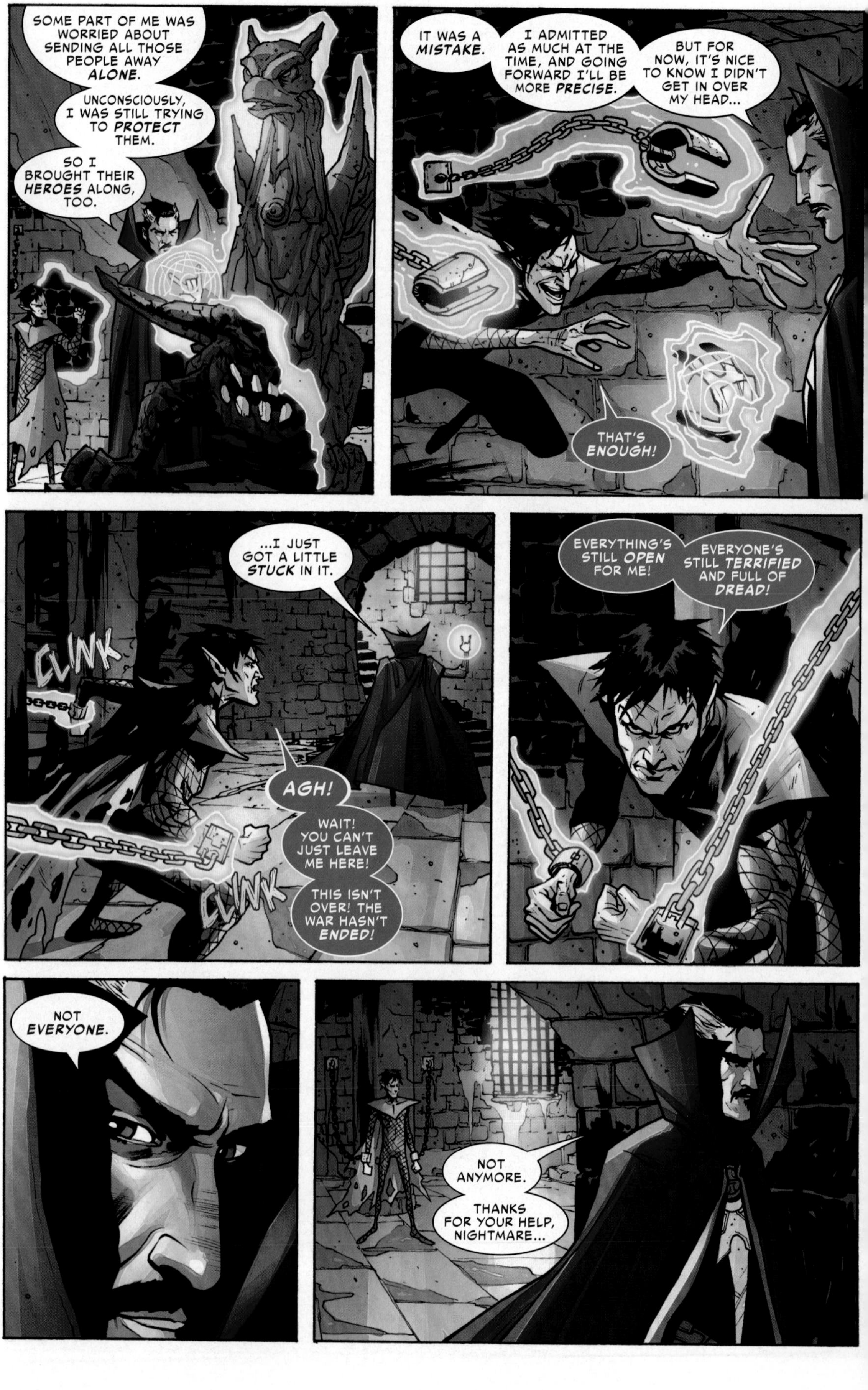

SOME PART OF ME WAS WORRIED ABOUT SENDING ALL THOSE PEOPLE AWAY *ALONE*.
UNCONSCIOUSLY, I WAS STILL TRYING TO *PROTECT* THEM.
SO I BROUGHT THEIR *HEROES* ALONG, TOO.
IT WAS A *MISTAKE*.
I ADMITTED AS MUCH AT THE TIME, AND GOING FORWARD I'LL BE MORE *PRECISE*.
BUT FOR NOW, IT'S NICE TO KNOW I DIDN'T GET IN OVER MY HEAD...
THAT'S *ENOUGH!*
...I JUST GOT A LITTLE *STUCK* IN IT.
CLINK
AGH!
WAIT! YOU CAN'T JUST LEAVE ME HERE!
THIS ISN'T OVER! THE WAR HASN'T *ENDED!*
CLINK
EVERYTHING'S STILL *OPEN* FOR ME!
EVERYONE'S STILL *TERRIFIED* AND FULL OF *DREAD!*
NOT *EVERYONE*.
NOT ANYMORE.
THANKS FOR YOUR HELP, NIGHTMARE...

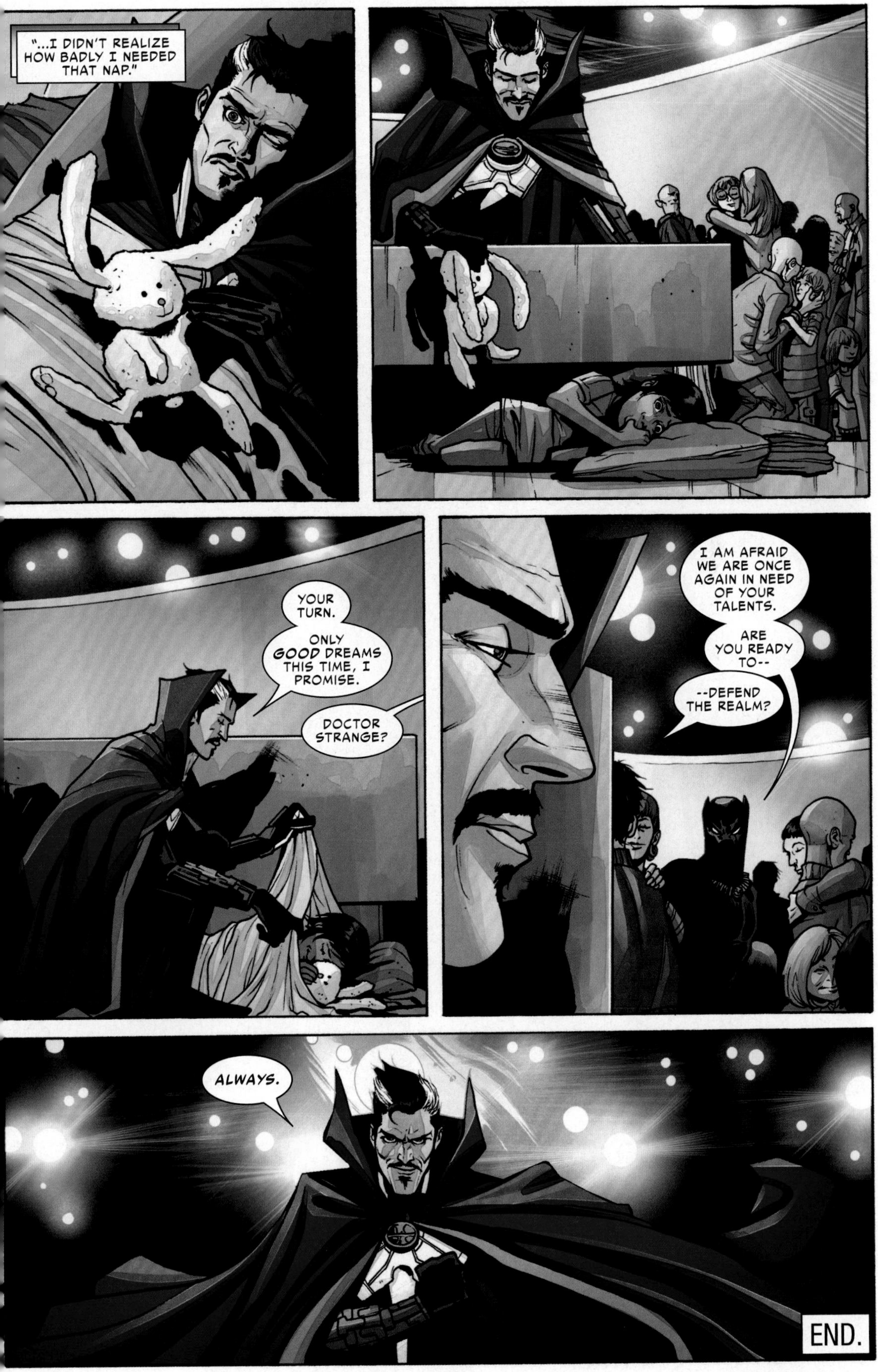
"...I DIDN'T REALIZE HOW BADLY I NEEDED THAT NAP."
YOUR TURN.
ONLY GOOD DREAMS THIS TIME, I PROMISE.
DOCTOR STRANGE?
I AM AFRAID WE ARE ONCE AGAIN IN NEED OF YOUR TALENTS.
ARE YOU READY TO--
--DEFEND THE REALM?
ALWAYS.
END.

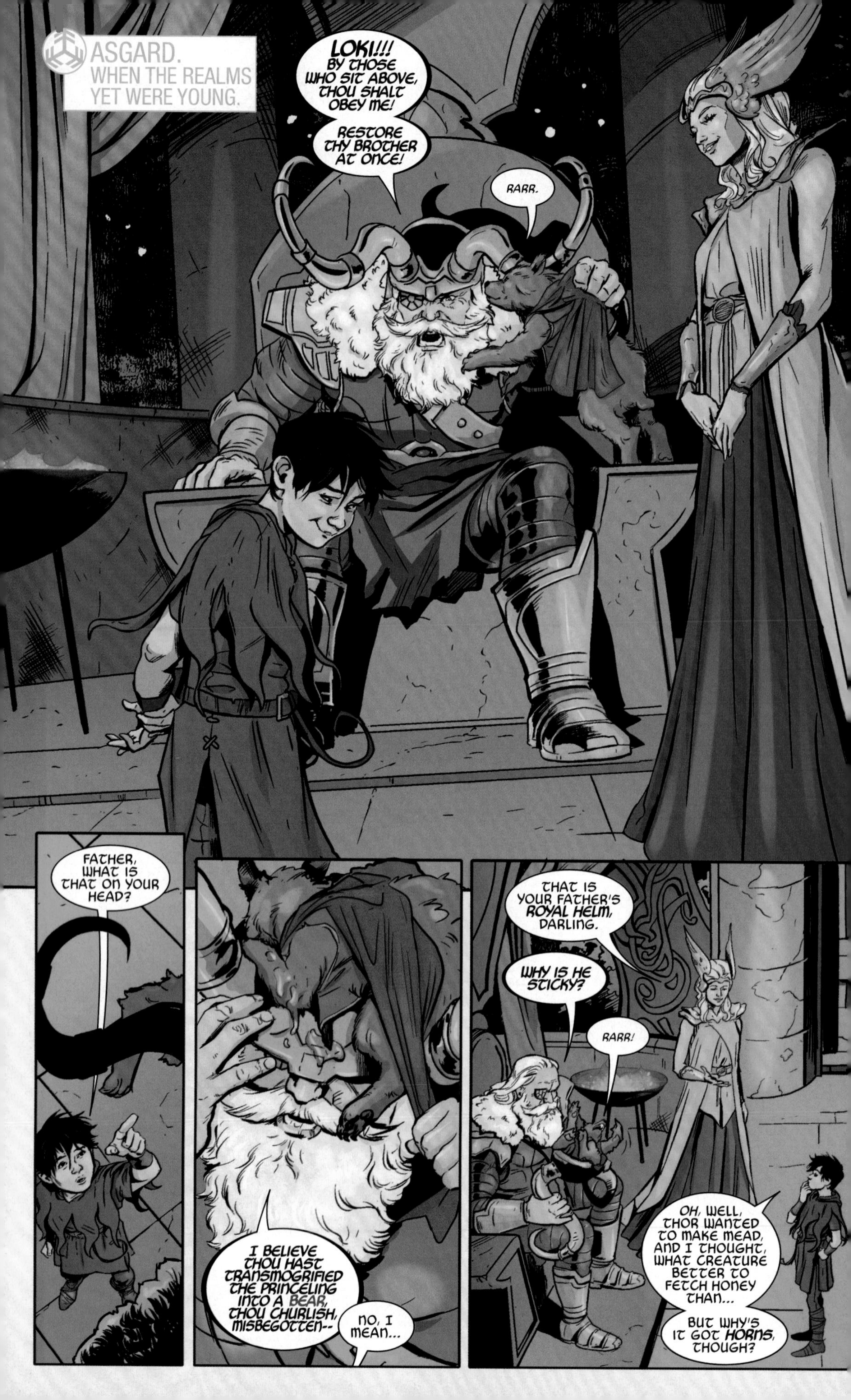
ASGARD.
WHEN THE REALMS YET WERE YOUNG.
LOKI!!! BY THOSE WHO SIT ABOVE, THOU SHALT OBEY ME!
RESTORE THY BROTHER AT ONCE!
BARR.
FATHER, WHAT IS THAT ON YOUR HEAD?
I BELIEVE THOU HAST TRANSMOGRIFIED THE PRINCELING INTO A BEAR, THOU CHURLISH, MISBEGOTTEN--
NO, I MEAN...
THAT IS YOUR FATHER'S ROYAL HELM, DARLING.
WHY IS HE STICKY?
BARR!
OH, WELL, THOR WANTED TO MAKE MEAD, AND I THOUGHT, WHAT CREATURE BETTER TO FETCH HONEY THAN...
BUT WHY'S IT GOT HORNS, THOUGH?

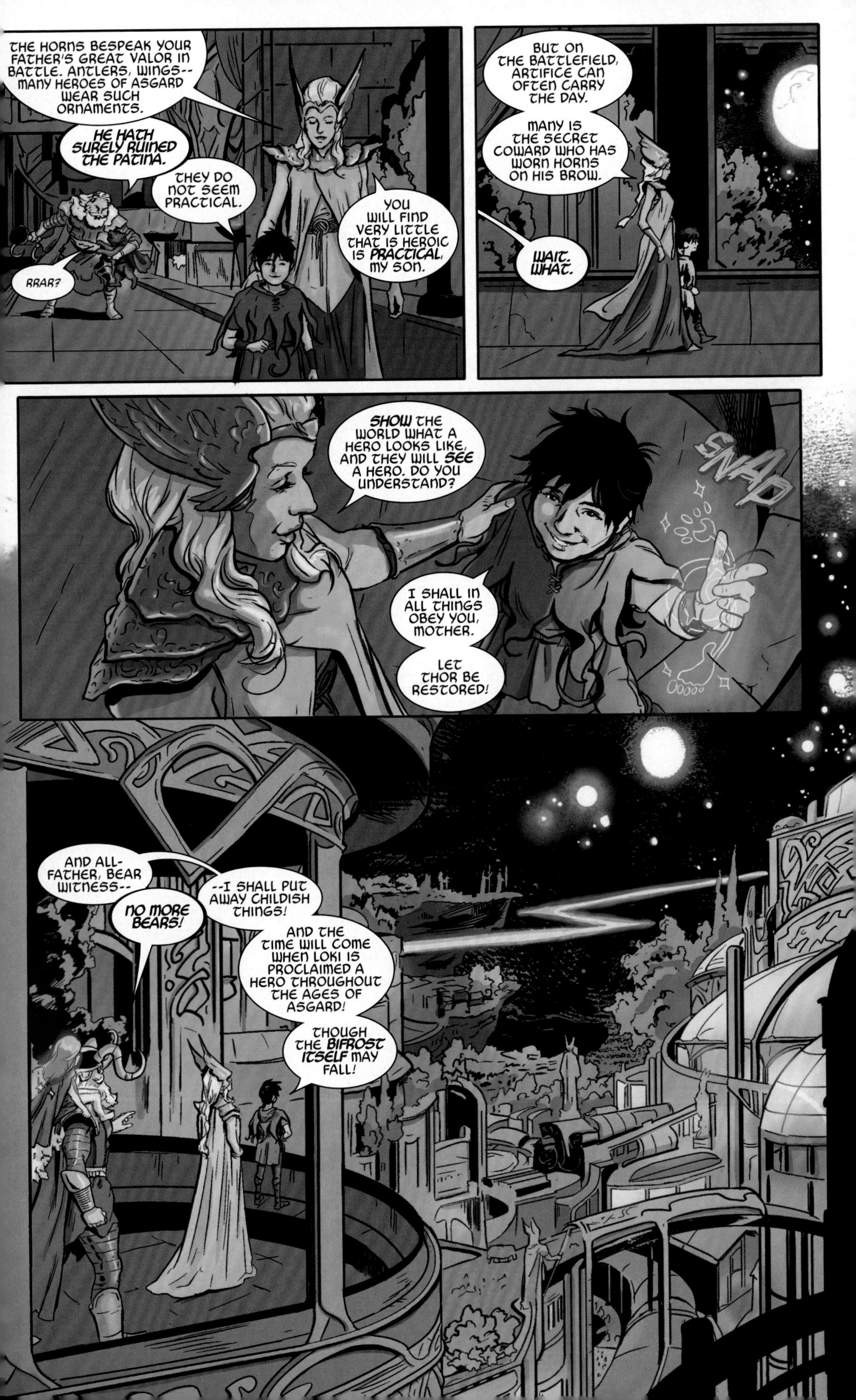
THE HORNS BESPEAK YOUR FATHER'S GREAT VALOR IN BATTLE. ANTLERS, WINGS-- MANY HEROES OF ASGARD WEAR SUCH ORNAMENTS.
HE HATH SURELY RUINED THE PATINA.
THEY DO NOT SEEM PRACTICAL.
YOU WILL FIND VERY LITTLE THAT IS HEROIC IS PRACTICAL, MY SON.
BRAR?
BUT ON THE BATTLEFIELD, ARTIFICE CAN OFTEN CARRY THE DAY.
MANY IS THE SECRET COWARD WHO HAS WORN HORNS ON HIS BROW.
WAIT. WHAT.
SHOW THE WORLD WHAT A HERO LOOKS LIKE, AND THEY WILL SEE A HERO. DO YOU UNDERSTAND?
SNAP
I SHALL IN ALL THINGS OBEY YOU, MOTHER.
LET THOR BE RESTORED!
AND ALL-FATHER, BEAR WITNESS--
--I SHALL PUT AWAY CHILDISH THINGS!
NO MORE BEARS!
AND THE TIME WILL COME WHEN LOKI IS PROCLAIMED A HERO THROUGHOUT THE AGES OF ASGARD!
THOUGH THE BIFROST ITSELF MAY FALL!

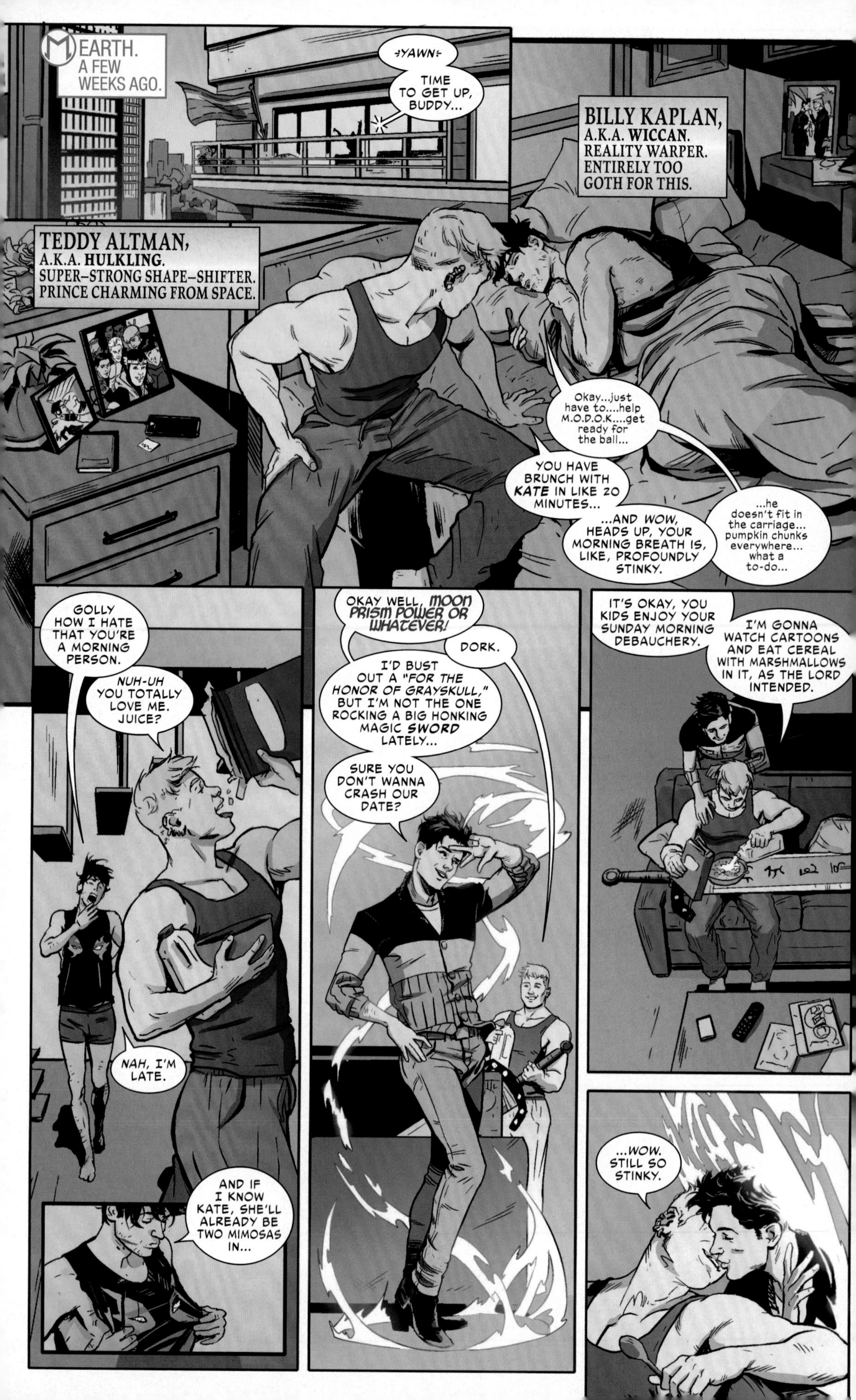
EARTH. A FEW WEEKS AGO.
YAWN
TIME TO GET UP, BUDDY...
BILLY KAPLAN, A.K.A. WICCAN. REALITY WARPER. ENTIRELY TOO GOTH FOR THIS.
TEDDY ALTMAN, A.K.A. HULKLING. SUPER-STRONG SHAPE-SHIFTER. PRINCE CHARMING FROM SPACE.
Okay...just have to....help M.O.D.O.K....get ready for the ball...
YOU HAVE BRUNCH WITH KATE IN LIKE 20 MINUTES...
...AND WOW, HEADS UP, YOUR MORNING BREATH IS, LIKE, PROFOUNDLY STINKY.
...he doesn't fit in the carriage... pumpkin chunks everywhere... what a to-do...
GOLLY HOW I HATE THAT YOU'RE A MORNING PERSON.
NUH-UH YOU TOTALLY LOVE ME. JUICE?
NAH, I'M LATE.
AND IF I KNOW KATE, SHE'LL ALREADY BE TWO MIMOSAS IN...
OKAY WELL, MOON PRISM POWER OR WHATEVER!
DORK.
I'D BUST OUT A "FOR THE HONOR OF GRAYSKULL," BUT I'M NOT THE ONE ROCKING A BIG HONKING MAGIC SWORD LATELY...
SURE YOU DON'T WANNA CRASH OUR DATE?
IT'S OKAY, YOU KIDS ENJOY YOUR SUNDAY MORNING DEBAUCHERY.
I'M GONNA WATCH CARTOONS AND EAT CEREAL WITH MARSHMALLOWS IN IT, AS THE LORD INTENDED.
...WOW. STILL SO STINKY.

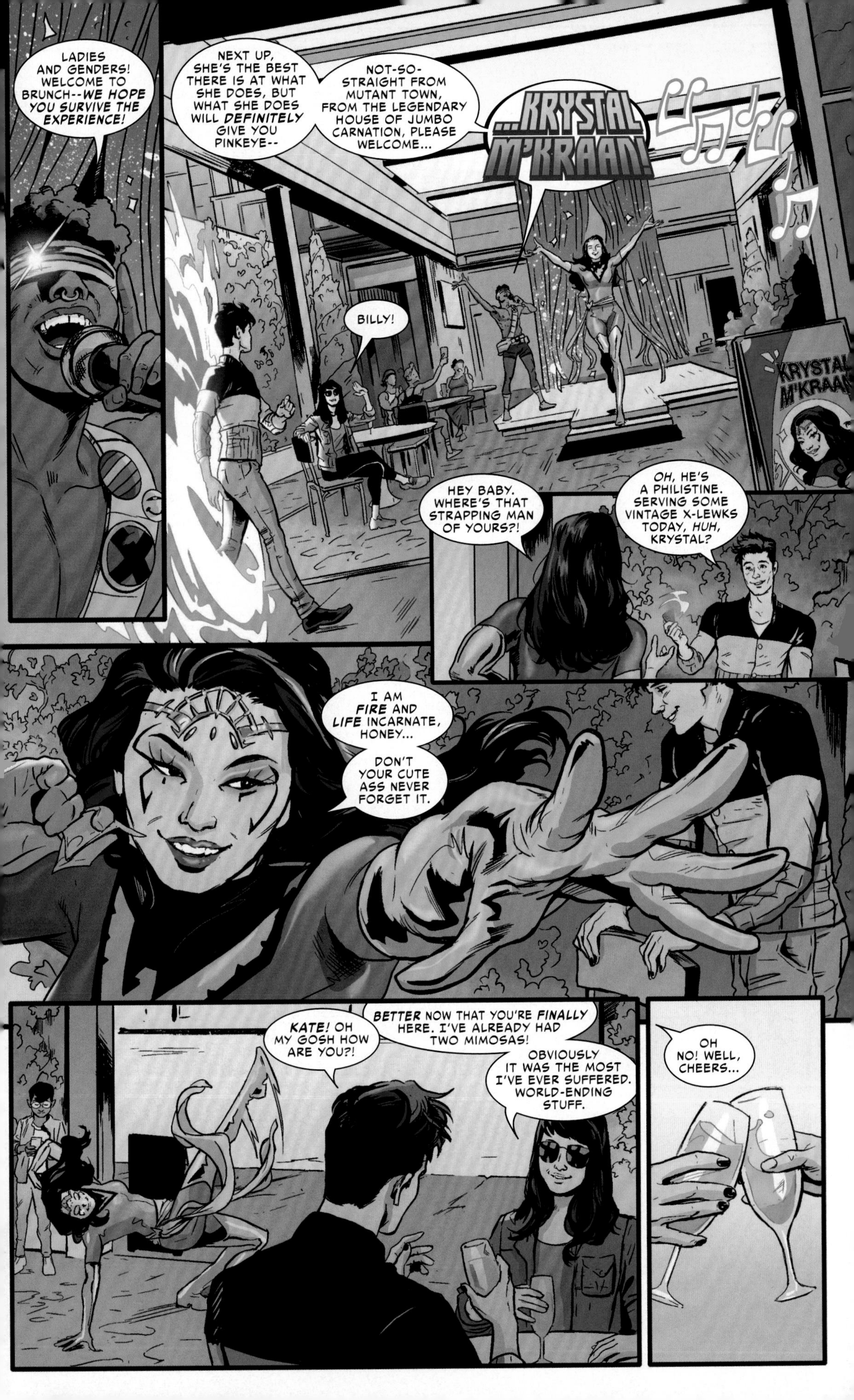

LADIES AND GENDERS! WELCOME TO BRUNCH--WE HOPE YOU SURVIVE THE EXPERIENCE!
NEXT UP, SHE'S THE BEST THERE IS AT WHAT SHE DOES, BUT WHAT SHE DOES WILL DEFINITELY GIVE YOU PINKEYE--
NOT-SO-STRAIGHT FROM MUTANT TOWN, FROM THE LEGENDARY HOUSE OF JUMBO CARNATION, PLEASE WELCOME...
...KRYSTAL M'KRAAN!
BILLY!
KRYSTAL M'KRAAN
HEY BABY. WHERE'S THAT STRAPPING MAN OF YOURS?!
OH, HE'S A PHILISTINE. SERVING SOME VINTAGE X-LEWKS TODAY, HUH, KRYSTAL?
I AM FIRE AND LIFE INCARNATE, HONEY...
DON'T YOUR CUTE ASS NEVER FORGET IT.
KATE! OH MY GOSH HOW ARE YOU?!
BETTER NOW THAT YOU'RE FINALLY HERE. I'VE ALREADY HAD TWO MIMOSAS!
OBVIOUSLY IT WAS THE MOST I'VE EVER SUFFERED. WORLD-ENDING STUFF.
OH NO! WELL, CHEERS...

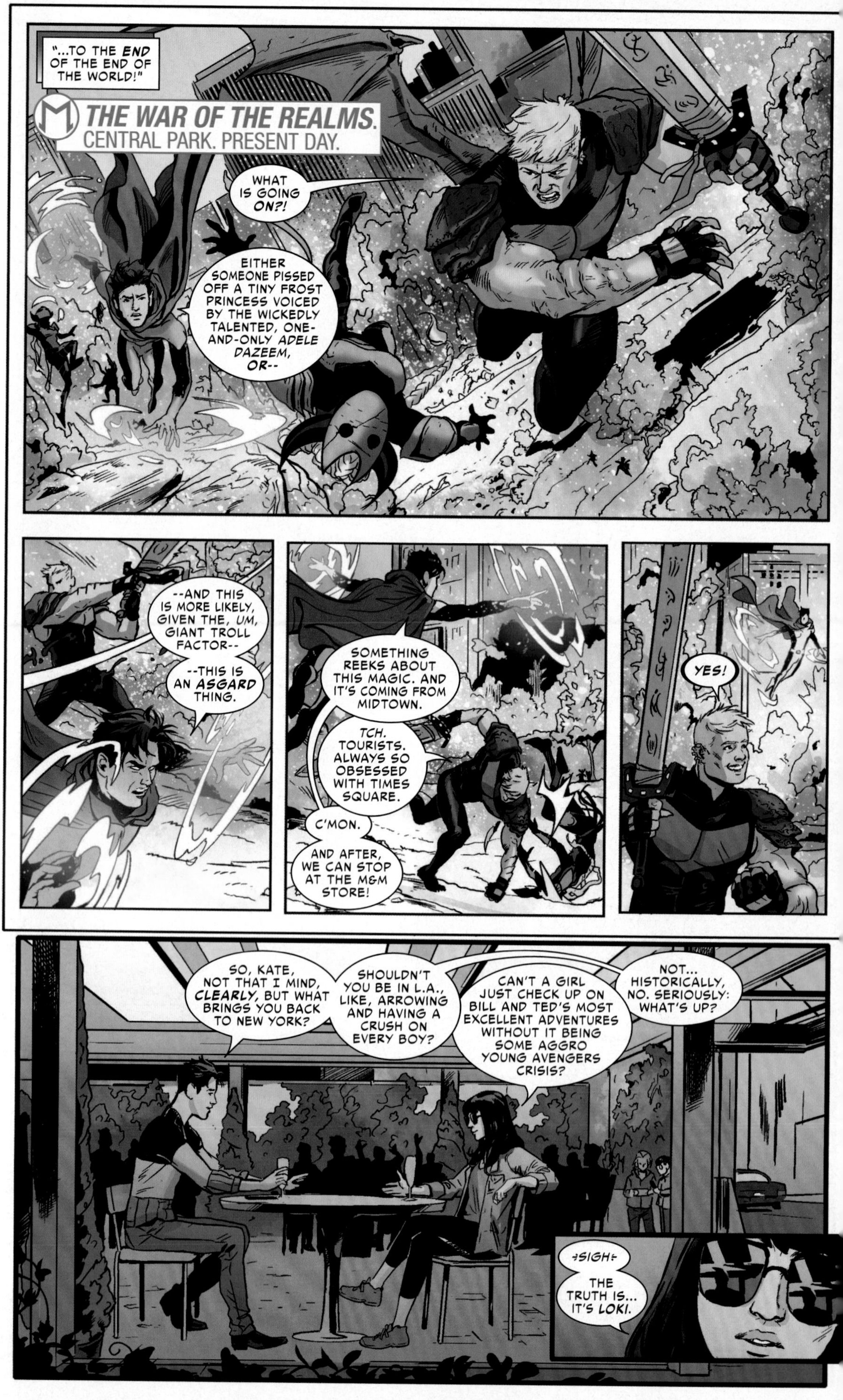
"...TO THE END OF THE END OF THE WORLD!"
THE WAR OF THE REALMS. CENTRAL PARK. PRESENT DAY.
WHAT IS GOING ON?!
EITHER SOMEONE PISSED OFF A TINY FROST PRINCESS VOICED BY THE WICKEDLY TALENTED, ONE-AND-ONLY ADELE DAZEEM, OR--
--AND THIS IS MORE LIKELY, GIVEN THE, UM, GIANT TROLL FACTOR--
--THIS IS AN ASGARD THING.
SOMETHING REEKS ABOUT THIS MAGIC. AND IT'S COMING FROM MIDTOWN.
TCH. TOURISTS. ALWAYS SO OBSESSED WITH TIMES SQUARE.
C'MON.
AND AFTER, WE CAN STOP AT THE M&M STORE!
YES!
SO, KATE, NOT THAT I MIND, CLEARLY, BUT WHAT BRINGS YOU BACK TO NEW YORK?
SHOULDN'T YOU BE IN L.A., LIKE, ARROWING AND HAVING A CRUSH ON EVERY BOY?
CAN'T A GIRL JUST CHECK UP ON BILL AND TED'S MOST EXCELLENT ADVENTURES WITHOUT IT BEING SOME AGGRO YOUNG AVENGERS CRISIS?
NOT... HISTORICALLY, NO. SERIOUSLY: WHAT'S UP?
SIGH
THE TRUTH IS... IT'S LOKI.

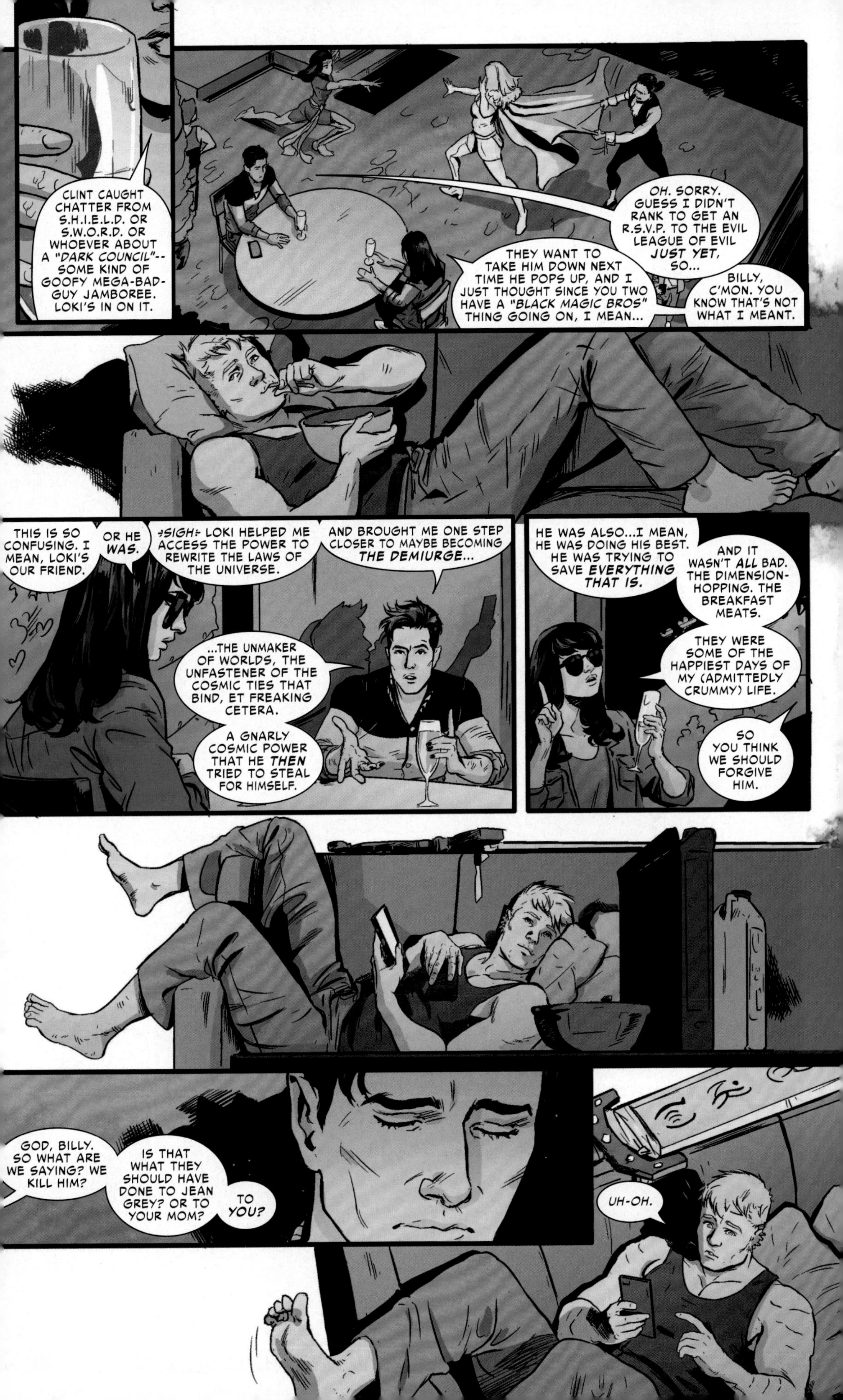
CLINT CAUGHT CHATTER FROM S.H.I.E.L.D. OR S.W.O.R.D. OR WHOEVER ABOUT A "DARK COUNCIL"-- SOME KIND OF GOOFY MEGA-BAD-GUY JAMBOREE. LOKI'S IN ON IT.
THEY WANT TO TAKE HIM DOWN NEXT TIME HE POPS UP, AND I JUST THOUGHT SINCE YOU TWO HAVE A "BLACK MAGIC BROS" THING GOING ON, I MEAN...
OH. SORRY. GUESS I DIDN'T RANK TO GET AN R.S.V.P. TO THE EVIL LEAGUE OF EVIL JUST YET, SO...
BILLY, C'MON. YOU KNOW THAT'S NOT WHAT I MEANT.
THIS IS SO CONFUSING. I MEAN, LOKI'S OUR FRIEND.
OR HE WAS.
=SIGH= LOKI HELPED ME ACCESS THE POWER TO REWRITE THE LAWS OF THE UNIVERSE.
AND BROUGHT ME ONE STEP CLOSER TO MAYBE BECOMING THE DEMIURGE...
...THE UNMAKER OF WORLDS, THE UNFASTENER OF THE COSMIC TIES THAT BIND, ET FREAKING CETERA.
A GNARLY COSMIC POWER THAT HE THEN TRIED TO STEAL FOR HIMSELF.
HE WAS ALSO...I MEAN, HE WAS DOING HIS BEST. HE WAS TRYING TO SAVE EVERYTHING THAT IS.
AND IT WASN'T ALL BAD. THE DIMENSION-HOPPING. THE BREAKFAST MEATS.
THEY WERE SOME OF THE HAPPIEST DAYS OF MY (ADMITTEDLY CRUMMY) LIFE.
SO YOU THINK WE SHOULD FORGIVE HIM.
GOD, BILLY. SO WHAT ARE WE SAYING? WE KILL HIM?
IS THAT WHAT THEY SHOULD HAVE DONE TO JEAN GREY? OR TO YOUR MOM?
TO YOU?
UH-OH.

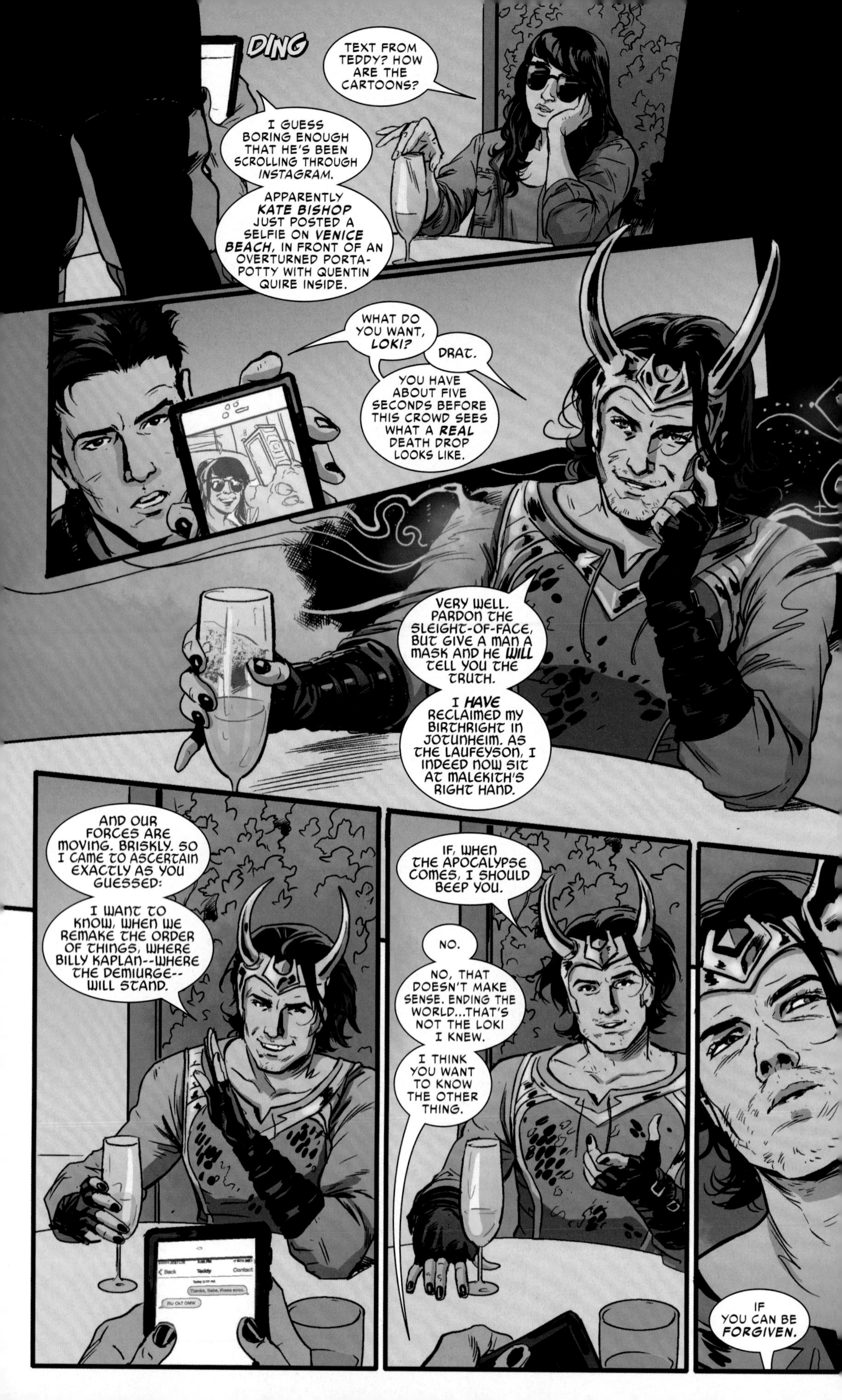
DING
TEXT FROM TEDDY? HOW ARE THE CARTOONS?
I GUESS BORING ENOUGH THAT HE'S BEEN SCROLLING THROUGH *INSTAGRAM.*
APPARENTLY ***KATE BISHOP*** JUST POSTED A SELFIE ON ***VENICE BEACH,*** IN FRONT OF AN OVERTURNED PORTA-POTTY WITH QUENTIN QUIRE INSIDE.
WHAT DO YOU WANT, ***LOKI?***
DRAT.
YOU HAVE ABOUT FIVE SECONDS BEFORE THIS CROWD SEES WHAT A ***REAL*** DEATH DROP LOOKS LIKE.
VERY WELL. PARDON THE SLEIGHT-OF-FACE, BUT GIVE A MAN A MASK AND HE ***WILL*** TELL YOU THE TRUTH.
I ***HAVE*** RECLAIMED MY BIRTHRIGHT IN JOTUNHEIM. AS THE LAUFEYSON, I INDEED NOW SIT AT MALEKITH'S RIGHT HAND.
AND OUR FORCES ARE MOVING. BRISKLY. SO I CAME TO ASCERTAIN EXACTLY AS YOU GUESSED:
I WANT TO KNOW, WHEN WE REMAKE THE ORDER OF THINGS, WHERE BILLY KAPLAN--WHERE THE DEMIURGE--WILL STAND.
IF, WHEN THE APOCALYPSE COMES, I SHOULD BEEP YOU.
NO.
NO, THAT DOESN'T MAKE SENSE. ENDING THE WORLD...THAT'S NOT THE LOKI I KNEW.
I THINK YOU WANT TO KNOW THE OTHER THING.
IF YOU CAN BE ***FORGIVEN.***

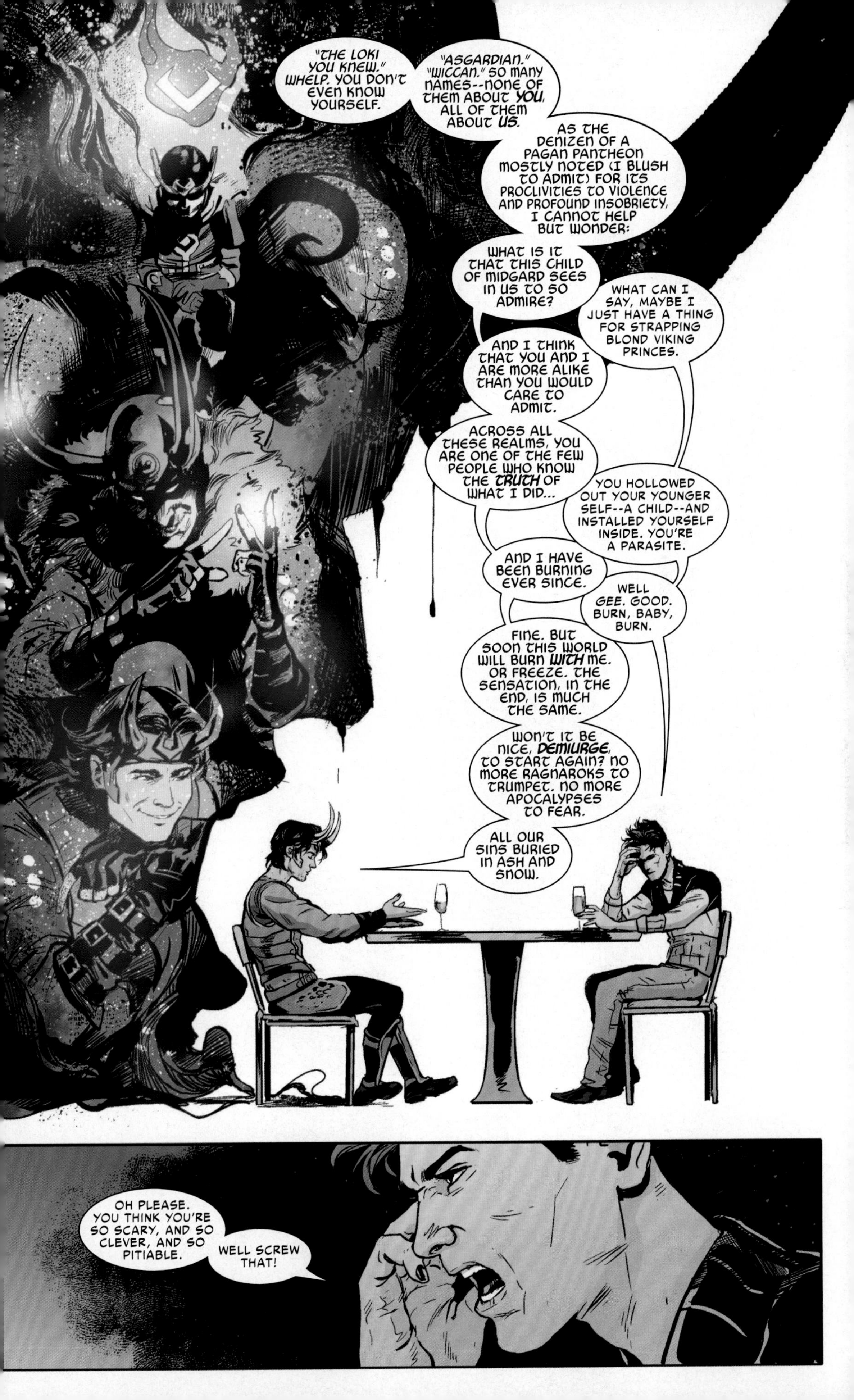
"THE LOKI YOU KNEW." WHELP. YOU DON'T EVEN KNOW YOURSELF.
"ASGARDIAN." "WICCAN." SO MANY NAMES--NONE OF THEM ABOUT YOU, ALL OF THEM ABOUT US.
AS THE DENIZEN OF A PAGAN PANTHEON MOSTLY NOTED (I BLUSH TO ADMIT) FOR ITS PROCLIVITIES TO VIOLENCE AND PROFOUND INSOBRIETY, I CANNOT HELP BUT WONDER:
WHAT IS IT THAT THIS CHILD OF MIDGARD SEES IN US TO SO ADMIRE?
WHAT CAN I SAY, MAYBE I JUST HAVE A THING FOR STRAPPING BLOND VIKING PRINCES.
AND I THINK THAT YOU AND I ARE MORE ALIKE THAN YOU WOULD CARE TO ADMIT.
ACROSS ALL THESE REALMS, YOU ARE ONE OF THE FEW PEOPLE WHO KNOW THE TRUTH OF WHAT I DID...
YOU HOLLOWED OUT YOUR YOUNGER SELF--A CHILD--AND INSTALLED YOURSELF INSIDE. YOU'RE A PARASITE.
AND I HAVE BEEN BURNING EVER SINCE.
WELL GEE. GOOD. BURN, BABY, BURN.
FINE. BUT SOON THIS WORLD WILL BURN WITH ME. OR FREEZE. THE SENSATION, IN THE END, IS MUCH THE SAME.
WON'T IT BE NICE, DEMIURGE, TO START AGAIN? NO MORE RAGNAROKS TO TRUMPET. NO MORE APOCALYPSES TO FEAR.
ALL OUR SINS BURIED IN ASH AND SNOW.
OH PLEASE. YOU THINK YOU'RE SO SCARY, AND SO CLEVER, AND SO PITIABLE.
WELL SCREW THAT!

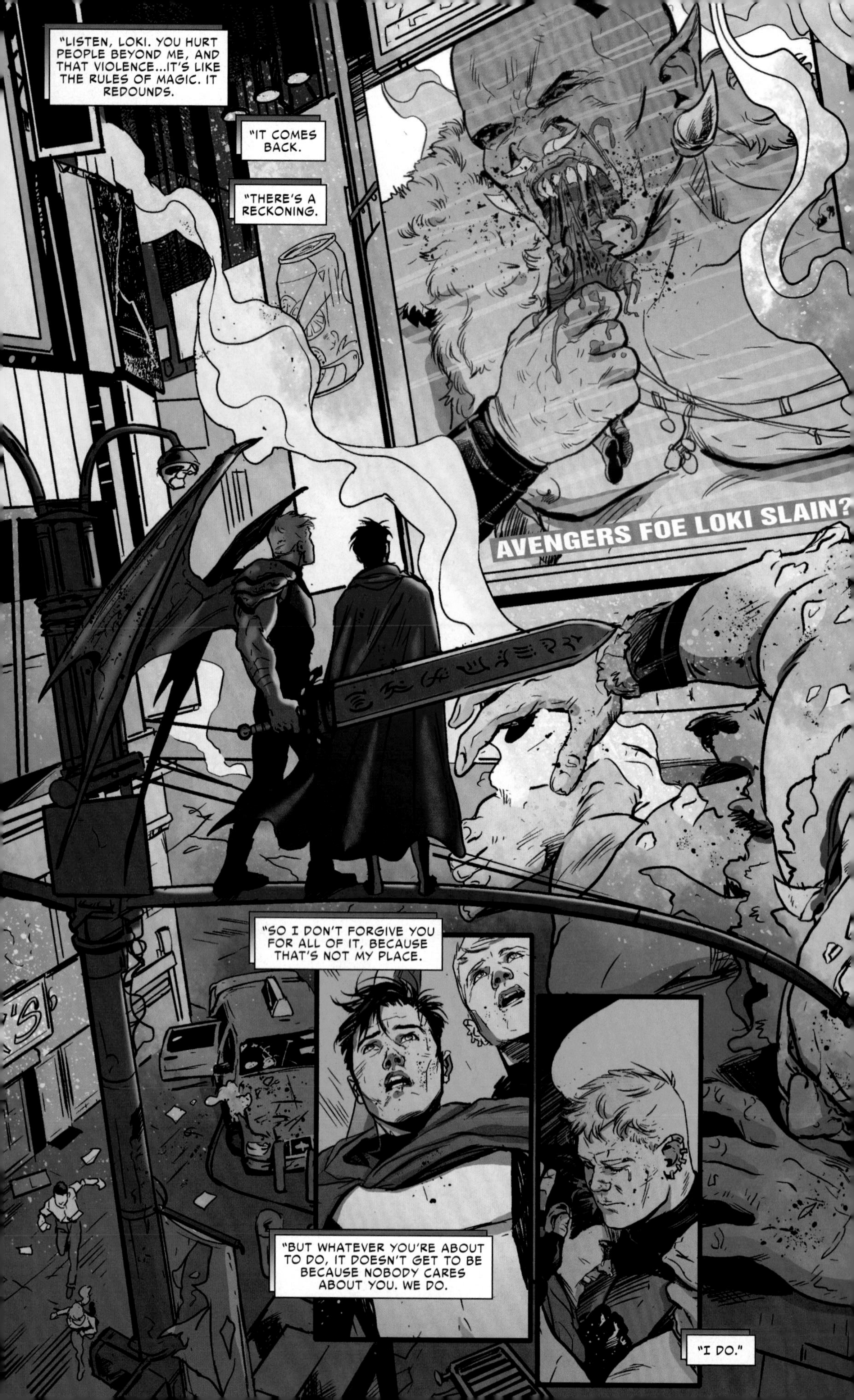
"LISTEN, LOKI. YOU HURT PEOPLE BEYOND ME, AND THAT VIOLENCE...IT'S LIKE THE RULES OF MAGIC. IT REDOUNDS.
"IT COMES BACK.
"THERE'S A RECKONING.
AVENGERS FOE LOKI SLAIN?
"SO I DON'T FORGIVE YOU FOR ALL OF IT, BECAUSE THAT'S NOT MY PLACE.
"BUT WHATEVER YOU'RE ABOUT TO DO, IT DOESN'T GET TO BE BECAUSE NOBODY CARES ABOUT YOU. WE DO.
"I DO."

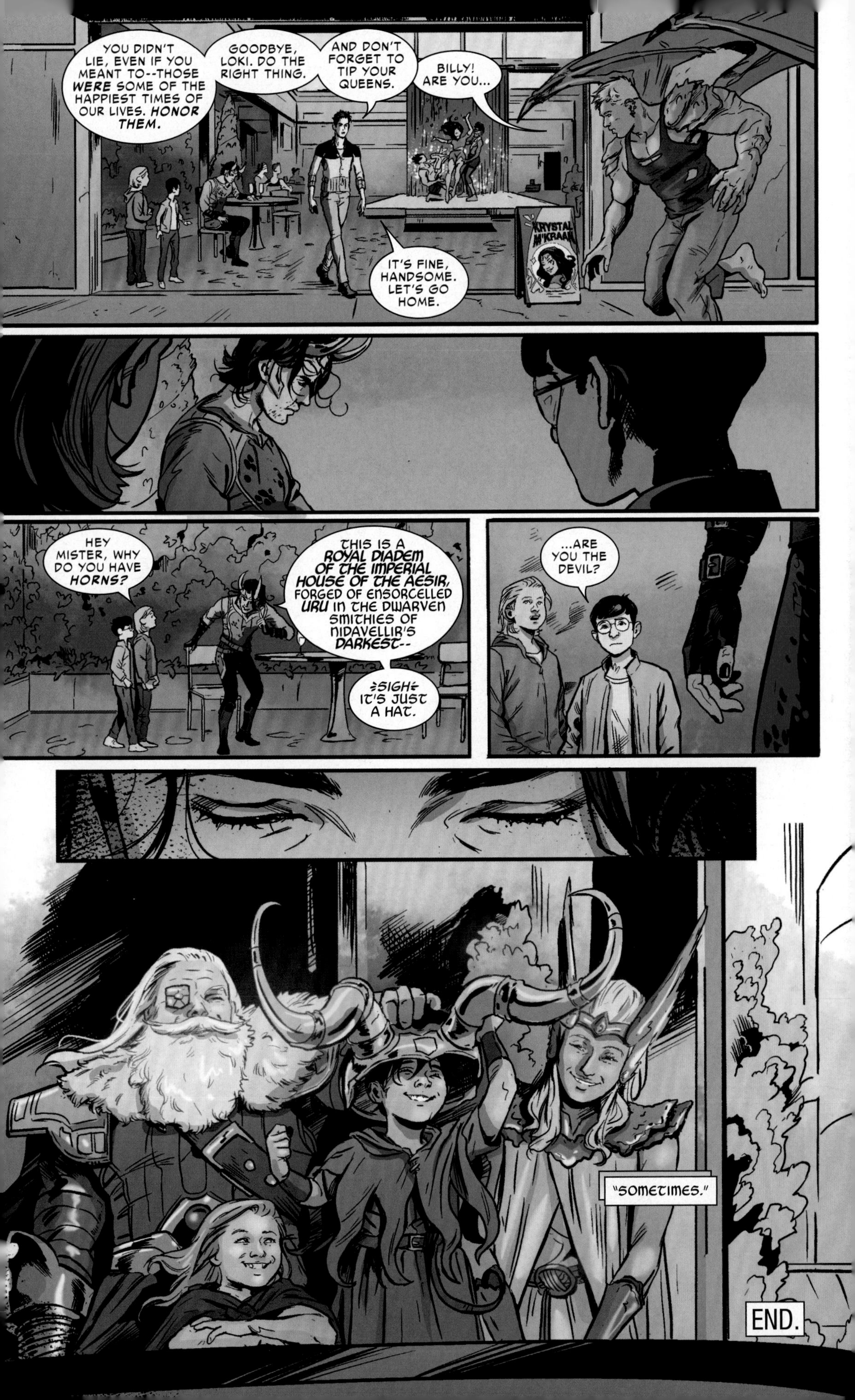

YOU DIDN'T LIE, EVEN IF YOU MEANT TO--THOSE *WERE* SOME OF THE HAPPIEST TIMES OF OUR LIVES. *HONOR THEM.*
GOODBYE, LOKI. DO THE RIGHT THING.
AND DON'T FORGET TO TIP YOUR QUEENS.
BILLY! ARE YOU...
KRYSTAL M'KRAAN
IT'S FINE, HANDSOME. LET'S GO HOME.
HEY MISTER, WHY DO YOU HAVE *HORNS?*
THIS IS A *ROYAL DIADEM OF THE IMPERIAL HOUSE OF THE AESIR,* FORGED OF ENSORCELLED *URU* IN THE DWARVEN SMITHIES OF NIDAVELLIR'S *DARKEST*--
SIGH IT'S JUST A HAT.
...ARE YOU THE DEVIL?
"SOMETIMES."
END.

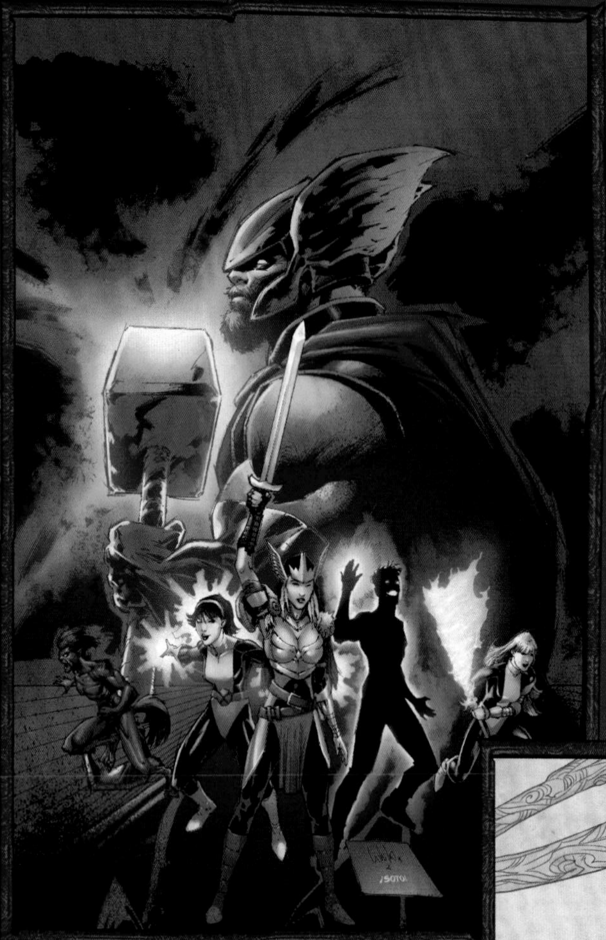

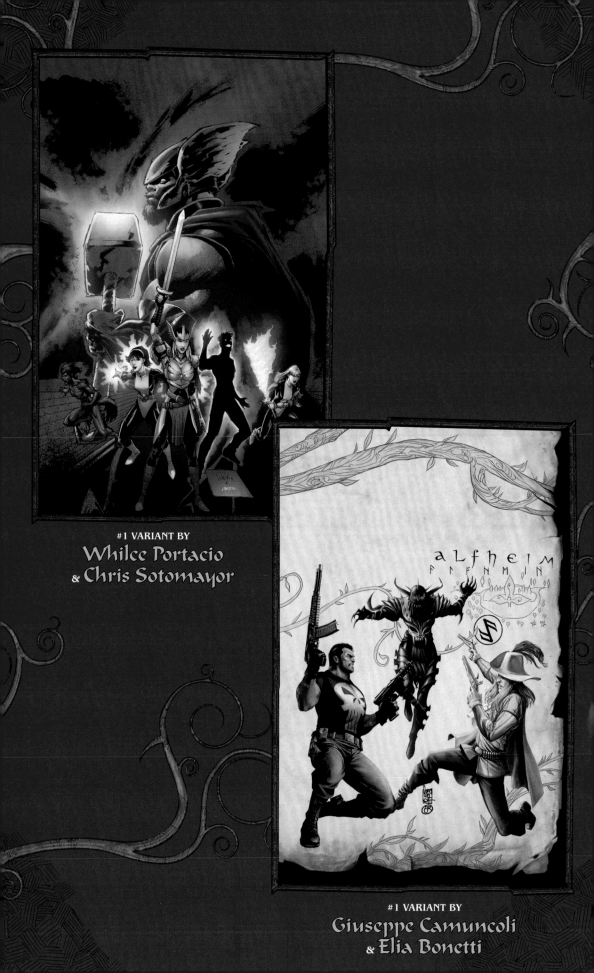

#1 VARIANT BY
Whilce Portacio
& Chris Sotomayor

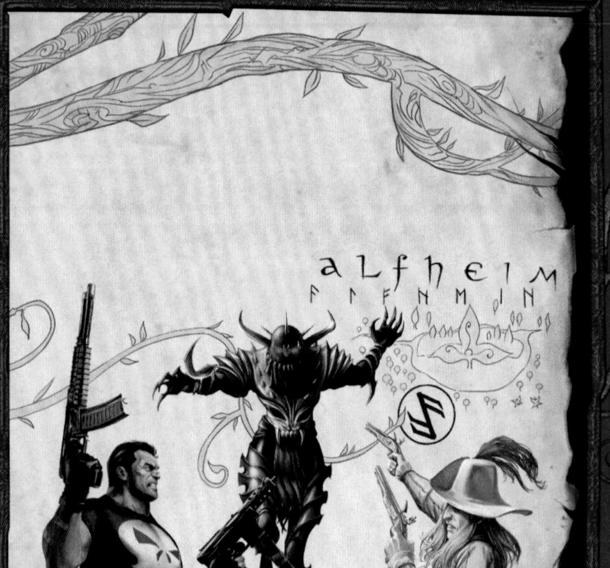
ALFHEIM

#1 VARIANT BY
Giuseppe Camuncoli
& Elia Bonetti

#2 VARIANT BY
Scott Williams
& Sunny Gho

#3 VARIANT BY
Ivan Shavrin

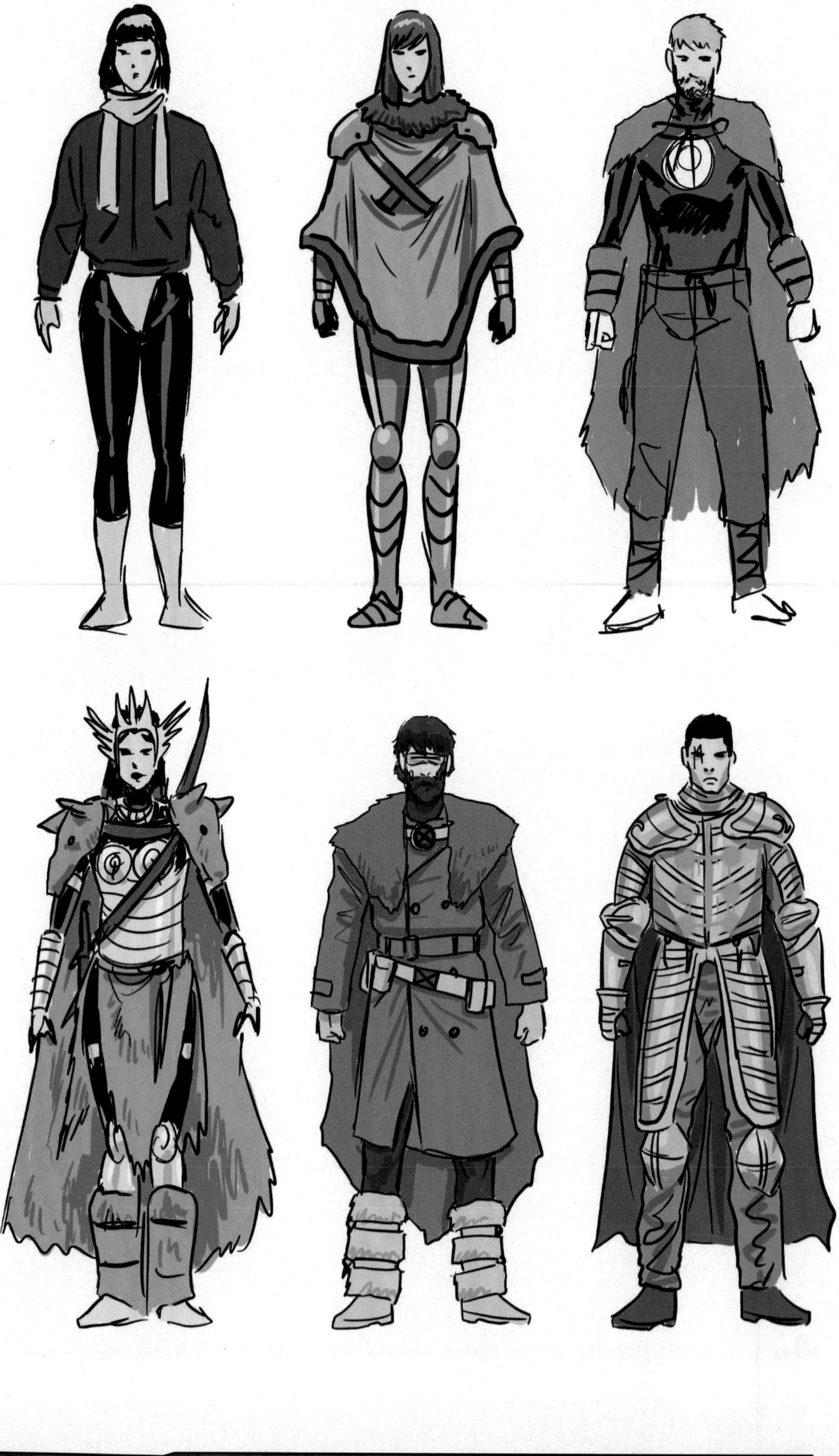

CHARACTER SKETCHES BY Pere Pérez